Inspiring Reading Success

Interest and Motivation
in an Age
of High-Stakes Testing

Rosalie Fink **S. Jay Samuels**

EDITORS

INTERNATIONAL
Reading Association
800 BARKSDALE ROAD, PO BOX 8139
NEWARK, DE 19714-8139, USA
www.reading.org

The International Reading Association attempts, through its publications, to provide a forum for a wide spectrum of opinions on reading. This policy permits divergent viewpoints without implying the endorsement of the Association.

Executive Editor, Books   Corinne M. Mooney
Developmental Editor   Charlene M. Nichols
Developmental Editor   Tori Mello Bachman
Developmental Editor   Stacey Lynn Sharp
Editorial Production Manager   Shannon T. Fortner
Design and Composition Manager   Anette Schuetz

Project Editors   Charlene M. Nichols and Cynthia L. Held

Cover   Design: Linda Steere; Photographs (from top): © 2007 Punchstock/Blend Images, © 2007 JupiterImages/Photos.com, © 2007 JupiterImages/Photos.com

The publisher would appreciate notification where errors occur so that they may be corrected in subsequent printings and/or editions.

Library of Congress Cataloging-in-Publication Data
Inspiring reading success : interest and motivation in an age of high-stakes testing / Rosalie Fink & S. Jay Samuels, editors.
     p. cm.
  Includes bibliographical references and indexes.
  ISBN-13: 978-0-87207-682-2
  1. Reading--United States. 2. Motivation in education--United States. I. Fink, Rosalie, 1942- II. Samuels, S. Jay.
  LB1573.I633 2007
  372.41--dc22
                                                                                            2007032951

To teachers everywhere who inspire and educate students,
To Gerry, who inspires me,
And to Julia, Uri, Jennifer, Sarah, Hal,
Adina, Maya, Alisa, Ben, and Nadia.
—*Rosalie*

To the teachers of children who struggle daily
to create a literate society.
—*Jay*

Contents

List of Figures and Tables

About the Editors

Rosalie Fink, EdD, is Professor of Literacy at Lesley University in Cambridge, Massachusetts, USA. Rosalie has been a teacher and reading specialist in public and private schools, where she taught reading and writing—as well as dance—to children and adults. She lectures internationally about the Interest-Based Model of Reading that she developed.

Rosalie earned the degree of Doctor of Education in Reading, Language, and Learning Disabilities from the Harvard Graduate School of Education. She has been recognized for her research by the National Academy of Education and the Spencer Foundation, which awarded her a Spencer Postdoctoral Research Fellowship. Rosalie was an invited Visiting Scholar in Education at the Harvard Graduate School of Education and served on the Executive Board of the Massachusetts Association of College and University Reading Educators (MACURE). She was elected president of MACURE, 2002–2003.

Rosalie was also elected to the International Academy for Research in Learning Disabilities and, in 2006, to the International Mind, Brain, and Education Society. She has published extensively in the field of reading. Rosalie's book, *Why Jane and John Couldn't Read—And How They Learned*, was chosen as the International Reading Association's April 2006 Book Club selection.

Jay Samuels started teaching elementary school shortly after the end of World War II. At that time, the schools were crowded and teachers were in short supply. Los Angeles needed teachers, so recruiters came to the New York area. Jay took a job offered by a recruiter because he knew that Muscle Beach, the Mecca for bodybuilding, would be conveniently located to where he would be teaching. He entered the University of California, Los Angeles, doctoral program, where he received a doctorate in educational psychology.

Jay later joined the Educational Psychology Department at the University of Minnesota and has been there for the last 40 years. Through Psychology Professor David LaBerge, Jay developed an interest in reading fluency. At the university, Jay received a Distinguished Teaching Award for his large teacher training lecture class on learning, cognition, and assessment. The National Reading Conference and the International Reading Association also have recognized Jay with research awards for reading. Jay was inducted into the Reading Hall of Fame in 1990.

Contributors

Janine Bempechat
Associate Professor
Human Development
Wheelock College
Boston, Massachusetts, USA

Rosalie Fink
Professor of Literacy
Lesley University
Cambridge, Massachusetts, USA

Kurt W. Fischer
Charles Warland Bigelow Professor
Director of Mind, Brain, & Education
Harvard Graduate School of Education
Cambridge, Massachusetts, USA

Maria Fusaro
Doctoral Candidate
Human Development and Psychology
Harvard Graduate School of Education
Cambridge, Massachusetts, USA

Irene W. Gaskins
Founder and Head of School Emeritus
Consultant for Staff and Program
   Development
Benchmark School
Media, Pennsylvania, USA

John T. Guthrie
Professor of Human Development
Director of Maryland Literacy Research
   Center
University of Maryland
College Park, Maryland, USA

Angela McRae
Doctoral Candidate
College of Education, Department
   of Human Development
University of Maryland
College Park, Maryland, USA

Timothy Rasinski
Professor of Education
Department of Teaching, Leadership,
   and Curriculum Studies
Kent State University
Kent, Ohio, USA

S. Jay Samuels
Professor of Educational Psychology
University of Minnesota
Minneapolis, Minnesota, USA

Ana Taboada
Assistant Professor, Literacy Program
College of Education & Human
   Development
George Mason University
Fairfax, Virginia, USA

Foreword

Most of the work done by reading researchers and most of the time invested in reading instruction is focused on the *how* of reading: how to build phonological awareness, how to ensure grasp and mastery of the alphabetic principle, how to build fluency, how to teach vocabulary, how to promote comprehension. This focus on *how* has led to real advances in our understanding of reading development and effective reading instruction. But it has produced at the same time a regrettable neglect of an equally important set of research questions and instructional focus: the *why* of reading. The chapters in this volume provide a useful corrective. They review research that indicates the importance to many developing readers, especially those for whom learning to read is hard, of knowing why they are being asked to read, what they are expected to get out of reading any particular text, how the reading they do might connect to their own lives and interests, and whether they will ever get to read something that answers their own burning questions. The research reviewed is overwhelmingly convincing that attending to the *why* of reading is crucial to the success of instructional strategies focused on the *how*.

Good teachers, of course, know about the role of motivation and interest in their students' success. This book will be of value to them, though, in a number of ways. First, the various chapters provide theoretical and research-based approaches to motivation that give teachers ideas for thinking about their own practice. Second, some of the chapters offer very practical suggestions for engaging student interest and embedding attention to motivation, relevance, and student interest into how-focused instruction. Third, and perhaps most important, this book offers teachers help in building the argument they may need to make to open up space for these activities in their teaching schedules. We are all responsible for convincing coaches, providers of professional development, principals, and other instructional leaders of the need to attend to the *why* of reading. For adults, alas, the motivation is all too often better performance on tests, but children are not taken in by such flimsy goals. They need authentic purposes and real relevance to their lives.

The issues raised in this volume apply with particular urgency to adolescent readers. Five-year-olds, in general, go happily to school expecting to learn to read and are motivated to persist by their small, incremental successes in mastering that domain. In the primary grades reading is, for most if not all students, intrinsically rewarding—they have a new and valuable skill, and they get to read all sorts of fun texts. In the middle grades, the rules change. Students are expected to be reading for learning, not just for practice. Even good readers face enormous challenges if they lack the vocabulary and background knowledge to tackle their history and science texts. Students with dyslexia, or those

Inspiring Reading Success: Interest and Motivation in an Age of High-Stakes Testing, edited by Rosalie Fink and S. Jay Samuels. © 2008 by the International Reading Association.

who somehow missed learning the required skills early on, of course struggle even more. If reading is not fun, then it needs to be purposeful. This book is about that simple claim and how to make purposeful reading a reality for every student.

—Catherine E. Snow
Henry Lee Shattuck Professor
Harvard Graduate School of Education
Cambridge, Massachusetts, USA

Preface

The No Child Left Behind Act of 2001 has had a profound impact on reading instruction; yet, many students continue to fail as readers and learners. This volume explains how teachers and others can engineer success for all types of students by focusing on an important aspect of reading: personal interest and motivation. Our goal is to present engaging ways to teach all types of students—English-language learners, children who struggle, typically developing learners, and advanced students.

Who Should Read This Volume?

Inspiring Reading Success: Interest and Motivation in an Age of High-Stakes Testing is for teachers, families, reading coaches, reading specialists, and tutors involved with students of all ages, backgrounds, and abilities. It will also be of interest to administrators, researchers, and policymakers. We hope that *Inspiring Reading Success* spurs educators to focus on approaches to teaching that capitalize on students' interests and spark each child's motivation to read.

How Is the Volume Organized?

We present a variety of perspectives from different populations and research traditions. Each chapter opens with prereading questions to spur readers' predictions and involvement prior to reading. In addition, each chapter concludes with questions for readers to consider after they have read the chapter. Many of the postreading questions are purposely open-ended in order to provide opportunities for deep reflection, critical thinking, and rich discussion. Many chapters contain reproducible materials designed for easy duplication and immediate classroom use. In addition, many chapters contain valuable resource lists of engaging books, websites, magazines, and activities organized by topic and grade level. Our purpose is to make it easy for teachers to locate materials that fit each student's interest and reading level.

Why Did We Write This Volume Now?

Over the years, many professional organizations have published books that emphasize different methods that seem to work in teaching reading and writing. Clearly, teaching methods are extremely important. However, we believe that if the emphasis is just on methods, the focus is too narrow. It is time to expand our approach and consider other factors that influence the success or failure of even the best reading methods.

Inspiring Reading Success: Interest and Motivation in an Age of High-Stakes Testing, edited by Rosalie Fink and S. Jay Samuels. © 2008 by the International Reading Association.

We are educating students today who have a variety of problems. Some students are not fluent in English; some are not motivated to do the work required for academic success. Some have fallen so far behind academically that they have lost the will and confidence in themselves to get on track, while some who have the desire to learn have neurological handicaps that make learning to read difficult. These problems are often so formidable that even the best methods are no match for the challenges that many students face.

However, research has shown that some struggling readers and others who face severe challenges can eventually become proficient and succeed in fields that demand sophisticated reading (Fink, 2006, 2007). *Inspiring Reading Success* describes the research and clinical findings of what works with unusual populations (including urban students, English-language learners, and individuals with dyslexia) in order to glimpse how to help all children learn to read in an age of high-stakes testing. Teachers and school staff need to know about aspects of education, such as motivation, attitude, and engagement, that can greatly enhance reading instruction for a broad array of students—struggling, typically developing, and advanced.

We address several intriguing questions. For example, What can teachers learn from research about students who struggled but eventually became successful readers, writers, and professionals? Why are students in some urban schools successful, while many are not? Some of the research that is reported here was conducted with students who had dyslexia but overcame their problems and attained high levels of success in fields that require skilled reading (Fink, 2006, 2007). Other students were raised under highly stressful conditions—such as extreme poverty, drug addiction, lack of adult supervision, and violence—yet they went on to high levels of school achievement. One of the components that drove these successful children was their strong motivation and desire to do well and move ahead with their lives. Another component had to do with the support they got from mentors. Still another component was traced to the materials they chose to read.

The purpose of this volume is to put together the pieces of an intellectual jigsaw puzzle that examines successful coping strategies from a variety of sources. By understanding common threads found in the diverse perspectives in this volume, we hope that teachers will come away with a new outlook on teaching and learning. We are especially excited about the creative approaches of each of the authors. We are also enthusiastic about the materials that each author recommends. We believe that the engaging strategies, activities, and resource lists in this volume will be useful in helping all types of students at all ages and stages of development to succeed.

—*Rosalie Fink and S. Jay Samuels*

REFERENCES

Fink, R. (2006). *Why Jane and John couldn't read—And how they learned: A new look at striving readers.* Newark, DE: International Reading Association.

Fink, R. (2007). What successful adults with dyslexia teach educators about children. In K.W. Fischer, J.H. Bernstein, & M.H. Immordino-Yang (Eds.), *Mind, brain, and education in reading disorders* (pp. 264–281). Cambridge, England: Cambridge University Press.

Acknowledgments

We want to thank each individual who contributed a chapter to this book—Janine Bempechat, Kurt W. Fischer, Maria Fusaro, Irene W. Gaskins, John T. Guthrie, Angela McRae, Timothy Rasinski, and Ana Taboada. We appreciate your unique perspectives, expertise, and insights. We are also grateful to Catherine E. Snow for writing the foreword.

Finally, we want to acknowledge our editors at the International Reading Association who worked tirelessly on drafts of the book to improve the final product: Dan Mangan, Teresa Curto, Shannon Fortner, Charlene Nichols, Corinne Mooney, Cindy Held, and Elizabeth Hunt. Thanks to each of you!

CHAPTER 1

Beating the Odds: Giving Kids a Chance to Win the Game of Life

S. JAY SAMUELS

Inspiring Reading Success: Interest and Motivation in an Age of High-Stakes Testing, edited by Rosalie Fink and S. Jay Samuels. © 2008 by the International Reading Association.

PREREADING QUESTIONS

◆ You have probably heard the expression that the playing field is not level for all of us. From the vantage point of your knowledge and experience, can you list three or four reasons involving guidance and coaching that might explain why children who come from the middle and upper classes have higher school achievement than children from the lower classes?

◆ Is there a solution to this problem, and, if so, what is it?

The underlying theme of this chapter, as well as some of the other chapters in this volume, is expressed in a song from the very popular musical *Miss Saigon*. In the musical, Kim has had an out-of-wedlock child with an American soldier who was forced to leave her during the chaos surrounding the fall of Saigon at the end of the Vietnam War. Because of the prejudice of the people of Saigon, Kim knows how bleak and unpromising the future is for her child. The dilemma for Kim is that she loves her son and wants to keep him with her, but she realizes that if he goes with his father, he will have a chance for a better life. She decides to give him up and sings, "I'll give you a million things I'll never own. I'll give you a world to conquer when you're grown. You will be who you want to be; you can choose whatever…. As long as you can have your chance, I swear I'll give my life for you." What Kim wants for her child is the theme of this chapter. She wants to give her child a chance to overcome the roadblocks that stand in his way so that he can try to create a happy and fulfilling life for himself.

Using research from several fields, in this chapter I identify some of the key buffering factors that help students overcome obstacles and problems so that they can have a chance in life. Some of the chronic problems the students face in their day-to-day living are so formidable that the best reading methods are no match. In other words, before these children can take advantage of even the best reading methods, we must help them solve some basic problems they encounter in their personal lives, such as having a relationship with mentors, and we must be certain that they do not have defeatist attitudes about their ability to forge a better life for themselves. As educators, we are seeking ways to help students cope with the problems they encounter in their day-to-day living so that they can have a chance in life (Cohen, 1993).

Barriers to Achievement

My research on reading has frequently brought me into contact with students who live in the inner cities of Minneapolis and St. Paul, Minnesota, USA, where teachers tell me about the problems their students face. Most of these inner-city children come from homes characterized by poverty, low level of parental education, frequent moves within the low-income housing zones to keep ahead of the bill collectors, and neighborhoods where the level of street violence is so high that many children are not allowed to play outside without supervision. At one school where I did my research, the food service workers noted that some of the students who received free cafeteria meals wasted the food. Thinking that there would be less food wasted if the students were served their favorite foods, the workers surveyed the children to find out which foods they preferred. The workers were surprised when a group of children said that Monday's was their favorite meal. Upon questioning, the workers found out that some of the children had so little food available over the weekend that on Monday they came to school hungry, and anything the school served that day, they liked. One teacher told me about how a student in her class slept in a car with his destitute mother each night because they were unable to find accommodations in a homeless shelter. Upon arriving at school each morning, the student was so exhausted that she kept falling asleep. When the teacher made a mattress to the side of the classroom so the student could sleep, the principal told the teacher that sleeping in class was not acceptable and the student had to sit at her desk and work.

The harsh winters we have in Minneapolis and St. Paul, the Twin Cities, bring even more problems to the classroom. Two years ago, thousands of Hmong people who had been living in the refugee camps of Thailand were told that they had to leave the camps. Due in large measure to the help the Hmong gave to U.S. troops during the secret war in Laos during the Vietnam War, the Hmong were told that they could relocate to the United States. Consequently, when forced out of refugee camps in Thailand, thousands of Hmong moved to the Twin Cities. Their children, who had never been to school and who could not speak English, came into the St. Paul schools with no warm winter clothing just as the weather began to turn cold. Using e-mail, I alerted faculty and staff at the College of Education at the University of Minnesota about this situation and requested that they leave gloves, hats, and coats outside my office door. For several weeks, I brought hundreds of pounds of clothing to a St. Paul Elementary School where the clothing was put on tables in the cafeteria and the Hmong parents were invited to come and take what they needed. Securing winter clothing for students was carried out by teachers in other schools as well. However, despite these efforts, teachers inform me that children continue to come to school inadequately dressed for the winter weather.

The Star Tribune, which is the most widely read newspaper in a metropolitan area of more than 2 million Minnesotans, had as its lead article a story about a high school girl who stabbed her newborn infant more than one hundred times after giving birth to the infant on her laundry room floor (Adams & Powell, 2007). When interviewed about the teenage mother who committed the crime, her longtime neighbor commented, "That girl didn't have a chance from the time she was born. She had a tough time growing up." The county attorney stated that what the teenage mother needed but never had was a trusted person who could help her get through this difficult time in her life. This teenage mother knew that she could have left her infant at any hospital within 72 hours of the birth without any legal consequence. What she did not have was a trusted relationship with an adult with whom she could confide, and who would help her work out a plan to overcome the problem. This teenager lived in a home with her own mother, but they did not have the desired trusting relationship. As the county attorney stated, "Instead, she destroyed two lives, hers and the baby's." State and local governments are aware of the research that has been done on stress resiliency in children. In an editorial entitled "Mentors, Intervention Help Kids and Society," Albright (2007) states,

> Connect kids with caring, involved adults and the children will be much better off.... That is why effective mentoring and other youth programs merit more support.... The Wilder Foundation and the University of Minnesota researchers found that Minnesota can expect a $2.72 return for every dollar spent on effective mentoring programs. (p. A14)

Stress-Resilient Children and Child Prodigies

Almost every inner-city student has a story to tell about the formidable obstacles that they face in their day-to-day living that they must overcome in order to do satisfactory schoolwork. Fortunately, many students from disadvantaged backgrounds have managed to overcome the obstacles strewn across their paths, and by doing well in school they have managed to build happy lives for themselves. The National Research Council recently concluded that although many young people survive and lead productive, happy lives, large numbers of others do not because the odds against them are too great. Scholars such as Norman Garmezy, Ann Masten, and Auk Tellegen (1984) have studied these successful resilient children to identify what factors allow them to overcome the negative influences that often seem to block achievement. Resilience research seeks to identify the environmental support variables that enable these students to escape the troubled situations in which they live, and the researchers have reported their findings on which factors have helped these stress-resilient students to succeed.

One might imagine that the road to success for children who are blessed with prodigious intellectual gifts is an easy one, but that is not necessarily the case.

However, as an educational psychologist who has seen many popular interventions come to nothing, I have developed a healthy caution about blindly accepting these breakthroughs. Before I suggest that anyone invest a lot of time and effort into applying an intervention, what I look for are sources of converging evidence that seem to be in agreement about what we must do to help students succeed in the big game of life. Converging evidence exists between the findings from stress-resilient children and from child prodigies. One might imagine that the road to success for children who are blessed with prodigious intellectual gifts is an easy one, but that is not necessarily the case. Some child prodigies fail to have happy, successful lives because some essential element necessary for building a happy life is missing in their upbringing. What is most interesting is that what helps a child prodigy succeed is almost exactly the same requirement as for helping children born into a hostile environment. When the lines of evidence converge, we can place greater confidence in their findings and feel more confident in trying to apply the findings to all children.

William Sidis (April 1, 1898–July 17, 1944), an Unsuccessful Prodigy

Before going into the converging research literatures on prodigies and resilient children, I would like to describe the rather sad ending to the life of William Sidis, who was one of the great prodigies of recent times (Wallace, 1986). A brief examination of his life is informative because it illustrates how a human life, like a chain, is only as strong as its weakest link. In the case of William Sidis, his major problem was his failure to develop healthy self-esteem. He believed that his sole worth as a human being was his prodigious intellect.

William Sidis was born near the beginning of the 20th century to two unusual parents who arrived in the United States as poor, uneducated Jewish Russian immigrants. When Sidis's father arrived in the Boston area, he focused on getting an education at Harvard College. What little money he earned, he spent on books and tuition. The famous Harvard psychologist William James encouraged William Sidis's father to get a doctorate in psychology, which he did, along with an MD degree. William Sidis's first name was given to him as a way to honor William James, the Harvard psychologist. Sidis's mother went on to get an MD degree as well.

The time period in which William was born was also the beginning of the study of behaviorism in United States. This psychological paradigm placed great emphasis on the power of the environment to mold human behavior. The child-rearing advice to parents was to keep children on a schedule. If children cried in between feedings, the parents were told to ignore the crying because picking up the child only reinforced more crying. As much as possible, Dr. Sidis, William's father, treated his infant son as an intelligent child rather than an infant. It quickly became apparent to his parents that William was gifted, and the parents attributed his early talents to their strict application of behaviorism and the way they treated him as an intelligent young person who could understand all the information they provided. By the time William was only 6 months old, he was speaking, and he could spell words by the age of 1 year. At age 3, he used the typewriter to write letters. Before his sixth birthday, he devised a calendar that would allow him to tell the day of the week of any date. By age 8, he had taught himself to speak eight languages. That year, he passed the Massachusetts Institute of Technology entrance examination in mathematics and the Harvard Medical School examination in human anatomy. William completed both elementary school and high school in one year. In his 11th year, he enrolled in Harvard in a new program they had for the gifted, and he was the youngest person they had ever enrolled. Other gifted students who were in the program were Norbert Wiener (originator of cybernetics), inventor R. Buckminster Fuller, and composer Roger Sessions.

William's fame spread and newspapers ran stories about this most unusual prodigy who excelled in mathematics, languages, biology, and mental computation. Newspaper reporters interviewed William and asked him how it felt to be an "egg head." The downside of all the attention William got as a child was that he began to feel that he had no worth as a human being other than his mind. Consequently, as an adult he decided he did not want to do any work that required higher level thinking. Despite having an IQ that was estimated to be between 250 and 300, he roamed the United States working at menial jobs and pursuing his hobby of collecting trolley car tickets. On one of William's visits to the Boston, Massachusetts, area, he had a chance to see a copy of Albert Einstein's theory of relativity that was still in the galley stage, and William discovered typographical errors in the manuscript that dealt with the mathematics.

Here was William, a child born into a family of scholars, born with a great intellect, who never took advantage of his talents. What was missing in his life? He wanted to be valued and loved as a human being. Instead, he grew up feeling his sole value was the great mind he was born with, and he rejected a life that put emphasis primarily on the intellect.

Starting in the late 1960s, the importance of helping all children feel loved for themselves was taken up by the highly popular children's television program *Mr. Rogers' Neighborhood*. This children's television series encouraged children to feel good about themselves by supporting a sense of self-worth. The song composed by Mr. Rogers that he sang to the children regularly tells them, "You've made this day a special day just by being you.... And people like you just because you're you." If young William Sidis had heard this message in his formative years, it is possible his life might have turned out better.

Key Factors That Contribute to the Success of Stress-Resilient Children

Mentoring. One of the key factors that accounts for the ability of students to overcome a hostile environment is the presence of a mentor in their lives (Garmezy & Rutter, 1983). The mentor can be a parent, relative, teacher, or friend. What mentors do for the child is to provide guidance, information, moral values, stability, emotional support that helps develop the child's sense of self-worth, and a helping hand through troubled times. If the child who is trying to beat the odds becomes discouraged, the mentor encourages the child to keep on trying.

All children need mentoring. Those children who are fortunate enough to be raised in a socially healthy and nurturing environment often have the advantage of being able to observe mentors who model appropriate behaviors. In addition to observing mentors who model appropriate behaviors, the child who grows up in a healthy environment usually has some adult mentor there to explain the steps one must take in order to climb the ladder of success on the way to creating a happy life.

Some years ago I invited a highly successful wrestling coach to talk to a class I was teaching to explain how he had taken a below average team and within five years coached them to a conference championship and later to a national championship. The coach said to my class that wrestling is just a game, but there are lessons from wrestling that can be applied to life. He said that he is a mentor to his athletes, and he tells them, "If you listen to me, I will help you to get through the minefields of life faster and more safely than if you try it on your own." This is precisely the kind of mentoring and guidance that children who are fortunate to have been raised in a nurturing environment receive. Unfortunately, many children who are raised in stressful environments seldom get an opportunity to observe situationally appropriate behavior, and often there is no one who will take the time to explain how to travel the rocky road to success and happiness.

For example, a young woman who was an excellent student and who had come from a background of poverty had won a scholarship to attend the University of Minnesota. Not knowing what kind of major to declare, the student explained her dilemma to a college guidance counselor. In an effort to help the student make a decision, the counselor asked her what kind of work she enjoyed doing. The student said that she once held a job she liked at a children's day-care center, and she might enjoy working with children in such a center again. When the counselor said that the problem with working at such a center was that the workers did not earn much money for the work they did, the student replied that she had no intention of starting at the bottom. She said she was an idea person and would start at the top of the organization. The college counselor had to explain to this young woman that if a person wants to climb the ladder of success, he or she does not start at the top of an organization. Instead, one starts at the lower levels, and over the course of many years of good work the worker can hope to get promotions and eventually work up to better paying jobs that carry more responsibility. To the college student who had grown up in poverty, this basic information about starting at the bottom and working upward was missing in her social upbringing.

Although mentors are usually adults, they can also be adolescents. For example, a high school student who was living under extremely adverse home conditions had become so depressed that she began cutting her wrists and covering up the wounds with bandages and long-sleeved shirts. A good friend of hers, another high school student, became suspicious of the long-sleeved shirts worn in hot weather and confronted her. While at first the suspicious student spent time talking to her depressed friend to find out more about her friend's problems, she soon realized that the problems her friend was experiencing were so serious that she could not help her. Consequently, the adolescent mentor convinced her friend that she should confide her problems to the school guidance counselor, who got help for the stressed student through a local community agency. This same wise teenage friend consistently acted in the role of a mentor by helping her stressed-out friend to maintain a study and homework schedule that allowed her to continue to make progress toward graduation despite her troubles.

Often, the resilient student has mentors who change over time. For example, as the resilient student goes through school, different teachers may take on the mentoring role. What some teachers do so well is to identify students living in stressful conditions who need their help, and the teachers mentor these students. However, there are two interrelated components to mentoring, and these components represent two sides of the same coin. On one side of the coin, we need a caring, informed coach or mentor who can guide the student. On the other side of the coin, as the sports expression says, we also need a person who is coachable, one who is capable of using and applying the advice that is given. Some resilient students actually seem to be aware of how much they need the help offered by teachers who are willing to take on the role of a mentor. One resilient student said she knew she needed help, and she looked for teachers who were sympathetic to her. Once the student identified a teacher who might take on the mentoring role for her, she then tried to become friendly with the teacher in order to establish a relationship. Over the course of many years, in the absence of any useful help from home, this strategy worked for the coachable student.

Belief System: Effort and Locus of Control. How students assign causality for the problems that they face and how they react to adversity are important factors in overcoming obstacles. For example, some students may believe that predestination controls their lives and that the problems they face in day-to-day living are so formidable and overwhelming that nothing they do will make a difference. This belief system is defeatist. It often leads to apathy, and the students may be unmotivated to try to improve their situations. On the other hand, if a student believes that through hard work and effort, he or she can rise above the hostile environment, there is at least a chance that the student will beat the odds (Garmezy, Masten, & Tellegen, 1984; Garmezy & Rutter, 1983).

Where does the power to alter a life reside? Is it within an individual or is it external? Research on resilient children has shown that the ones who surmount their problems and go on to live fulfilling lives are the ones who have an internal locus of control. Locus of control may be thought of as where one believes the power to affect a life is found. Some believe the power is external to a person, that it is the outside forces of fate, which no one can control, that determine destiny. On the other hand, some believe the power to affect life is internal to a person, and that the effort put into building a better life determines destiny. That is, successful resilient children tend to believe that in the end it is not fate or destiny that determines their future but the effort they put into bettering their condition that will make a difference. In essence, the students who beat the odds are the ones who believe that the power to change lives resides in them and that if they work hard and do well in school, they have a chance to build a better life.

Key Factors That Contribute to the Success of Child Prodigies

Child prodigies are those who have mastered a complex skill in areas such as chess, music, mathematics, or sports usually before their adolescent years. Some prodigies are well known, such as Wolfgang Amadeus Mozart (music), William Sidis (mathematics), Pablo Picasso (art), John Stuart Mill (philosopher), Wayne Gretzky (hockey), and Tiger Woods (golf). Many prodigies have gone on to have highly successful adult lives. What characterizes those who enjoyed success was the following (Feldman, 1979).

Mentoring. Each prodigy had a parent or some responsible adult who recognized the extraordinary talent the child possessed and acted as a mentor. The mentor then took on the responsibility of getting outstanding teachers to nurture the talent. In many instances, nurturing the talent was done at significant personal expense and sacrifice to the parent. For example, Tiger Woods's father invested many years of his time and energy in helping his son become a world-famous athlete. He spent considerable time inspiring and motivating his son to develop the talents he displayed at a young age.

Likewise, if the child is in a sport such as figure skating, the mentor or parent has to transport the child on a regular basis to early morning practices in order to get time on the ice. In addition, the parent must find a way to pay for the considerable costs of coaching and expensive dance costumes, and at times this might require one parent to live in one city in order to earn money and the other parent to live in another city, where the best figure skating coach may be found. In gymnastics, the parents may have the child live in the home of a well-known coach; thus, the parents lose the companionship of their child. In music, parents may move to the area of the country where the best music instruction may be found.

Personal Effort and Time in Developing Talent. Even though the prodigy has enormous natural inborn talent, the child puts great effort and time into developing that skill. For example, in chess the child devotes endless hours memorizing some of the great moves and strategies used in the game. In gymnastics, a well-known college coach estimated that to perfect a complex and dangerous move may require 2,000 repetitions over several years before the trick is mastered.

What is most interesting about the time and effort that many prodigies put into developing their inborn talent is that much of their effort is driven by self-determination and motivation to succeed. In essence, child prodigies believe that only through hard work and effort will their skill and talent be developed to its maximum. Furthermore, the many hours the prodigy spends nurturing and practicing that talent are often done with the help, guidance, and supervision of great coaches and teachers. These prodigies are a pleasure for the coach or teacher to work with because the prodigies are so coachable. However, that is not the entire story. Not all of the drive to develop talent is internal to the prodigy. Many gifted prodigies seem to benefit by the additional encouragement provided by their teachers, coaches, and mentors.

Converging Factors That Contribute to the Success of Stress-Resilient Children and Child Prodigies

When two lines of research findings such as the work on stress-resilient children and child prodigies converge, we can have greater confidence that the findings are valid. The common factors that account for the success of stress-resilient children and child prodigies include the need for mentoring and a belief that it is not fate that controls the future, but the effort and hard work that children spend in improving their lives that in the end will make a difference. Given these lines of converging evidence, if we want all of our students to develop high levels of reading skill, it is important that we ensure that all of our students have mentoring and a belief in an internal locus of control.

What One Teacher Does to Help Her Inner-City Students Beat the Odds

The 2000 National Reading Panel report (National Institute of Child Health and Human Development) emphasized that teacher quality was one of the most important factors in raising reading achievement. In the many years that I have been researching in schools, I have worked with numerous high-quality teachers, and I want to share what one particularly excellent teacher does to help her inner-city students. This teacher cooperated with me on the condition that I not identify her or her school. Consequently, I refer to her under a fictitious name, Ms. Shane.

Ms. Shane is highly educated. She has an undergraduate degree from Emory University in sociology, a master's degree from Georgia State, and has completed all the course work for the doctorate in curriculum and instruction at the University of Minnesota. She has been teaching fifth grade for the last 20 years and has seen the racial composition of her school change during that period. Currently, about 70% of the students at her school are Hmong, with other groups represented such as African Americans, Hispanics, and Caucasians. All the students at her school qualify for free breakfast because the income level is so low. Some students in Ms. Shane's class speak no English and have never been in a school before. These are the students who were living in the refugee camps in Thailand, whose parents, when forced to leave Thailand, decided to come to the Twin Cities.

Daily Oral Language (DOL)

Ms. Shane told me that she recognizes how important mentoring is to her students, and during the year that students are in her class she tries to mentor them. One way that she mentors them is through the use of a technique that many teachers use, called Daily Oral Language (DOL). Actually, a better name for this procedure would be Daily Written Language. Each morning before students come into the classroom there is a text on the board that contains grammatical, spelling, or punctuation errors. Here is an example of what the students might see:

> Some studentz think that because they were borne poor they will be poor all of their livez
>
> thay think there is nothing they can do to make a better lif four thimselves som other studentz think that if they get a good education, they can bild a better life four themselves
>
> what do you think.

Students have to correct the paragraph on the board and then write their opinion on whether fate or effort determines their futures. When using this DOL technique, the teacher reads the passage orally to the students. This is a necessary first step for several reasons, particularly because the spelling might be altered enough that students have difficulty reading the passage. The second step is for the students to correct the spelling and punctuation of the written assignment on the board. The third step is for the students to write down their opinion on fate versus effort and education that will be most important in determining their future. It is the fourth step that is most crucial for mentoring. Ms. Shane has the students read their answers to the class, with brief discussion after each presentation. During the discussions, Ms. Shane tries to steer the opinions so that students realize that through education and effort it is possible to build a happy life.

There are several examples of well-known Americans such as Abraham Lincoln, Bill Clinton, Booker T. Washington, Harriet Tubman, Sojourner Truth, and Frederick Douglass who were born into adverse circumstances and who managed to build a better life for themselves through hard work and education. For example, few realize that shortly before Bill Clinton was born in the tiny town of Hope, Arkansas, USA, his father died in an automobile accident, leaving Clinton's mother with no money and little chance of finding a good job because at the time she had no marketable skills. Realizing how important training would be to earn a living, Clinton's mother left her son in the care of relatives while she got a nursing degree in another city.

> During the discussions, Ms. Shane tries to steer the opinions so that students realize that through education and effort it is possible to build a happy life.

Clinton was lucky that his relatives provided excellent mentoring, instilling in him important social values and the realization that education held the key to his future. Ms. Shane reads books to her class about Americans who rose out of poverty and asks her class to identify how these children overcame their problems and became renowned people. A comment she made to me was enlightening. She said she knows she cannot save all of her students, but if she can help even one student develop the attitudes that will give that child a chance, she is satisfied.

Ms. Shane also told me she realizes how important it is for her students to develop good moral values. Middle class children are often exposed to good values from their parents or from church, but Ms. Shane has found that the values her students have often come from the street and are not conducive to beating the odds and building a good life. Therefore, she uses questions from *The Kids' Book of Questions* (Stock, 1988) as part of her Daily Oral Language. Here is a sampling of questions she uses from Stock's book to help her students develop good moral values:

- Who are your heroes? Why do you think they are so terrific?
- If you knew that by practicing hard every Saturday you could become the best in your school at whatever you wanted, what—if anything—would you work on? Now imagine looking back on your choice in twenty years; do you think you would wish you had picked something else to work on?
- If a rich kid wanted to buy your parents, how much would you ask for them—assuming you were willing to sell? Would you trade parents with any of your friends?
- When was the last time you were generous to a stranger just because you wanted to be nice?

- If you knew it would save the lives of ten starving children in another country, would you be willing to go without new clothes for the next year? What about bad acne for a year?

- When did you get yourself in the biggest mess by telling a lie? What do you think would have happened if you had just told the truth?

- How would you act differently if you had a younger sister who idolized you and tried to copy everything you did? What things do you think your parents do only because they want to set an example for you? (n.p.)

University Scholarships for Low-Income Students

Another thing that Ms. Shane does as a mentor is to take her class as well as other classes from her school on a field trip to visit the University of Minnesota. The parents and guardians of these students are urged to attend as well. There is good reason for wanting the parents to attend. The university has a policy of providing financial support to low-income inner-city students who have taken the desired courses and have good grades. Virtually none of the students who Ms. Shane brings with her have ever been to the University of Minnesota campus, or any college campus, before. The university takes them on a tour, during which they see the basketball and hockey arenas, the athletic facilities that are open to all students at the university, a science laboratory, classrooms and lecture halls, and the atrium in the College of Education where the entire ceiling is highlighted from a stained glass covering. After the tour, the students are brought into an auditorium where students from economically poor homes tell how they got to the university, and the students who have beaten the odds also describe the kinds of jobs they hope to get when they graduate. These students all have scholarships, and the parents of the students from Ms. Shane's school are usually very interested to learn what their children must do to qualify for a scholarship. Following the talks, the students are treated to lunch in one of the dorm cafeterias, and then they go back to their own school.

This half-day visit by inner-city children to the University of Minnesota is a wonderful, mind-broadening experience for them. Until their visit, most of them have no idea of what a university is like, nor do they realize that if they take the right courses and do well, they could attend the university. The books that Ms. Shane reads to her class about Americans who were born in difficult circumstances and who beat the odds, combined with the visit to the University of Minnesota, starts a process in which the inner-city students begin to think that perhaps they too can go to the university some day.

As a follow-up activity to the University of Minnesota visit, Ms. Shane invites the parents back to her classroom, and they review the requirements for getting financial aid to attend the University of Minnesota. In addition, Ms. Shane describes what the parents can do at home to help their children meet the standards of the university. In essence, when the culture of the home is similar to the culture of the classroom, children tend to do well academically. Following is a list of things that Ms. Shane suggests that parents can do to help their children in school:

- Regularity of time. Classrooms and schools run on schedules. At home the children know when it is time to wake up, when they must be ready to walk out the door to be on time for school, and when it is time to come inside and do homework. Children also have a time limit on how much television to watch. In successful homes, there is a regular time set aside for homework and for book reading.

- Regularity of place. Classrooms have a place for books, for papers, and for clothing, and the teachers strive to maintain neat rooms. When the same idea is carried to the student's home, the home has a place for eating, book storage, doing homework, and reading for enjoyment.

- Free time spent on cultural activities. Economically poor African American parents that had children who did well at school spent at least some of their free time visiting the library and taking out books, going to museums and zoos, and making sure that some of the television time was on educational topics.

- Interest in what children are learning in school. Parents regularly ask their children what they are learning in school. They also ask their children if they are having problems.

- Speech register. Formal speech, such as the speech used at work with a superior, is the same type of speech that is used in the classroom. On the other hand, informal speech can be used with one's friends. In successful homes, parents often use formal speech.

Parents who try to incorporate these characteristics in their homes often find that it helps their children at school.

Establishment of Personal Relationships

Ms. Shane claims that there are numerous dimensions to mentoring students, and one of them requires that the student and the teacher establish a personal relationship. Establishing a relationship is difficult to accomplish when the teacher is spending almost all of her time with the students under the instructional conditions of No Child Left Behind, in which the emphasis is on raising academic achievement. Consequently, Ms. Shane eats lunch by herself in her room, and that is a time when students can come and visit with her. Earlier I had written about mentoring being a two-sided coin with coachability representing the other side of the coin. Students who are the most coachable and in need of a personal relationship with their teacher come and visit with Ms. Shane. It is during these talks that some of the closest personal bonds are formed. In addition, students who suddenly find themselves in crisis situations come to Ms. Shane during the lunch periods to talk with her. I think that Ms. Shane has recognized an important requirement for efficient mentoring. That important requirement is the need to have some time outside of instruction when students can come and sit down to talk to her.

The final aspects of Ms. Shane's mentoring are in the realm of motivation. The two motivational approaches have to do with the use of Accelerated Reader (Renaissance Learning, 2000) and the use of stuffed animals. Ms. Shane believes that the article "If They Don't Read Much, How They Ever Gonna Get Good?" (Allington, 1977) captures an important component of developing competent and skillful readers, that is, the need for students to get a lot of practice reading appropriately leveled books.

The Accelerated Reader Program

Patricia Harvey, the former superintendent of schools at St. Paul, required that every student in the district read a minimum of 25 books in the academic year. By using the Accelerated Reader program, Ms. Shane has her students reading many times the number of books required by the school superintendent. Accelerated Reader is a computer-managed system that tests a student's comprehension of library books that the student has read independently. Part of the Accelerated Reader program is the STAR Reading Test (Renaissance Learning, 1999). This self-administered instrument determines each student's grade level of reading skill. The split–half reliability of the STAR Reading Test ranged from .89 to .93. The test–retest reliability of the STAR Reading Test ranged from .79 to .94.

Having information on each student's level of reading ability is important because it allows the students and the teacher to know what level of text difficulty is appropriate when selecting books from the library. The books in the school library are all color coded by grade level of text difficulty. Once the student's reading ability is determined by the STAR Reading Test, the student is encouraged to read books from the library that are color coded to represent the student's reading skill. In order to read as many books as possible, some students may rush through the books. To prevent this type of casual reading, the students are encouraged to read each book carefully, the goal being to get a score above 90% on the computer-administered quiz on the book the student has finished. When the student is finished reading a book, the student may go to the computer, log on, and take a comprehension test. As soon as the last test item on the quiz is answered, the computer gives immediate feedback to the student. If the student gets a 100% score, no matter what else is happening in the class, the student may yell out, "Yes!" and that is a signal to fellow students and Ms. Shane that the student got a perfect score. For a brief moment, all else in the class comes to a halt and everyone claps to show support for that student's achievement. Does the program work? Apparently so, because the students are reading their library books carefully, getting top scores, and reading far more than the 25 books mandated by the superintendent. As educators, we must realize that the Accelerated Reader program is not an instructional system. It is simply an efficient way to encourage and motivate students to read. Whereas most teachers agree that motivation is an important component in the instructional sequence, it is a badly neglected aspect of instruction. Accelerated Reader is a valuable tool teachers can use to get students to read a lot. One of the nice features of the program is that once it is in place, without an investment of time from the teacher, students can test themselves and get immediate feedback on the books they read.

Reading to Stuffed Animals

We come now to what is arguably the most innovative aspect of Ms. Shane's mentoring activities, and that is her use of small stuffed animals that the students believe enjoy having a student read orally to them. Figure 1.1 shows a picture of Humphrey, a tiny stuffed camel with his camel jewelry, who happens to belong to Ms. Shane. Each student in Ms. Shane's room is encouraged to bring in a small stuffed animal. If you walk down the hall outside of her class, you may see boys and girls sitting on the floor reading a book to their own stuffed animal friend. If you walk into her classroom during instruction you may see her ask a question and the children raise the paws of their animals to indicate they want to respond to the question. Use of these animals has become one of the dominant unifying forces in the room. Its popularity is such that second graders start a three-year personal campaign to get assigned to her room upon finding out how much fun Ms. Shane's fifth graders have with their animals.

FIGURE 1.1
Stuffed Animal Reading Partner From Ms. Shane's Classroom

Other teachers who have tried to duplicate the process using other stuffed animals have had far less success. I have observed Ms. Shane at work with her students and their animals and I have observed the other teachers who are trying to use her technique. Through these observations I think I understand what the magic ingredient is that spells success or not. It has nothing at all to do with the breed of the stuffed animal. It has to do with the ability to suspend reality and to build a world in which these stuffed animals are treated not like inanimate toys but like real living animals that can understand what is going on. More than this, the animals are endowed with the ability to understand spoken language, and they like it when their owners read books to them. Have you ever watched children at play with their dolls as they talk to them as though they were living infants? That is what takes place in Ms. Shane's room. The students have learned to treat their stuffed animals as if they were living things. As she has tried to explain, it takes time to develop this suspension of reality and to treat the stuffed animals as if they can feel, think, and understand, and not every teacher has the ability to interact with stuffed animals and children in such a way that that reality is suspended. In addition, Ms. Shane's interactions with the stuffed animals are spread over the entire time the students are in school, whereas the less successful teachers limit their animal interactions only to the block of time allocated to reading.

When the students read a book, they read it orally to the animals. Ms. Shane explained that under the usual classroom conditions when struggling readers read silently to themselves, they may skip hard words. However, if they are reading orally to stuffed animals that are capable of understanding, it is important to read every word so that the animal will understand the story. It is interesting to observe the children read to the animals. The children are careful to read every word. If the student is a struggling reader, the student often will go back and reread a section to the animal so that it is read with expression. These animals understand the stories most easily when they are read with expression. Reading a story accurately and with expression to their stuffed animals is important because when the student is satisfied that he or she understands the story, the student will go to the computer and take the Accelerated Reader test on the book that was read independently.

Interestingly, Ms. Shane is not the only educator who has discovered how useful reading to an animal, stuffed or real, can be. *The New York Times* (Engel, 2007) reported that Ms. Brennan, a third-grade teacher, decided that a student of hers was showing little progress because he did not get enough practice actually reading stories to improve. This child would not read to a person because he was so poor at reading that he was embarrassed, but reading to a pet terrier that was kept in her room was fun. Every day the student would walk over to a bookshelf and select a book. He then read the book to the dog, pointing to each word as he read and looking over the pictures. By June the boy was reading from a wide range of picture books and eagerly volunteering for read-aloud times. By this time he was accurate and reading with expression.

Conclusion

In closing this chapter, what message do I want to leave? There are many excellent reading methods teachers can use to develop reading skills. However, even the best methods are no match for some of the problems that students bring to school with them that are part of their personal lives. Before we can help our students learn to read with skill, we have to help them overcome their personal problems, and this aid comes in the form of a mentor. If we want to help students beat the odds and succeed in the game of life, all students need a mentor and a belief system in which students are convinced that hard work and education are the keys for overcoming the obstacles in order to lead productive and happy lives.

POSTREADING QUESTIONS

◆ I have often compared teaching to running and advise teachers to pace themselves. Teaching is not a 100-yard dash. It is a marathon, and one has to pace oneself to last a long time. This chapter states that all students need a mentor. Is this asking too much of teachers? If they try to emulate Ms. Shane, will teachers wear themselves out prematurely? Is it possible to be a mentor to children in your class and still go at a pace that allows you to sustain your efforts over a long haul, or is that asking too much?

◆ If you had to choose one thing that you could do to mentor your students, what would you choose to do first, and why would you choose that one item? Remember, the longest journey starts with the first step. What would this first step be?

REFERENCES

Adams, J., & Powell, J. (2007, April 13). A newborn's grisly death in Oakdale. *Star Tribune*, p. A1.

Albright, S. (2007, April 20). Mentors, intervention help kids and society. *Star Tribune*, p. A14.

Allington, R. (1977). If they don't read much, how they ever gonna get good? *Journal of Reading, 21*, 57–61.

Cohen, D.L. (1993). Schools beginning to glean lessons from children who "defy the odds." *Education Week, 12*(37), 18–19.

Engel, S. (2007, January 10). For a boy stumbling over words, a dog is the ideal reading partner. *The New York Times*, p. B7.

Feldman, D. (1979). The mysterious case of extreme giftedness. In A.H. Passow (Ed.), *The gifted and the talented: Their education and development* (78th yearbook of the National Society for the Study of Education, part I, pp. 335–351). Chicago: University of Chicago Press.

Garmezy, N., Masten, A., & Tellegen, A. (1984). The study of stress and competence in children: A building block for developmental psychopathology. *Child Development, 55*, 97–111.

Garmezy, N., & Rutter, M. (1983). *Stress, coping and development in children*. New York: McGraw-Hill.

National Institute of Child Health and Human Development. (2000). *Report of the National Reading Panel. Teaching children to read: An evidence-based assessment of the scientific research literature on reading and its implications for reading instruction* (NIH Publication No. 00-4769). Washington, DC: U.S. Government Printing Office.

Renaissance Learning. (1999). *The Standardized Test of Assessment of Reading* (Version 2.0) [Computer software]. Wisconsin Rapids, WI: Author.

Renaissance Learning. (2000). *The Accelerated Reader Program* (Version 5.12) [Computer software]. Wisconsin Rapids, WI: Author.

Stock, G. (1988). *The kids' book of questions*. New York: Workman.

Wallace, A. (1986). *The prodigy: A biography of William James Sidis, the world's greatest child prodigy*. New York: Macmillan.

High-Interest Reading Leaves No Child Behind

Rosalie Fink

Inspiring Reading Success: Interest and Motivation in an Age of High-Stakes Testing, edited by Rosalie Fink and S. Jay Samuels. © 2008 by the International Reading Association.

PREREADING QUESTIONS

◆ What level of success do you think striving readers can ultimately achieve?

◆ What factors do you consider most important for helping all kinds of readers succeed in literacy? In life?

◆ What are your views regarding the role of testing and assessment?

Teachers Under Pressure

Teachers today are under enormous pressure to ensure that all students pass state-mandated reading tests. The pressure is felt at all grade levels in diverse communities across the United States. A consequence of this high-stakes testing atmosphere is an emphasis on certain aspects of literacy at the expense of others. Overall, cognitive skills have been emphasized, often to the exclusion of literacy's motivational components. Yet based on my experience, getting students motivated and eager to read is crucial to their ultimate achievement. As a teacher of first graders as well as adolescents, I discovered that one of the best ways to generate excitement about reading is through texts about students' individual interests—whether their interests are typical school topics and genres like biography, science, and history or nonacademic topics like sports, pets, cars, drugs and alcohol, terrorism, and so forth.

As a classroom teacher and Title I reading specialist in rural upstate New York, I taught low-income children who came to school under extraordinarily difficult conditions—some were malnourished and came to school hungry; some lacked running water in the home and came to school dirty; some were victims of abuse and came to school damaged by physical and emotional scars. Yet, despite these formidable obstacles, many of my students ultimately succeeded in reading, a skill that opened a world of opportunities to them. I worked hard to get my students fired up and eager to read and, simultaneously, to raise their reading test scores. Early on I noticed that their motivation and skill performance seemed to go hand in hand.

Recently, a powerful body of research has supported what I observed. Several studies have shown that students' interests play a pivotal role—both in motivating them to read and in enhancing their reading levels (Fink, 2006, 2007; Hidi & Renninger, 2006; Lipstein & Renninger, 2007; Renninger, 1992, 2000; Renninger & Hidi, 2002; Schiefele, 1996). In fact, new research suggests that the motivational aspects of reading are *equal in importance to* the cognitive aspects. Lipstein and Renninger (2007) explicitly categorized interest as "both a cognitive and affective motivational variable" (p. 138). Likewise, Verhoeven and Snow (2001) juxtaposed reading attitudes and beliefs with cognitive reading skills, indicating that the two are virtually inseparable.

Because reading motivation and reading skill are closely linked, the question for teachers is, How can I get my students excited about reading and, simultaneously, improve their scores on state-mandated exams? Teachers know that there is not a single magical answer because they know that different students learn to read differently (Fink, 2006, 2007; Fischer & Fusaro, this volume). Research conducted at the Harvard Graduate School of Education documents several developmental pathways that different children follow as they learn to read (see chapter 3, this volume). Yet, regardless of the specific pathway that a particular student follows, research has shown that intrinsic motivation trumps external motivation and has a longer lasting effect on ultimate reading outcomes (Ryan & Deci, 2000). And, interest in a topic spurs children's intrinsic motivation to read (Csikszentmihalyi, 1991; Fink, 1995/1996, 1998, 2002, 2003, 2006, 2007).

A national study that I began at the Harvard Graduate School of Education in the 1990s and later expanded (with support from the National Academy of Education and the Spencer Foundation) provides insight into the relationships among interest in a topic, intrinsic motivation, and high reading test scores. The study included 66 successful men and women who had struggled with severe reading problems as children yet ultimately succeeded in fields that demand sophisticated reading—fields such as medicine, law, business, theater, art, psychology, education, biology, physics, and so forth. Many of the individuals were outstanding professionals; some were the "movers and shakers" in their fields. For example, the group included Baruj Benacerraf, a Nobel laureate in medicine and physiology; George Deem, an internationally known artist; Lora Brody, a television/radio personality and author of Cooking With Memories (1989); Tania Baker, a professor of biochemistry at the Massachusetts Institute of Technology; G. Emerson Dickman, III, an attorney and president of the International Dyslexia Association; James R. Bensinger, a Brandeis University professor of physics; Florence Haseltine, a gynecologist and director of the Center for Population Research at the National Institutes of Health; and many others. Table 2.1 shows the name, profession, and workplace of each individual who participated in the study. All of them had overcome severe reading difficulties. All but one individual gave me permission to use his or her real name in the hope of inspiring and informing others. I used real names in all cases except three, in which pseudonyms were used to protect individuals' privacy due to the sensitive nature of the information.

The study compared reading development in the group of 66 successful readers who had struggled with a comparison group that was equally successful but had not struggled with reading. Equal numbers of men and women participated. The sample was not random but rather was selected based on level of educational and career achievement, field of expertise, gender, age, and socioeconomic level. Participants were considered successful if (1) they demonstrated professional competence recognized by peers in fields that require sophisticated reading and (2) they were financially self-supporting. Selection criteria met the International Dyslexia Association research definition of dyslexia (1994) and the Responsiveness to Intervention definition of a striving reader (Gresham, 2002).

TABLE 2.1
Successful Striving Readers

Name	Profession and Workplace
Men	
J. William Adams	Headmaster, The Gow School, South Wales, New York
S. Charles Bean	Neurologist, Clinical Associate Professor, Jefferson Hospital, Philadelphia, Pennsylvania
Baruj Benacerraf	Immunologist, Professor of Immunology and Chair, Dept. of Pathology, Harvard Medical School, Cambridge, Massachusetts
James R. Bensinger	Physicist, Brandeis University, Waltham, Massachusetts
William Brewer	Psychologist, Professor of Psychology, University of Illinois, Champaign, Illinois
Michael L. Commons	Psychometrician, Lecturer/Research Associate, Dept. of Psychiatry, Harvard Medical School, Cambridge, Massachusetts
Heriberto Crespo	Social Worker, Latino Health Institute, Boston, Massachusetts
Roy Daniels*	Biochemist, Director, Stanford DNA Sequencing/Technology Center, and Professor, Stanford University School of Medicine, Stanford, California
George Deem	Graphic Artist, Adjunct Professor of Art, University of Pennsylvania, Philadelphia, Pennsylvania
G. Emerson Dickman	Attorney at Law, Maywood, New Jersey
Charles Drake	Founding Director, The Landmark School, Beverly, Massachusetts
H. Girard Ebert	Interior Designer and Chief Executive Officer, H. Girard Ebert, Inc., Baltimore, Maryland
Donald Francis	Virologist/AIDS Researcher, Genentech, Inc., and Founder and President, VaxGen, Inc., San Francisco, California
Miles Gerety	Attorney at Law, State Public Defender, Bridgeport, Connecticut
Daniel Gillette	Learning Specialist and Coordinator of Advising, Boston Architectural Center, Boston, Massachusetts
Alexander Goldowsky	Program Developer, New England Aquarium, Boston, Massachusetts
David Gordon	Marketing Consultant, Adaptive Computing, Beverly, Massachusetts
Philip Hulbig	Tutor, Walpole, Massachusetts
Robert Knapp	Gynecologist, Professor and Chair, Dept. of Gynecology, Harvard Medical School, Cambridge, Massachusetts
John Moore	Social Worker, Boston, Massachusetts
Jonathan Pazer	Attorney at Law, Law Offices of Pazer & Epstein, New York, New York
Bart Pisha	Computer Specialist, Director of Research, Center for Applied Special Technology (CAST), Peabody, Massachusetts
Cruz Sanabria	Early Childhood Educator, Boston, Massachusetts
Michael Schweitzer	General and Vascular Surgeon, Virginia Surgical Specialists, Richmond, Virginia
David Selib	Sales Manager, Reebok International, Medfield, Massachusetts
Larry B. Silver	Psychiatrist and Writer, Clinical Professor of Psychiatry, Georgetown University School of Medicine, Washington, DC
Hilary Smart	Chief Executive Officer, Industrial Products Company, Boston, Massachusetts
James Soberman	Dentist, Clinical Assistant Professor of Prosthodontics, New York University, New York, New York
Michael Spock	Codirector/Researcher, Chapin Hall Center for Children, University of Chicago, Chicago, Illinois
Michael Van Zandt	Research Scientist, Institute for Diabetes Discovery, Branford, Connecticut
A. McDonald Vaz	Writer, Miami Beach, Florida
Thomas G. West	Writer, Visualization Research Institute, Washington, DC
Glenn Young	Learning Disabilities Program Specialist, Washington State Dept. of Social & Health Services, Seattle, Washington

(continued)

TABLE 2.1 (continued)
Successful Striving Readers

Name	Profession and Workplace
	Women
Hannah Adams	Elementary Teacher, Cambridge, Massachusetts
Tania Baker	Biochemist and Professor, Massachusetts Institute of Technology (MIT), Cambridge, Massachusetts
Barbara Bikofsky	Special Educator, Adjunct Instructor, Lesley University, Cambridge, Massachusetts
Lori Boskin	Director of Alumni Relations, Special Projects & Promotions, University of California Los Angeles School of Law, Los Angeles, California
Lora Brody	Cookbook Author, TV and Radio Personality, Newton, Massachusetts
Terry Bromfield	Special Educator, Adjunct Assistant Professor, Lesley University, Cambridge, Massachusetts
Dale S. Brown	Program Manager, The President's Committee on Employment of People With Disabilities, Washington, DC
Susan E. Brown	Filmmaker, New York, New York
Ann L. Brown (deceased)	Researcher/Educator, Professor of Education, University of California, Berkeley, California
Jane Buchbinder	Fiction Writer, Boston, Massachusetts
Susan Cobin	Administrator/Principal, Talmud Torah Day School, St. Paul, Minnesota
C. Ellen Corduan	Theater Set Designer/Teacher, The Walnut Hill School, Natick, Massachusetts
Ellen Gorman	Social Worker, New Haven Adult Education, New Haven, Connecticut
Stacey Harris	Attorney at Law, Brookline, Massachusetts
Florence Haseltine	Gynecologist and Director, Center for Population Research, National Institutes of Health, Washington, DC
Marlene Hirschberg	Arts Administrator/Director, Jewish Community Center, Milwaukee, Wisconsin
Melissa Holt	Head Teacher, South Shore Day Care, Quincy, Massachusetts
Annette Jenner	Neurobiologist, Biology Teaching Fellow, Harvard University, Cambridge, Massachusetts
Sylvia Law	Attorney at Law, Professor of Law, Medicine, & Psychiatry, New York University School of Law, New York, New York
Nancy Lelewer	Writer, Research Associate in Neurology, Harvard Medical School, Cambridge, Massachusetts
Joanne Lense	Social Worker, Bronx Lebanon Hospital & Knight Education, New York, New York
Susan Marlett	Artist, Clearway Technologies, Fort Lee, New Jersey
Robin Mello	Storyteller/Actress, Adjunct Instructor, Tufts University & Lesley College, Boston and Cambridge, Massachusetts
Fiona Moore	Social Worker, Human Resource Institute, Brookline, Massachusetts
Tania Phillips	Elementary Teacher, Northampton, Massachusetts
Priscilla Sanville	Arts Educator, Adjunct Assistant Professor, Lesley University, Cambridge, Massachusetts
Maureen Selig*	Social Worker, Easton Hospital, Easton, Pennsylvania
Charlann Simon	Author & Program Developer, Speech/Language and Learning Specialist, Tempe, Arizona
Amy Simons	Attorney at Law, Assistant State Attorney, Dade County State Attorney's Office, Miami, Florida
Jane Smith*	Anthropologist, American University, Washington, DC
Beth Steucek	Manager, Executive Vice President, New England Innkeepers, Portsmouth, New Hampshire
Lezli Whitehouse	Speech/Language Specialist, Boston, Massachusetts
Kathleen Yellin*	Hotel Manager, Boston, Massachusetts

* Indicates a pseudonym.

Reprinted from Fink, R. (2006). *Why Jane and John couldn't read—And how they learned: A new look at striving readers* (pp. 3–5). Newark, DE: International Reading Association.

(For additional details about selection criteria and methodology, see *Why Jane and John Couldn't Read—And How They Learned* [Fink, 2006].)

Questions About Striving Readers

Several questions intrigued me about these successful readers who had struggled: (1) How did they eventually learn to read despite years of failure and reading difficulties? (2) What factors contributed to their resilience? (3) What level of reading ability did they ultimately achieve? (4) At what age had they developed basic fluency? (5) Are they fluent readers today and, if so, according to what definition of fluency? (6) Were there any gender differences and, if so, what were they? (7) What instructional materials and strategies can be used with students with diverse interests at different ages?

Interviews and Reading Test Results

I interviewed each of the 66 participants individually in lengthy, face-to-face interviews (3–9 hours each). Interviews were audiotaped and transcribed in their entirety in order to preserve rich descriptive detail and ensure accuracy. I also administered six formal and informal reading assessments to each individual. The reading assessments included the Diagnostic Assessments of Reading With Trial Teaching Strategies (DARTTS); the Nelson–Denny Reading Test of Vocabulary, Reading Comprehension, and Reading Rate, Form H; the Pig Latin Test; the Florida Nonsense Passages; the Graded Nonword Reading and Spelling Test; and the Adult Reading History Questionnaire. (See *Why Jane and John Couldn't Read—And How They Learned* [Fink, 2006] for additional details about the methods used in the study.)

Becoming Highly Skilled Readers

Avid Readers. The interviews and reading tests were full of surprises about how each individual had learned to read. The first thing I noticed was a surprising pattern that I had not expected—they were all avid readers. They did not (as I had expected) bypass reading in order to learn; instead, they read a lot as children.

> You'd start reading a lot—because you like it.
> —Roy Daniels, biochemist

Skilled, Lifelong Readers. The second thing I discovered was that they all became highly skilled, lifelong readers (see Table 2.2). According to the results of reading tests administered to them in adulthood, these men and women understood complex, sophisticated texts and scored high on all upper level skills, including vocabulary knowledge and silent reading comprehension. In fact, their mean reading comprehension score equaled 16.9 GE on the Nelson–Denny Reading Test (a grade equivalent above the fourth year of college).

TABLE 2.2
Reading Test Results

A. Performance on Literacy Tests and Adult Reading History Questionnaire*

	Nondyslexic Controls (*n* = 10)	Individuals With Dyslexia			Contrasts**	
		Fully Compensated (*n* = 17)	Partially Compensated (*n* = 43)	Total Dyslexics (*n* = 60)	Controls v. Total Dys.	Full v. Partial
DARTTS (% Adults Obtaining GE < 12th Grade)*						
Word Recognition	0	0	30.2	21.7	.103	.010
Oral Rdg. Accuracy	0	0	55.8	40.0	.014	.001
Silent Comp'n	10	0	6.9	5.0	.528	.264
Spelling	40	0	79.0	57.0	.327	<.001
Word Meaning	0	0	6.9	5.0	.470	.264
Nelson–Denny						
Vocabulary						
Raw Score *M* (SD)	79(.6)	75.9(4.4)	73.9(5.0)	73.5(6.3)	.008	.155
GE *M*	18.9	17.5	16.9	16.9		
GE Range	18.9–18.9	14.6–18.9	11.6–18.9	11.6–18.9		
Comprehension						
Raw Score *M* (SD)	75.2(4.4)	70.5(3.9)	67.7(5.6)	68.7(6.7)	.004	.056
GE *M*	18.9	18.6	17.1	171		
GE Range	16.4–18.9	13.2–18.9	9.6–18.9	9.6–18.9		
Rate (% With *s.s.* < 180)	0	0	33.0	23.3	.088	.007
% Using Extended Time	0	53	60	58	.001	.594
Adult Reading History Questionnaire						
Total Score *M* (SD)	.07(.04)	.57(.09)	.61(.09)	.60(.09)	.0001	.126
Range	.01–.15	.38–.75	.38–.82	.38–.82		
Florida Passages						
# Seconds *M* (SD)	25.3(8.4)	78.5(17.8)	106.7(38.9)	98.7(36.5)	.0001	.0060
Range	17–50	51–112	51–225	51–225		
# Errors *M* (SD)	1.5(1.0)	8.8(3.0)	14.5(6.0)	12.9(5.9)	.0001	.0004
Range	0–4	4–13	4–27	4–27		
Pig Latin Test						
# Correct *M* (SD)	44.2(5.6)	40.4(7.5)	30.0(11.9)	33.0(11.8)	.005	.002
Range	30–48	24–48	1–47	1–48		
Graded Nonword Tests						
Reading *M* (SD)	19.8(.4)	17.1(1.9)	15.0(3.5)	15.6(3.3)	.0002	.0231
Range	19–20	13–20	6–20	6–20		
Spelling *M* (SD)	18.8(1.3)	16(2.4)	13.0(4.6)	13.8(4.3)	.0007	.0136
Range	16–20	11–20	2–19	2–20		

(continued)

* Full data set available upon request (participants' identities withheld)
** Observed probability levels from the statistical contrasts; the first column of contrasts shows comparisons between the nondyslexic comparison group and the total number of individuals with dyslexia; the second column of contrasts shows comparisons between fully compensated and partially compensated individuals with dyslexia.
*** GE = grade equivalent; maximum performance on the DARTT is 12th-grade level (Roswell & Chall, 1992).

TABLE 2.2 (continued)
Reading Test Results

B. Adult Self-Reported Reading Habits, Using a Scale of 0 to 4 From the Adult Reading History Questionnaire*

| | Nondyslexic Controls ($n = 10$) | Individuals With Dyslexia | | | Contrasts** | |
		Fully Compensated ($n = 17$)	Partially Compensated ($n = 43$)	Total Dyslexics ($n = 60$)	Controls v. Total Dys.	Full v. Partial
Work-Related Reading						
(% Reporting a Great Deal)	100%	88%	67%	73%	.063	.101
Mean Response (SD)	3.7(.5)	3.5(1.0)	3.0(.9)	3.1(.9)	.0683	.0652
Range	3–4	0–4	1–4	0–4		
Pleasure Reading						
(% Reporting a Great Deal)	80%	53%	37%	42%	.025	.265
Mean Response (SD)	3.4(.8)	2.5(1.1)	2.2(1.3)	2.3(1.2)	.0081	.4049
Range	2–4	0–4	0–4	0–4		
Book Reading						
Mean Response (SD)	3.7(.6)	2.5(1.2)	2.4(1.4)	2.4(1.3)	.0046	.7966
Range	2–4	0–4	0–4	0–4		
Magazine Reading						
Mean Response (SD)	3.2(1.2)	2.0(1.3)	2.0(1.4)	2.0(1.4)	.0113	1.0
Range	0–4	0–4	0–4	0–4		
Daily News Reading						
Mean Response (SD)	3.5(1.0)	2.9(1.4)	2.7(1.4)	2.8(1.4)	.1142	.6199
Range	1–4	0–4	0–4	0–4		
Sunday News Reading						
Mean Response (SD)	3.8(.4)	2.9(1.0)	2.7(1.0)	2.8(1.0)	.0019	.4879
Range	0–1	1–4	0–4	0–4		

* Full data set available upon request (participants' identities withheld)

** Observed probability levels from the statistical contrasts; the first column of contrasts shows comparisons between the nondyslexic comparison group and the total number of individuals with dyslexia; the second column of contrasts shows comparisons between fully compensated and partially compensated individuals with dyslexia.

Reprinted from Fink, R.P. (1998). Literacy development in successful men and women with dyslexia (pp. 322–323). *Annals of Dyslexia, 48,* 311–346. Used with kind permission of Springer Science and Business Media.

Also previously published in Fink, R. (2006). *Why Jane and John couldn't read—And how they learned: A new look at striving readers* (pp. 15–16). Newark, DE: International Reading Association.

The third thing I learned was that the 66 individuals in my study developed most of the characteristics of Chall's Stage 5—the highest level of skilled reading (Chall, 1996). Stage 5 entails reading for one's own personal and professional purposes and reading materials that are "highly difficult, specialized, technical, and abstract" (Chall, 1983, p. 100). The striving readers in this study demonstrate each of these skills. Their high performance on the reading assessments attests to their ability to read, understand, make inferences, and create meaning from text—all Stage 5 skills. Moreover, many of the individuals have written major books and articles. Their impressive publications demonstrate the creation of new knowledge in their fields of expertise—a hallmark of skilled reading at the highest possible level. (A Stage 5 skill that many of them still lack is rapid reading speed. Many of them read slowly—even today.)

Passionate Interests

How had these individuals eventually succeeded as readers despite years of reading failure? I discovered a common motivational pattern from their stories: Each individual had had a burning desire to know more about a topic of passionate personal interest. Spurred by personal passion, curiosity, and intrinsic motivation, they all read voraciously, engaging in what Chall called "reading to learn" (1983, 1994, 1996). As children, they read everything they could find in order to learn more about a topic that fascinated them.

> I did a lot of reading; I loved reading about physics, so I got lots of physics magazines and books, and I just read about physics on my own.
>
> —James Bensinger, physicist

Although topics and genres of passionate interest varied, avid reading about a specific, fascinating topic was a common theme. Through lots of reading about topics of personal interest, these striving readers became familiar with the specific vocabulary, syntax, themes, and scripts of their favorite types of texts. Consequently, they developed deep background knowledge and became "little experts" about their favorite topics. The repetition and redundant text material itself provided some of the requisite drill and practice they needed to develop fluency and increasingly sophisticated reading ability. Table 2.3 summarizes their topics and genres of high-interest reading.

TABLE 2.3
Topic/Genre of High-Interest Reading

Women		Men	
n = 30		*n* = 30	
Novels	23	Novels	14
Biographies	2	Biographies	2
Science	2	Science	5
Social Studies	1	Social Studies	6
Cooking	1	Automechanics	1
No Data	1	Sailing	1
		Poetry	1

Gender differences in topics of high-interest reading were statistically significant (chi square = 5.71, *p* = .017).
Reprinted from Fink, R. (2006). *Why Jane and John couldn't read—And how they learned: A new look at striving readers* (p. 9). Newark, DE: International Reading Association.

TABLE 2.4
Ranges of Interests and Ages When Avid Reading Began

Name	Genre/Interest	Age
B. Benacerraf	Biography	age 7
R. Knapp	History	age 7
R. Daniels	Science	age 8
J. Bensinger	Physics	age 10
A. Simons	Math	age 10
E. Corduan	History	age 11
S. Bean	Poetry	age 12
A. Brown	Novels	age 13
B. Bikofsky	Novels	age 17
G. Deem	Novels	~age 22

Reprinted from Fink, R. (2006). *Why Jane and John couldn't read—And how they learned: A new look at striving readers* (p. 10). Newark, DE: International Reading Association.

Ages When Avid Reading Began

The ages when these striving readers began to read avidly varied considerably. Overall, those who began their avid, high-interest reading the earliest became the highest achievers. This finding fits with results from early intervention studies that suggest that the earlier a child receives intervention, the more likely it is that the child will eventually close the achievement gap and catch up to normally developing peers (Foorman, Francis, Beeler, Winikates, & Fletcher, 1997; Torgesen, Wagner, & Rashotte, 1997). Table 2.4 shows a range of the individuals, their interests, and the range of ages when they began to read avidly about a favorite topic (range = age 7 to age 22). The wide age range suggests that it is never too late to learn to read. And, as Nobel laureate Baruj Benacerraf's experience implies, it is never too late to hone and refine literacy skills to higher and higher levels:

> My problems were earlier.... And from about 11 or 12, I surmounted it; I surmounted my reading problem.
>
> —Baruj Benacerraf, immunologist

Fascination and Flow

The 66 individuals became increasingly fluent and ultimately were transformed by reading their favorite types of texts. Many became so deeply engrossed while reading that they lost awareness of everything else around them, so much so that they were unlikely to hear a parent call, "Time for dinner!"—even though the parent was standing inches away in the same room. Czikszentmihalyi (1991) calls this total immersion and enjoyment a "flow experience"—the feeling of being carried away by a current, which often results in a loss of self-consciousness. For these striving readers, who became visibly anxious in many reading situations, this feeling of flow while reading about a topic of personal interest was truly liberating.

Late Fluency

All of these readers showed a consistent pattern of delay in fluency. On average, they developed basic fluency (or smoothness and accuracy in reading with appropriate expression, intonation, and comprehension) between the ages of 10 and 12. This is approximately 3 to 4 years later than typically developing peers, who usually develop basic fluency between ages 7 and 8 (Chall, 1983, 1996). Fluency development represented a major turning point for each of the individuals in this study. No matter how long it took them, all of them remembered when, and with whose help, they had finally learned to read. They recalled the experience with vivid emotion and poignant memories of important mentors.

> In fifth grade, I finally learned to read; it was a big change! I remember it clearly: Mrs. King helped me.
> —James Bensinger, physicist

Ongoing Problems

Although they eventually became skilled readers, many individuals in this study continued to fail courses—especially in middle school, high school, college, and graduate school, when the curriculum demands got tougher. And many continued to grapple with ongoing problems in word recognition and sound analysis—lower level skills that for some remain weak in adulthood. Despite years of instruction and practice in phonemic awareness and phonics, some who had learned the sound–symbol relationships of English still have trouble applying this knowledge due to ongoing problems with blending and sequencing. So, they use phonics, but not very effectively.

> I can look at a letter and tell you what the sound is, but I can't put it together into a word.
> —Marlene Hirschberg, arts administrator

> My phonetic sounds don't always fit with everybody else's. Yet it's not important to me; it's the idea that's important.
> —S. Charles Bean, neurologist

Schema Knowledge and Context Clues

The striving readers in this study were aware of the ultimate goal of reading—making meaning from text. How could they make meaning and think about ideas (higher level skills) despite their continuing problems with lower level skills such as letter identification, word recognition, and phonics? I analyzed the interviews and reading assessments and found that they relied on context.

Even today, when I can't figure out a word, I guess from the context. I guess what makes sense and usually have it right.

—Baruj Benacerraf, immunologist

These striving readers use the context to guess at words and monitor their own understanding, and they usually "have it right"—a finding that fits with Lefly and Pennington's (1991) discovery that compensated adults with dyslexia read unfamiliar words nearly as accurately as other skilled readers. But I wondered: How had they *become* accurate? I found that, by reading avidly about a favorite topic, they had developed deep background knowledge and schema familiarity, which enabled them to fill in the blanks correctly, because context clues were more reliable in a familiar schema. According to schema theory, a reader's prior knowledge creates a powerful advantage that facilitates accuracy and comprehension (Recht & Leslie, 1988; Rumelhart, 1980; Samuels, 2002). For example, a child's familiarity with the components of narrative schema (e.g., characters, setting, plot, problem, resolution) enables prediction and fulfillment of expectations. So, the more narratives a child reads, the better the child's ability to read new narratives with increasing ease and comprehension. Likewise, a child immersed in reading about science develops familiarity with the schema of science (i.e., the specialized vocabulary, technical concepts, experimental designs). This schema familiarity enables the child to read future science texts with increasing ease, accuracy, and comprehension.

Three Groups of Striving Readers

According to the reading test results, three groups of striving readers emerged from this study. Each group revealed a distinct profile, shown in Figure 2.1. One group, called *compensated readers*, showed few, if any, ongoing weaknesses, scoring high in every category of reading (one third of the individuals). In contrast, there were two groups of *partially compensated readers* (two thirds of the individuals) who showed jagged, uneven profiles of strengths and weaknesses. Both groups scored high in upper level, meaning-making skills (such as vocabulary knowledge and silent reading comprehension). However, one group of partially compensated readers showed weaknesses mainly in spelling (about one third); the other group showed weaknesses in a variety of basic, lower level skills, including word recognition and oral reading as well as spelling (about one third).

Table 2.2 (see page 25) compares the striving readers with a matched comparison group and summarizes the assessment results. As might be expected, the comparison group outperformed all of the striving readers on all measures of reading. Perhaps most striking, however, ongoing jagged profiles persisted into adulthood for both groups of partially compensated readers. Furthermore, on the Nelson–Denny Reading Test, 58% of the striving readers were slow readers who used extended time to complete the test (refer to Table 2.2). Apparently, without the accommodation of extended time, many of them would have scored lower. They needed the extra time to process text information, repair and reconsider their understanding, and answer test questions accurately. This result fits with other re-

FIGURE 2.1
Profiles of Compensated and Partially Compensated Individuals With Dyslexia

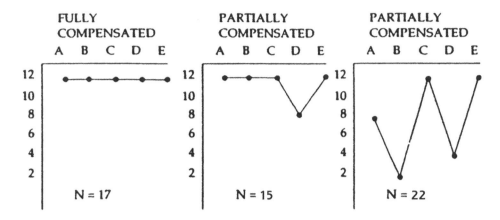

The numbers on the vertical axis represent the grade equivalent score. Maximum performance on this test (DARTT) is 12th-grade level.
A = word recognition, B = oral reading, C = silent reading comprehension, D = spelling, E = knowledge of word meanings. Six individuals did not fit into these types.
Adapted from Fink, R.P. (1998). Literacy development in successful men and women with dyslexia (p. 329). *Annals of Dyslexia, 48,* 311–346. Used with kind permission of Springer Science and Business Media.
Also previously published in Fink, R. (2006). *Why Jane and John couldn't read—And how they learned: A new look at striving readers* (p. 13). Newark, DE: International Reading Association.

search on testing outcomes and the benefits of struggling readers' use of additional time to utilize compensatory strategies effectively (Walczyk & Griffith-Ross, 2007).

The 66 striving readers in this study attended school prior to the age of high-stakes testing ushered in with the No Child Left Behind Act. What would have happened to these individuals had they been in school today and been subject to passing state-mandated tests? How would they have fared in today's testing atmosphere? Would they have graduated with high school diplomas, completed college and graduate school, and succeeded in their various professions? Given their jagged, uneven skills, would they have been given testing accommodations? We can only guess about answers to these questions. However, given some of their ongoing difficulties with basic, lower level skills, it seems likely that some of these individuals would have failed today's high-stakes tests and, consequently, been denied high school diplomas.

The jagged, uneven profiles of ongoing strengths and weaknesses in two thirds of the group (the partially compensated readers) suggests that a subset of these striving readers may have followed a different developmental pathway from that of most skilled readers. Instead of following a steady, forward-moving ladder-like pathway on which the rungs of the ladder represent the step-by-step hierarchy in which one skill builds incrementally upon another, they followed something akin to Fischer's web-like pathway, moving simultaneously forward and backward in a messy, multidirectional pathway (see chapter 3, this volume). Their ongoing problems with basic, lower level skills suggests that they would have had great difficulty passing the state-mandated tests required for high school graduation in many states in the United States today.

Jagged Profiles: An Individual Case Study

Nowhere is the concept of a jagged, uneven profile more apparent than in the case of Roy Daniels, an eminent scientist and professor of biochemistry and genetics at Stanford University School of Medicine. Despite his severe struggles with reading, Roy Daniels became a world leader in science and one of the youngest members elected to the U.S. National Academy of Sciences. Currently, he conducts cutting-edge genomics research on muscular dystrophy, cystic fibrosis, and other devastating diseases and has written over 175 articles and a major textbook. However, Daniels's early years did not foreshadow a stellar career in science.

> I was at the bottom in reading skills and spelling. I was a very, very slow reader and couldn't read out loud or silently...throughout grade school. I had to repeat first grade because of my reading problems.
>
> —Roy Daniels, biochemist

Daniels received extensive tutoring in reading and, eventually, at the age of 11, developed basic fluency. However, he continued to have difficulty identifying letters and their corresponding sounds and, as an adult, still has trouble distinguishing between letters that look alike (e.g., *b, d, p, q*). Yet, despite these weaknesses, Daniels was an avid science reader as a child, voraciously reading science books and magazines. He was propelled by his intense interest—what Winner (1996) calls a "rage to master" a subject (p. 4). Driven by passionate interest, he read many advanced science books and journals despite his difficulties with lower level visual–graphic and phonological decoding skills.

> When I was a freshman in high school, I read quite a few college texts. I became fascinated with nitrogen chemistry, so I got organic chemistry textbooks and read them and various aeronautic journals.
>
> —Roy Daniels, biochemist

Hands-On Activities. Hands-on activities were also pivotal to Daniels's ultimate success. In addition to scientific reading, Daniels immersed himself in stimulating, hands-on science activities: He designed experiments, ordered chemical supplies, and conducted chemistry investigations for fun. These active, playful hands-on activities helped him develop deep scientific background knowledge and self-confidence.

> I set up a lab in my basement and did experiments.... That early experience was useful, building your own confidence by doing these things.
>
> —Roy Daniels, biochemist

Early on, Daniels made an astute observation: He noticed a disparity between his own capabilities and the assessments of people in authority.

> In grade school I could estimate in math...instantly, better than other kids. This gave me confidence. Yet people would tell me that I couldn't do it. Now that immediately questions their credibility. You begin to question their wisdom and trust yourself more.
> —Roy Daniels, biochemist

While Daniels was learning to trust himself, his high school guidance counselor discouraged him from pursuing science and forbade him to take elementary algebra due to his reading difficulties and low score on an intelligence test (administered under standard timed conditions). Unfortunately for Daniels, unitary notions of intelligence prevailed at the time; intelligence was considered a single trait that individuals either possessed or lacked. More complex, dynamic concepts of intelligence were still in the future—for example, Gardner's theory of multiple intelligences (1983), which acknowledges the coexistence of different types of intelligences at different levels within the same person. Daniels's guidance counselor focused on Daniels's score of 90 (low normal range) on a single IQ test and concluded that Daniels was a slow learner, incapable of all abstract reasoning regardless of the subject. So he forbade Daniels to take elementary algebra, urging him to take shop instead, saying, "You can't be a chemist; you don't even qualify to be a chemist's assistant washing dishes. Your aptitude is not high enough even for that. With an IQ of 90, you'll never pass algebra. Forget the algebra, and major in shop."

Daniels's father was a carpenter and would have been happy to have his son major in shop and become a carpenter—just like dad. Both parents were loving but had only completed the eighth grade, so they lacked the educational background to recognize their son's scientific talents. But Daniels was fascinated by science and knew that he wanted to go to college to become a scientist. Keenly aware that algebra was a requirement for college, Daniels defied his counselor, saying, "'Okay, I'll take shop, but I'm going to take the algebra class too'.... We argued, and then he said, 'Okay, go and take it, and when you flunk out, I'm going to tell you I told you so.'" Undaunted, Daniels borrowed the algebra textbook over the summer and read it slowly and haltingly, in a manner typical of many striving readers when they encounter unfamiliar material. Reading slowly and methodically in this way, he gradually mastered the concepts and, eventually, earned a final grade of 95%—the highest grade in the class.

Yet, despite his algebra success, several teachers concluded that Daniels was not "college material" due to his slow reading and "horrendous" spelling. They refused to write him recommendations, telling him that the college requirements for English classes were far too stiff for him, his IQ was too low, and so forth. Nevertheless, Daniels decided to apply anyway, demonstrating the same kind of gritty persistence reported in other studies of successful readers who struggled but did not give up (Gerber & Reiff, 1991). He applied to a community college (where recommendations were not required), was accepted, attended for a few semesters, and then transferred to a four-year university. Ultimately Daniels graduated from college, earning straight A's in all his science courses.

Uneven Reading Abilities. Daniels earned straight A's in science from grade school through graduate school, which reflects his interest and proficiency in scientific reading (which he loved and did avidly). However, Daniels avoided doing most assigned reading in English, history, and other noninterest subjects. As a result, he got less practice and fell further and further behind in those subjects, sometimes even failing courses.

> I got an F in English Comp. So I researched all the English teachers and figured one who would give me a passing grade, given my spelling problems.
>
> —Roy Daniels, biochemist

Ultimately, Daniels passed English composition the second time around by using a problem-solving approach that Gerber and Reiff (1991) call "reframing." Reframing is a realistic, positive approach that involves naming, facing, and acknowledging a problem—then creatively seeking alternative solutions. Daniels's solutions included applying to colleges where recommendations were not required and seeking a college professor more likely to understand his spelling difficulties.

Testing and Accommodations. Daniels's goal was to become a PhD-level scientist. After graduating from college, he applied to doctoral programs, which meant taking the Graduate Record Examination (GRE). The GRE consists of timed silent reading comprehension questions. Even the chemistry section tests reading comprehension (see sample questions at www.ets.org/Media/Tests/GRE/pdf/Chemistry.pdf). Daniels's jagged, uneven profile was evident in his GRE test results, which showed high skill peaks and low skill valleys. In chemistry, Daniels scored in the top 99.9th percentile nationally on the Graduate Record Exam. However, in sharp contrast, he scored in the lowest 16th percentile in English and was consequently rejected by several graduate schools. Nevertheless, the California Institute of Technology admitted him to its doctoral chemistry program, taking a chance on him despite his discrepant test scores. Once at Cal Tech, Daniels excelled in science courses and hands-on laboratory experiments.

However, he had a serious problem as a graduate student: Daniels failed the required French proficiency exam at Cal Tech—not once, but several times. He was told that he would flunk out if he did not pass the French exam. Consequently, he studied hard and took special test preparatory courses; however, he continued to take—and fail—the French test. Eventually, a special mentor advocated for Daniels. Norman Davidson, Daniels's thesis advisor, recognized Daniels's talent as an experimentalist and argued for special accommodations for him in French.

> He went to bat for me and convinced the graduate committee to let me do a translation project instead of the test. And they let me use a dictionary for the translation. They sent me a letter that said, "The Graduate Committee accepted your translation. Congratulations." It was the happiest day of my life! I owe it to Norman Davidson.
>
> —Roy Daniels, biochemist

Without accommodations and help from Norman Davidson, his mentor, Daniels would have flunked out of graduate school. His dream of becoming a scientist would have been shattered, and we would not have benefited from his discoveries—discoveries that have spawned major advances in modern medicine and saved lives. We can only surmise how Roy Daniels would fare in today's high-stakes testing climate given the peaks and valleys in his reading skills.

Daniels's Reading in Adulthood. Today, Roy Daniels reads at college and graduate school levels with regard to upper level, meaning-making skills such as vocabulary knowledge and silent reading comprehension. However, he still has gaps in basic lower level skills such as word recognition (out of context), word analysis, spelling, and oral reading, as shown by results on the Diagnostic Assessments of Reading With Trial Teaching Strategies (DARTTS). Based on results of this test, Daniels's spelling is at a sixth-grade level, his oral reading at an eighth-grade level. (Figure 2.2 shows additional DARTTS test results.) As an adult, Daniels still moves his lips when reading silently the way children do when they are first learning to read. This slows him considerably (Nelson–Denny Reading Rate SS = 181). Daniels's slow reading speed indicates his poor integration of visual–graphic, phonological, and semantic meaning-making skills. Clearly, he has not developed the seamless automaticity of most skilled readers. However, his overall functioning as a reader is high. He comprehends and writes at very high levels, suggesting that he developed his reading ability through a different developmental pathway from that of most readers. Like one third of the individuals in this study, Daniels did not follow a normative pathway in which visual–graphic, phonological, and semantic skills became seamless, instantaneous, and automatic. For him, the elements of visual–graphic, sound analysis, and meaning-making skills remain poorly integrated.

Is Daniels a Fluent Reader? Daniels still lacks speed and automaticity when reading unfamiliar material. He could not automatically distinguish between *horse* and *house* when I tested him on the Matching Words subtest of the DARTTS (refer to Figure 2.2 for Daniels's DAR test summary). In contrast, when reading science texts, Daniels reads with apparent ease, speed, and automaticity. He comprehends complex science books and articles at the highest possible level due to the wealth of science background knowledge from which he draws. However, in less familiar content areas such as English literature, history, and foreign languages, Daniels shows clear evidence of dysfluency: an extremely halting, hesitant oral style, lack of appropriate expression and prosody, and frequent decoding errors. So Daniels's fluency as a reader varies, depending on the content area or genre. He reads different types of texts with varying degrees of fluency—depending on the text, its interest to him, its structure, familiarity, concepts, and vocabulary.

Content Area–Dependent Fluency

Roy Daniels's case study suggests that the more a student reads in one content area (such as science), the richer or better at reading the student becomes in that domain. This

FIGURE 2.2
DAR Interpretive Profile

Student Roy D. _____ Date of Birth _____ Grade Not Applicable

DAR Administrator Rosalie Fink   Teacher Not Applicable   (Adult)

DAR Test	DAR Level
Word Recognition	12
Word Analysis (Check if mastery is achieved.) √ **Consonant Sounds** -missed soft c √ **Consonant Blends** -missed drip √ **Short vowel Sounds** -missed short e & short u out of context; √ **Rule of Silent *E*** misread *sit* for *set* √ **Vowel Digraphs** √ **Diphthongs** √ **Vowels with R** √ **Polysyllabic Words** **Pre-Reading Subtests:** Simple matching task √ **Naming Capital Letters** √ **Naming Lowercase Letters** – confuses b/d √ **Matching Letters** √ **Matching Words** – very slow to figure out same or not the same; reported reading them twice to figure it out	
Oral Reading	8
Silent Reading Comprehension Subvocalized while spelling and reading silently.	12
Spelling See mistakes in spelling booklet	6
Word Meaning	12

1. For Word Recognition, Oral Reading, Silent Reading Comprehension, Spelling, and Word Meaning, enter the highest level for which the student achieved mastery.

2. For Word Analysis, check the subtests for which the student achieved mastery.

Note: See the TTS *Teacher's Manual,* especially "Part 2: Introduction to the Trial Teaching Strategies" And "Part 3: Preparing for Teaching," for information on reporting DAR results to students and Using results to plan and implement the TTS session with the student.

Reprinted from Fink, R. (2006). *Why Jane and John couldn't read—And how they learned: A new look at striving readers* (p. 78). Newark, DE: International Reading Association.

raises an intriguing question: Should the concept of fluency be expanded to embrace a more flexible concept similar to the way Gardner (1983) expanded the notion of intelligence to a more dynamic theory that included multiple intelligences? Perhaps there are multiple fluencies. A more flexible, intraindividual concept of fluency could help teachers understand how children like Roy Daniels read personally appealing texts at high readability levels with more ease and skill than they read other texts.

Test Failure and Persistence

The striving readers in this study sometimes failed important tests yet succeeded at high levels due in part to their hard work and persistence. Their ability to bounce back after failure, to keep on trying despite obstacles, helped them develop resilience and positive attitudes and habits, which enabled them to try new solutions and accommodations and, ultimately, develop their talents. In addition to developing persistence as an enduring personality trait, many striving readers in the study also revealed empathy, or the ability to feel *with* another person. They explained that they could empathize with others who struggle because they had been there and knew how it felt. This empathic trait probably helped them develop strong interpersonal connections—connections that turned out to be important when they needed assistance from mentors.

Mentoring

All 66 individuals attributed their success to help from marvelous mentors—adults who took a special interest in guiding them and providing invaluable encouragement and instruction. Who were these mentors? During the elementary school years, both the men and the women were mentored by parents (mostly by mothers). However, men in the study received academic help and guidance from extended family members such as grandparents, uncles, cousins, and so forth. In contrast, none of the women in this study received help from extended family.

Both the men and the women recalled equal numbers of elementary teachers who were marvelous mentors. However, beginning in middle school and extending through high school, college, graduate school, and the workplace, the men had twice as many mentors as the women. This was the case at home, at school, and at the workplace. This stark imbalance fits with other research findings that show mentoring disparities at home and at school based on gender (Whitehead & Maddren, 1974; Young, 2000). Men in this study received more attention at home.

> My brother has almost all the same learning problems that I have, but he got lots of attention. I didn't. My mother didn't even realize that I couldn't read until I was almost 11.
>
> —Florence Haseltine, gynecologist

> It was kind of like the whole world revolved around my brother Bob, who was dyslexic. My mother spent so much time with him! She ignored my sister Arlene and me, even though we were both dyslexic, too.
>
> —Kathleen Yellin, hotel manager

Teachers were crucial mentors for all of the striving readers in this study. Most important, teachers were essential mentors for students who lacked family support due to poverty and other difficult life circumstances. One example is Cruz Sanabria, who was born in Spanish Harlem in New York City, the son of poor Puerto Rican immigrants. One of seven children, Sanabria was raised by a single mom who was a high school dropout. Sanabria's mother loved him, but putting food on the table for seven growing children was a constant struggle for her. Consequently, she was unable to encourage her son in his education, let alone help him with his reading problems. However, Sanabria was supported at school by a very important teacher, a truly memorable mentor.

> Mr. Tilman is a teacher I'll never forget. He used the newspaper, which I was interested in from my paper route. And he got me psyched about reading by using comics and art, which fascinated me.
> —Cruz Sanabria, early childhood educator

The key importance of teachers as mentors of disadvantaged students in my study echoes Eric Cooper's crusade on behalf of African American students, whom he calls "school-dependent, not deficient" (Cooper, 2007). For these students, teachers matter enormously and can make the difference between failure or success, both in literacy and in life.

Summary of Findings

By reading avidly about a topic of passionate, personal interest, all of the striving readers in this study ultimately became high-level readers—even though it took them three to four years longer than their peers. Motivated by intrinsic interest in a favorite topic, they read extensively, developing deep background knowledge, schema familiarity, and contextual understanding. Familiarity with domain-specific vocabulary, themes, and typical text structures provided the scaffolds that supported their development of increasingly sophisticated literacy skills. Although they received instruction and tutoring in phonological decoding skills, two thirds of these striving readers never mastered spelling, and one third did not master spelling or other phonological decoding skills. Yet, all 66 individuals became skilled readers—scoring at the highest levels on silent reading comprehension and vocabulary tests. Some individuals (such as Roy Daniels) followed nonlinear developmental pathways and showed variable fluency, depending on the content area or genre. These results fit with other research that shows that not all children learn to read in the same way, and not all follow a traditional pathway in which the components of reading are highly integrated and seamless (Fink, 2006; Fischer & Knight, 1990; Mascolo, Li, Fink, & Fischer, 2002).

Teaching With the Interest-Based Model of Reading

The results of this study led to an interest-based model of reading instruction that explains how striving readers, who may continue to lack strong integration of basic, lower level phonological decoding skills, nevertheless can *and do* construct higher level meaning-making skills. The Interest-Based Model of Reading can be used to promote resilience and success for all types of children—typically developing students, English-language learners (ELLs), gifted and talented students, and struggling readers.

Key elements of the model include the following:

- A passionate, personal interest that spurs sustained reading
- Avid, topic-specific reading
- Deep schema knowledge
- Contextual reading strategies
- Mentoring support

Based on the Interest-Based Model of Reading, there are specific things that teachers and families can do to help all students develop into highly motivated skilled readers:

1. Discover each student's personal interests; then select motivating materials accordingly. Create content area libraries in classrooms with lots of enticing materials to spark a wide array of students' interests.

2. Look for underlying abilities and talents in each student—consider multiple intelligences and content area–dependent fluency.

3. Encourage hands-on activities at every age and stage of development.

4. Balance the reading program. Give equal time to three components: (1) motivational activities with high-interest materials, (2) explicit skills instruction, and (3) open-ended, thought-provoking discussions and activities.

5. Use identity-rich materials to enhance cultural pride and literacy growth in all students, including ELLs, typically developing students, gifted and talented learners, and striving readers.

Reading Interest Inventories

Based on the results of this study, teachers and families should provide compelling materials that match each child's individual interests. Students are likely to be enthusiastic and consequently read more books that explore a favorite topic—regardless of whether the topic is science, history, sports, auto mechanics, or romance.

How can busy teachers and families discover what interests and motivates each child? One way is to use a reading interest inventory, such as the reproducible adapted from Burns, Roe, and Ross (1992; see the reproducible Reading Interest Inventory on page 40). Reading interest inventories are quick and easy to administer and are easily modified to fit each student's age and developmental stage. Teachers can include questions about students' favorite media, which provide a great way to tap into the dormant interests of disadvantaged students, who often lack opportunities to develop interests through museum visits, ballet classes, music lessons, and so forth.

Reading Interest Inventory

- What is the best book that was ever read to you?

- What is the best book that you ever read yourself?

- What are your favorite hobbies?

- What after-school activities do you like best?

- What are some of your favorite movies?

- What television programs do you like the most?

- What are your favorite television specials, videos, DVDs, computer games, and Internet websites?

- What school subjects do you find most interesting?

- What pets, sports, or art activities do you like best?

- If you could take a trip, where would you go?

- What careers interest you?

Adapted from Burns, P.C., Roe, B.D., & Ross, E.P. (1992). *Teaching reading in today's elementary schools* (5th ed.). Boston: Houghton Mifflin.

Bio-Poems

Bio-poems are also superb for discovering students' interests. In bio-poems students write about themselves and draw self-portraits. Bio-poems are great because they can be used at all ages and grade levels. I have used bio-poems with young children and graduate students alike—and met with enthusiastic success in all cases. Not only did I learn what interests each student, but my students learned to appreciate one another's diverse interests as well. A bio-poem can be used with a whole class, a small group, or as a one-on-one activity. It can be used at any time but provides an especially fitting beginning-of-the-year activity to help students and teachers get to know each other. Included on page 42 is a reproducible Bio-Poem Protocol adapted by Florida middle school teacher Minnie Gross (personal communication, May 2, 2004).

"I" Poems

Like bio-poems, "I" poems, originally developed by Levstik and Barton (1997), provide a supportive structure to help students think, imagine, write about themselves, and get to know each other. I experimented with using an "I" poem in a class of graduate students, who liked it so much that they used it with their own elementary and middle school students. Their students were motivated to think deeply and write about themselves. They enjoyed sharing their poems with a partner and, later, with the whole class. In some cases, students then performed their poems for other classes and for parents and grandparents. See page 43 for the reproducible "I" Poem Protocol from Kucan (2007).

Locating Literature of Interest

Several resources are available to help busy teachers and parents find books to interest each student. *A to Zoo: Subject Access to Children's Picture Books* (Lima & Lima, 1993) is an excellent resource that reflects the interests of young children. This concise book lists preschool and elementary books alphabetically by topic. If a child is fascinated by dinosaurs, just look under "D" to find good books about dinosaurs. Another good resource is *100 Best Books for Children* (Silvey, 2004), which includes a plot summary and age range for each title. In addition, Children's Choices, a joint project of the International Reading Association (IRA) and the Children's Book Council, is a superb list of new books each year selected by children (see resources in Table 2.5 on page 44).

Leveled Books. Leveled books provide another source of interesting titles. To find titles for young children, consult *Matching Books to Readers: Using Leveled Books in Guided Reading, K–3* (Fountas & Pinnell, 1999). For titles for intermediate and middle school children, consult *Leveled Books for Readers, Grades 3–6: A Companion Volume to* Guiding Readers and Writers (Fountas & Pinnell, 2001) and *Guided Comprehension: A Teaching Model for Grades 3–8* (McLaughlin & Allen, 2002). In addition, the Degrees of Reading Power (DRP) system also lists interesting books by readability level. It is available as a CD-ROM and DRP-Booklink online under "Readability of Literature and Popular Titles" (www.tasaliteracy.com).

Bio-Poem Protocol

Line 1: First name only _____

Line 2: Four traits that describe you _____, _____, _____, _____

Line 3: Sibling of _____ (or son/daughter of _____)

Line 4: Loves _____, _____ _____ (3 people or things)

Line 5: Who feels _____, _____, _____ (3 items)

Line 6: Who needs _____, _____, _____ (3 items)

Line 7: Who gives _____, _____, _____ (3 items)

Line 8: Who fears _____, _____, _____ (3 items)

Line 9: Who would like to see _____, _____, _____ (3 items)

Line 10: Resident of (your city), (your street)

Line 11: Your last name (draw a picture of yourself)

"I" Poem Protocol

I am _____

I wonder _____

I hear _____

I see _____

I want _____

I am _____

I pretend _____

I feel _____

I touch _____

I worry _____

I cry _____

I am _____

I understand _____

I say _____

I dream _____

Reprinted from Kucan, L. (2007). "I" poems: Invitations for students to deepen literary understanding. *The Reading Teacher, 60,* 518–525.

TABLE 2.5
Choices Titles and Other Favorites

Refer to Choices Booklists at www.reading.org/resources/tools/choices.html

Grades K–2

Bano, M. (1999). *When Sophie gets angry—Really, really angry*. New York: Blue Sky Press.
Cronin, D. (2003). *Diary of a worm*. New York: HarperCollins.
Durant, A. (2003). *Dear Tooth Fairy*. Cambridge, MA: Candlewick.
Falconer, I. (2003). *Olivia...and the missing toy*. New York: Atheneum.
Reiss, M. (2003). *Late for school*. Atlanta, GA: Peachtree.

Grades 3–4

Davies, N. (2004). *Poop: A natural history of the unmentionable*. Cambridge, MA: Candlewick.
Flood, P.H. (2004). *It's test day, Tiger Turcotte*. Minneapolis, MN: Carolrhoda.
Pilkey, D. (1994). *Dog breath: The horrible trouble with Hally Tosis*. New York: Blue Sky Press.
Sharmat, M.W. (2004). *Nate the great*. New York: Dell.

Grades 5–6

Derby, K. (2004). *The top 10 ways to ruin the first day of 5th grade*. New York: Holiday House.
Estes, E. (1990). *Ginger Pye*. New York: Odyssey/Harcourt.
Mercado, N.E. (Ed.). (2004). *Tripping over the lunch lady and other school stories*. New York: Dial.
Nevins, C. (2004). *Karate hour*. New York: Marshall Cavendish.
Packer, T. (2004). *Tales from Shakespeare*. New York: Scholastic.

Grade 7–Adult

Byng, G. (2003). *Molly Moon's incredible book of hypnotism*. New York: HarperCollins.
Johnson, A. (2003). *The first part last*. New York: Simon & Schuster.
Mackler, C. (2003). *The Earth, my butt, and other big round things*. Cambridge, MA: Candlewick.
Paulsen, G. (2003). *The Glass Café*. New York: Wendy Lamb Books.
Spinelli, J. (2003). *Milkweed*. New York: Knopf.

Adapted from Fink, R. (2006). *Why Jane and John couldn't read—And how they learned: A new look at striving readers* (pp. 30–33). Newark, DE: International Reading Association.

Internet Searches. Internet searches are excellent for locating interesting materials. Students benefit from direct instruction on databases, websites, keyword search strategies, and criteria for evaluating the quality of Web information. *The Mysteries of Internet Research* (Cohen, 2003) is a helpful resource for grades 4–12 that uses a mystery format to teach students how to check facts on the Internet. (It also teaches the research process using print sources.) In addition, Story-Huffman's *Caldecott on the Net: Reading & Internet Activities* (2002a) for grades K–5 and *Newbery on the Net: Reading & Internet Activities* (2002b) for grades 4–8 have excellent suggestions for integrating award-winning literature with Internet activities and websites.

TABLE 2.6
Magazines and Newspapers for Children, Teens, and Adults

Arts

ASK (grades 1–4)
Dramatics: The Magazine for Students and Teachers of Theatre (grades 9–12)

Fiction

Cricket (grades 4–9)
Highlights for Children (grades 1–6)
Literary Cavalcade (grade 9–adult)

Multicultural Studies

Faces: People, Places, Cultures (grades 4–9)
Skipping Stones (grade 2–adult)

Social Studies

LibrarySparks (grades 3–9)
National Geographic (grades 2–adult)
TIME for Kids (K–6)
Weekly Reader (pre-K–grade 8)

Sports

Sports Illustrated for Kids (grades 3–10)

Science and Nature

ChicaDEE (K–grade 4)
Discover Magazine (grade 9–adult)
Kids Discover (grades 1–9)
OWL (grades 4–8)
Ranger Rick (grades 2–8)

Adapted from Fink, R. (2006). *Why Jane and John couldn't read—And how they learned: A new look at striving readers* (pp. 33–35). Newark, DE: International Reading Association.

Magazines. Student magazines and newspapers provide another highly motivating way to lure readers. Many students find the shorter articles less overwhelming than full-length books (see additional resources in Table 2.6 for an annotated list of children's periodicals organized by topic and genre).

Sustained Silent Reading (SSR)

Free reading is easy to integrate into any literacy program. Teachers can incorporate a widely used traditional approach, such as Sustained Silent Reading (SSR), in which each student selects and reads a book silently at a regular time each day. While students read, the teacher also reads silently, modeling good reading behavior. Usually, no work is assigned with SSR; students simply list the title of the books they read.

Voluntary Reading as Social Practice (VRSP)

A similar approach called the Voluntary Reading as Social Practice method (VRSP) includes an added conversational component in which students discuss their books with a peer, tutor, parent, or teacher. The added conversational component increases enthusiasm for reading and spurs students to borrow more library books (Parr & Maguiness, 2005). Both SSR and VRSP fulfill the National Research Council's recommendation that "*time, materials, and resources be provided daily for independent reading of texts of interest to each student*" (Snow, Burns, & Griffin, 1998, p. 324, author's emphasis).

Rhythm Walks

Rhythm Walks are exciting, highly motivating activities that use dance and body movement to support fluency development for a whole class, small groups, or pairs (see the reproducible Steps for Conducting a Rhythm Walk on page 47). Rhythm Walks provide opportunities for intensive instruction in repeated reading, a method that is key to success for all types of students (Samuels & Farstrup, 2006; see also chapters 1 and 6, this volume). As students repeat the Rhythm Walk, they incorporate increasing use of gesture, intonation, and expression. The result is an elaborate line dance that motivates students to read and, simultaneously, builds their fluency. Pairing skilled readers with less skilled readers who walk and read in unison is an excellent way to support students with learning disabilities and ELLs (Chard, Vaughn, & Tyler, 2002).

L1/L2 Books, Websites, and Activities

An exciting way to motivate students' identity development, cultural pride, and literacy development is simultaneously to build on the funds of knowledge that immigrant children bring from their home languages and cultures. Many ELLs struggle with learning academic literacy in the language of their adopted country (Cummins, 1994; Li & Zhang, 2004). Yet, some ELLs succeed despite their initial difficulties. One factor that contributes to their eventual success is their development of cultural pride and knowledge of their dual cultural and linguistic heritage (see Fink, 2006). Teachers can promote successful reading by utilizing children's knowledge and development of two languages simultaneously. According to recent work in bilingual literacy (Botelho, 2007; Chow & Cummins, 2003; Cummins, Chow, & Schecter, 2006), teachers should provide opportunities for speaking, reading, writing, and performing in L1, the child's home language, at the same time the child is developing speaking, reading, writing, and performing skills in L2, the main language of the predominant culture.

Maria José Botelho and her colleagues have developed intriguing ways to capitalize on immigrant children's home languages to build their English literacy skills—even when the teacher does not know the home language. They publish identity texts created and written by children in two languages—the home language and English. They use L1 to scaffold meaning, activate the child's prior knowledge, affirm and respect the child's multiple identities, and extend language development simultaneously in L1 and in L2. For

Steps for Conducting a Rhythm Walk

1. Before beginning, model the process for students.

2. Have the class choose a short poem, story, or informational text.

3. Analyze the text; decide where there are natural breaks and chunks through punctuation, line breaks, or context clues.

4. Write each "chunk" of text on a large rectangular cardboard strip. Write in large letters (about an inch and a half high).

5. Place strips in order—either in a curved or straight pathway on the floor. Place each strip a distance of one child-size step away from the other strip.

6. Have students line up in single file.

7. The first student reads the first strip aloud, steps to the next strip, reads this aloud, and so on until completing the passage.

8. Each student begins when the student in front has completed the first three strips.

9. Students who get to the end of the Rhythm Walk line up at the beginning and begin the process again (3–10 times).

10. To facilitate and monitor comprehension, students end with response journal writing and discussion questions.

Adapted from Peebles, J.L. (2007). Incorporating movement with fluency instruction: A motivation for struggling readers. *The Reading Teacher, 60*, pp. 578–581.

example, Canadian immigrants have simultaneously used their home languages and English to produce dramas, paintings, webpages, PowerPoint presentations, music, CDs, and other artifacts. Students work collaboratively, divide up tasks, and give and receive constructive feedback on their work. They tape record their presentations of the same story in two languages and also publish their written texts in two languages on the Web. Student pieces include stories, dramas, essays, and poems written in English and Urdu, English and Hebrew, and so forth. These activities affirm identity, promote literacy learning, and are both challenging and fun. Fascinating examples of these activities and samples of student work are available on several websites (see Table 2.7 for a list of resources).

TABLE 2.7
Multicultural Books and Websites

Books

Faeli, R. (2006). *Student exchange: Exploring cultures through school*. Clayton South VIC, Australia: Blake Education Pty Ltd.

Faeli, R. (2006). *The beat of the drums: African rhythms*. Clayton South VIC, Australia: Blake Education Pty Ltd.

Faeli, R. (2006). *Hinduism: History, beliefs, worship, and celebrations*. Clayton South VIC, Australia: Blake Education Pty Ltd.

Underwood, G. (2006). *Spirit of the Incas: Music from the Andes*. Clayton South VIC, Australia: Blake Education Pty Ltd.

Underwood, G. (2006). *Celebration of life: Indian culture and customs*. Clayton South VIC, Australia: Blake Education Pty Ltd.

Websites

Australian Multicultural Foundation: Blake Education
www.blake.com.au

City Lore
www.citylore.org

Doing Oral History
gcah.org/oral.htm

The Future We Want: Building an Inclusive Curriculum
www.gobeyondwords.org/splash.htm

The Multicultural Project Website
www.multiliteracies.ca

Parent Involvement in Education Project
www.yorku.ca/foe.Research/pie/2information.htm

Peel District School Board
thornwood.peelschools.org

Story Arts Online
www.cindislist.com/oral.htm

Urban Legends Reference Pages
www.snopes2.com

Readers Theatre

Readers Theatre is a highly motivating approach for developing fluency and deep comprehension. It emphasizes vivid oral reading and accurate interpretation of lines. Students do not memorize scripts; instead they read aloud and concentrate on voice interpretation and characterization. Readers Theatre provides practice in oral reading and emphasizes communication of meaning through voice intonation, expression, cadence, and speed. Readers perform with the script in hand, while the audience listens, provides feedback, and sometimes improvises endings (see Figure 2.3). By engaging students in short, dramatic scenes from great literary works, Readers Theatre can inspire students to read an entire literary work later on. This lively approach is for students of all ages, levels, and interests; I have used Readers Theatre to engage my own students, grades 3 to graduate school—and met with enthusiasm at every level. A wide variety of Readers Theatre resources are available as books or on websites (see additional resources in Table 2.8). Readers Theatre enactments can be turned into multicultural literacy experiences by using scripts based on folk tales from across the globe (see Table 2.9). In addition, after a story has been dramatized in English, the teacher can ask, "Who wants to retell the same story in your own native language?" By moving between two languages, students develop higher levels of literacy and, at the same time, develop pride in their ongoing rich and complex formation of identity—who they are in the process of becoming.

FIGURE 2.3
Students Involved in Readers Theatre

TABLE 2.8
Readers Theatre Resources, K–Adult

Early Grades

Marx, P. (1997). *Take a quick bow: 26 short plays for classroom fun*. Glenview, IL: Good Year Books.

Talbot, A.R. (1994). The Lost Cat *and other primary plays for oral reading*. Billerica, MA: Curriculum Associates.

Wolfman, J. (2004). *How and why stories for Readers Theatre*. Englewood, CO: Teacher Ideas Press.

Intermediate Grades

Black, A., & Stave, A.M. (2007). *A comprehensive guide to readers theatre: Enhancing fluency and comprehension in middle school and beyond*. Newark, DE: International Reading Association.

Fredericks, A. (2001). *Silly salamanders and other slightly stupid stuff for Readers Theatre*. Englewood, CO: Teacher Ideas Press.

Jenkins, D.R. (2004). *Just deal with it! Funny Readers Theatre for life's not-so-funny moments*. Englewood, CO: Teacher Ideas Press.

Laughlin, M.K., Black, P.T., & Loberg, M.K. (1991). *Social studies Readers Theatre for children: Scripts and script development*. Englewood, CO: Teacher Ideas Press.

Laughlin, M.K., & Latrobe, K.H. (1989). *Reader's Theatre for children: Scripts and script development*. Englewood, CO: Teacher Ideas Press.

Worthy, J. (2004). *Readers Theater for building fluency: Strategies and scripts for making the most of this highly effective, motivating, and research-based approach to oral reading*. New York: Scholastic.

Reader's Theatre Website

Aaron Shepard's RT Page: Scripts and Tips for Reader's Theater
www.aaronshep.com/rt/

Middle School–Adult

Blank, C., & Roberts, J. (1996). *Live on stage: Teacher resource book, performing arts for middle school*. New York: Dale Seymour Publications.

Latrobe, K.H., & Laughlin, M.K. (1997). *Readers Theatre for young adults: Script and script development*. Englewood, CO: Teacher Ideas Press.

Adapted from Fink, R. (2006). *Why Jane and John couldn't read—And how they learned: A new look at striving readers* (pp. 40–41). Newark, DE: International Reading Association.

Open-Ended Questions

To promote motivation, interest, and deep comprehension, research underscores the importance of higher level, critical thinking questions (De Temple & Snow, 2001). These are usually questions of the open-ended variety—not simple, factual, yes–no, right–wrong queries. Examples of open-ended types of questions include the following:

What if _____?

Why do you think _____?

What might have happened if _____?

How could the story have ended differently?

TABLE 2.9
Folk Tale Books

Worldwide Tales

Adler, N. (1996). *The Dial book of animal tales from around the world*. New York: Dial.

MacDonald, M.R. (1992). *Peace tales: World folktales to talk about*. Hamden, CT: Linnet Books.

Mayo, M. (1993). Magical tales from many lands. New York: Dutton.

Latin American Tales

Aldana, P. (1996). *Jade and Iron: Latin American tales from two cultures*. Toronto, ON: Groundwood.

Delacre, L. (1996). *Golden tales: Myths, legends, and folktales from Latin America*. New York: Scholastic.

González, L.M. (1997). *Señor Cat's Romance and other favorite stories from Latin America*. New York: Scholastic.

Soros, B. (1998). *Grandmother's song*. Brooklyn, NY: Barefoot Books.

Middle Eastern Tales

O'Connor, K. (1996). *A Kurdish family*. Minneapolis, MN: Lerner.

Sunami, K. (2002). *How the fisherman tricked the genie: A tale within a tale within a tale*. New York: Atheneum.

African Tales

Janisch, H. (2002). *The fire: An Ethiopian folk tale*. Toronto, ON: Groundwood.

Paye, W., & Lippert, M.H. (2002). *Head, body, legs: A story from Liberia*. New York: Henry Holt.

Asian Tales

Fang, L. (1995). *The Ch'i-Lin purse: A collection of ancient Chinese stories*. New York: Farrar, Straus and Giroux.

Mochizuki, K. (1993). *Baseball saved us*. New York: Lee & Low.

Uchida, Y. (1993). *The bracelet*. New York: Philomel.

Uegaki, C. (2004). *Suki's kimono*. Tonawanda, NY: Kids Can Press.

Indian Tale

So, M. (2004). *Gobble, gobble, slip, slop: A tale of a very greedy cat*. New York: Knopf.

Adapted from Fink, R. (2006). *Why Jane and John couldn't read—And how they learned: A new look at striving readers* (pp. 59–63). Newark, DE: International Reading Association.

Teachers can create higher level, open-ended questions themselves and also involve children in developing their own thought-provoking questions for discussion. This approach should begin as early as possible—preferably during preschool and kindergarten—then continue consistently in first, second, third, and fourth grade through middle school, high school, and graduate school. Deep comprehension requires learning thoughtful, questioning habits of mind as early as possible—preferably before children can read independently.

The type of questions and discussions matter for literacy, both in the short term and years later. Research on discussions and book talk conducted by De Temple and Snow (2001) supports this view. De Temple and Snow found that as early as preschool, children whose mothers engaged in open-ended, thought-provoking book discussions that went beyond the pictures and facts of the text performed significantly better on reading tests than children whose mothers stuck closely to lower level, factual questions. Even several years later, these results were consistent regardless of the mothers' socioeconomic or educational backgrounds.

Decoding and Vocabulary Activities

Educators know that phonological decoding should be taught in the early grades until students demonstrate mastery. But how can we teach decoding to older students? And how can we do so without holding them back? Several approaches have been tried successfully.

Syllabication for Decoding and Vocabulary Building. This visual, auditory, and kinesthetic strategy aids decoding of multisyllabic words and enables weak decoders to keep up with the content that their peers are learning. The Syllabication for Decoding Strategy (SDS) uses sound and rhythm to help students tap, hear, feel, and write the beats in syllables as a way of decoding long words. I created the strategy for my own middle school students and have used it successfully with high school and college students as well. It is a lively, fun way to approach syllabication for the purpose of decoding. Each teacher can modify the steps to meet her or his own students' needs (see the reproducible Syllabication for Decoding Strategy on page 53).

Small Puppies Syllabication Activity. This visual and auditory strategy for teaching decoding, fluency, and vocabulary has been used to teach students in low-income urban settings. It consists of several steps that I have adapted from Tatum (2003, pp. 106–110), focusing on syllables or "small puppies" and multisyllable words or "big dogs" (see the reproducible The Small Puppies Approach on page 54).

In conjunction with these decoding strategies, teachers should discuss word meanings in context and include a variety of rich, engaging vocabulary activities. One excellent approach is the semantic impressions vocabulary method (Richek, 2005, 2007). Semantic impressions facilitate text comprehension by deepening vocabulary understanding and building schematic background before students read. And, instead of the traditional method of writing words in isolated sentences, students work in groups and use all the new words in a coherent story of their own creation.

Rate Your Knowledge Vocabulary Activity. Another great vocabulary strategy is called Rate Your Knowledge Reading Vocabulary Strategy (see reproducible on page 55), based on work by Blachowicz and Fisher (1996) and Ogle (1986). Rate Your Knowledge is an excellent way for students to tap their prior knowledge, make predictions, and monitor their vocabulary development.

Vocabulary Card Games. Educators know that repeated encounters with words are necessary before students internalize meanings and make new words their own (Just & Carpenter, 1987; McKeown & Curtis, 1987; Pearson, Hiebert, & Kamil, 2007).

Syllabication for Decoding Strategy (SDS)

1. As if beating a drum, the teacher taps her desk according to the syllables in her name and each student's name. Students do the same and guess the number of taps (or syllables) they hear. For example: Ros/a/lie Fink (4); Jac/kie Rob/in/son (5); Mar/i/an An/der/son (6).

2. The teacher selects and writes on the board words from the student's most challenging reading assignments (e.g., social studies, science). Words should be underlined by the teacher and written in the meaningful context of a phrase or sentence, which can come directly from the reading assignment.

3. The student draws a line between letters to indicate each new beat or syllable. Syllable divisions are accepted as correct for decoding purposes even if they do not follow the dictionary rules of syllabication—as long as the divisions help the student to pronounce the word. For example, the teacher should accept the following divisions of the word *civilization*: ci/vi/li/za/tion or civ/il/iz/a/tion.

4. In parentheses, the student writes the number of beats or syllables heard in each word. For example: ci/vi/li/za/tion (5); E/gypt (2); gene (1); ge/no/mics (3); ba/cil/li (3).

5. After pronouncing the word, the student guesses its meaning from the context or looks up the meaning in a dictionary. The teacher should explain that SDS is primarily for decoding purposes and that traditional rules for syllabication have more constraints.

Inspiring Reading Success: Interest and Motivation in an Age of High-Stakes Testing, edited by Rosalie Fink and S. Jay Samuels. © 2008 by the International Reading Association. May be copied for classroom use.

The Small Puppies Approach

1. Create a word wall easily visible to all that lists 25 words from a text that is about to be assigned for reading. (Select 5 words at the beginning of the year and incrementally add up to 25 words per week as students become familiar with the strategy.)

2. Students capitalize the first letter of each syllable individually at their seats. Example: redundant = Re Dun Dant (3).

3. Students stand up, eliminating a seated "position of passivity." Then, in unison, students call out the syllabicated versions of the words aloud. (*Indefatigable* would sound like: big I, little n, big D, little e, big F, little a, and so forth.)

4. Students take turns reciting the syllabicated versions aloud individually at a fast pace. Together, students reach consensus about the pace beforehand (for example, 1 second per word).

5. Students earn the right to sit down by reciting the list individually at the agreed-upon pace.

6. Students who have difficulty keeping up the pace work in pairs and use an echo reading approach.

7. Students sing excerpts from songs that demonstrate the meaning of a word.

8. Students read words on a word wall every other day to build their sight vocabulary.

9. Students take dictation of a three- or four-sentence paragraph containing the words in a meaningful context. The teacher selects dictation words to demonstrate common spelling patterns or emphasize essential vocabulary to enhance understanding of the next reading assignment. (Dictation example: People *usually associate* the word *prejudice* with *intolerance* of a particular race or *creed*. In addition, *prejudice* can exist within a *minority* group that is the *victim* of *discrimination*.)

10. Open-ended, thought-provoking questions typically follow dictation and are used for discussion as a prereading activity. Discussion question examples: (a) Why do you think members of minority groups sometimes demonstrate prejudice toward themselves and each other? (b) What circumstances lead to discrimination?

Adapted from Tatum, A.W. (2003). Breaking down barriers that disenfranchise African-American adolescents in low-level tracks. In P.A. Mason & J.S. Schumm (Eds.), *Promising practices for urban reading instruction* (pp. 98–118). Newark, DE: International Reading Association.

Rate Your Knowledge Reading Vocabulary Strategy

Before Reading

- The teacher chooses salient words from the text and presents them in the first column of a four-column table (referred to as the Rate Your Knowledge sheet).

- Students individually read the words and approximate meanings by writing their guesses in the second column.

- In pairs, students group the words in simple categories and make a prediction about the text to follow.

During Reading

- The teacher collects the Rate Your Knowledge sheets and reminds students that they can find the words as they read.

- Students may take notes while reading and may use the notes when they return to their sheets at the end of the reading period.

After Reading

- The teacher distributes the Rate Your Knowledge sheets, directing students to fill out the third column with the correct definition based on the reading.

- In the fourth column, students write and reflect on the difference between their first guess and their final answer as to the word's meaning.

Inspiring Reading Success: Interest and Motivation in an Age of High-Stakes Testing, edited by Rosalie Fink and S. Jay Samuels. © 2008 by the International Reading Association. May be copied for classroom use.

To experience repeated word encounters, students can play vocabulary card games for additional word practice and reinforcement. Many games are available commercially, or they can be easily made. In one teacher-made game, each student (1) locates the card containing a word that the teacher (or a student) says out loud, (2) gives a correct definition, and (3) creates a sentence using the word orally. Games of this sort not only provide drill and practice but also enliven the lessons and make vocabulary learning fun.

Conclusion

When it comes to teaching, the power of a reader's passionate, personal interest cannot be overstated. The striving readers in this study told poignant tales of struggles and frustrations—struggles that eventually resulted in resilience and success based on their interests. The study resulted in the Interest-Based Model of Reading, which explains how students who struggle can learn to read well and succeed at high levels—even if they learn later than their peers. Mentoring by family members and teachers was a key component of the model. Perhaps most important, teachers were crucial mentors for poor students from disadvantaged life circumstances. Teachers made a major difference in their lives.

We can only guess how individuals such as Roy Daniels would fare in today's atmosphere of high-stakes testing. Would Daniels be permitted the accommodation of extra time? If not, would his scores be aggregated? Would his poor test scores in language-based subjects jeopardize his school's adequate yearly progress record? If so, how would his school district respond? Would Roy Daniels be permitted to earn a high school diploma if he passed all his courses yet failed the high-stakes exams required for a high school diploma in many states today? Answers to these questions are a matter of conjecture.

> When it comes to teaching, the power of a reader's passionate, personal interest cannot be overstated.

In the wake of No Child Left Behind, many school districts have seen an increasing number of students drop out of high school lacking essential skills and feeling hopeless and defeated. Yet, the No Child Left Behind legislation was intended to help more students learn to read and succeed in U.S. schools, especially in poor urban areas. One problem of No Child Left Behind has been the paucity of funding for professional development to provide teachers with essential knowledge of effective methods and approaches. Another problem is that No Child Left Behind is primarily system centered, rather than child centered. Furthermore, it is based primarily on formal assessment instruments and lacks the benefits that informal assessments have to offer.

What are some alternative approaches? One alternative is to set up an informal assessment system that focuses on each child's individual development and progress. The purpose of this approach would be to enable students to set goals; understand their interests, strengths, and weaknesses; and work toward self-improvement. Analyzing individual student performance and growth at key times throughout the school year offers the opportunity for students to compete with their own previous performance, develop their skills, and grow academically.

I am not arguing against all formal testing; however, a single test score alone should never be used as the sole indicator of successful performance. Ongoing formal and informal assessments should be used—and used in equal measure. One resource that I recommend is *Reading Assessment and Instruction: A Qualitative Approach to Diagnosis* (Flippo, 1997). This excellent book provides numerous checklists and forms that enable thorough, concise record keeping. It contains specific questions to help teachers conduct informal qualitative assessments of students' specific reading strengths and weaknesses—information that can be used to plan effective instruction (see sample assessment questions in Table 2.10). (In addition to the other resources in this chapter, see Table 2.11 for further recommended resources for professionals and parents.)

Based on the results of my study, teachers should use a variety of qualitative assessments and capitalize on each student's personal interests and strengths to plan a highly motivating, effective reading program for each child. The stories of the remarkably successful men and women in this study send a powerful resounding message: Striving readers can learn to read well, even if they learn differently from others—especially if we use motivating materials about their interests. I hope that this chapter inspires teachers, parents, and other mentors to instill in each student the motivation, beliefs, and strategies to succeed in literacy and in their life pursuits.

TABLE 2.10
Sample Questions for Qualitative Reading Assessment

1. Can the student give reasons to support his or her answers to comprehension questions?
2. What follow-up procedures does the student use to facilitate comprehension?
3. To what extent is the student aware of his or her metacognitive strategies for comprehension monitoring?
4. When the student realizes that comprehension is momentarily lagging, how effective is the student in going back to the text to find relevant information?
5. What strategies does the student use to regain understanding?
6. How well does the student use information from the text to support answers?
7. Does the student use general impressions or specific excerpts from the text?
8. Does the student understand the connotation of specific words as they are used in particular contexts?
9. Does the student use prior knowledge to support answers?
10. Does the student consider whether or not the author substantiates claims?
11. To what extent do the student's personal feelings about the topic influence responses, and is the student aware of the effect of his or her own feelings and perspectives on the interpretation?

Adapted from Flippo, R.F. (1997). *Reading assessment and instruction: A qualitative approach to diagnosis.* Fort Worth, TX: Harcourt Brace.

Previously published in Fink, R. (2006). *Why Jane and John couldn't read—And how they learned: A new look at striving readers* (p. 132). Newark, DE: International Reading Association.

TABLE 2.11
Recommended Resources for Professionals and Parents

Teaching Girls and Boys

Fink, R. (2006). *Why Jane and John couldn't read—And how they learned: A new look at striving readers.* Newark, DE: International Reading Association.

Keene, E.O. (2002). *Misreading masculinity: Boys, literacy, and popular culture.* Portsmouth, NH: Heinemann.

Sprague, M.M., & Keeling, K.K. (2007). *Discovering their voices: Engaging adolescent girls with young adult literature.* Newark, DE: International Reading Association.

Teaching With Poetry and Dance

Ambrosini, M., & Morretta, T.M. (2003). *Poetry workshop for middle school: Activities that inspire meaningful language learning.* Newark, DE: International Reading Association.

Durica, K.M. (2007). *How we "do" school: Poems to encourage teacher reflection.* Newark, DE: International Reading Association.

Tortora, S. (2006). *The dancing dialogue: Using the communicative power of movement with young children.* Baltimore: Paul H. Brookes.

Teaching for Motivation and Interest

Bempechat, J. (1998). *Against the odds: How "at-risk" students exceed expectations.* San Francisco: Jossey Bass.

Verhoeven, L., & Snow, C.E. (Eds.). (2001). *Literacy and motivation: Reading engagment in individuals and groups.* Mahwah, NJ: Erlbaum.

Teaching Gifted and Talented Students

Feldman, D.H., Csikszentmihalyi, M., & Gardner, H. (1994). *Changing the world: A framework for the study of creativity.* Westport, CT: Praeger.

Winner, E. (1996). *Gifted children: Myths and realities.* New York: Basic Books.

Teaching Urban and ELL Students

August, D., & Shanahan, T. (Eds.). (2006). *Developing literacy in second-language learners: Report of the National Literacy Panel on language-minority children and youth.* Mahwah, NJ: Erlbaum.

Bear, D.R., Helman, L., Templeton, S., Invernizzi, I., & Johnston, F. (2007). *Words their way with English language learners: Word study for phonics, vocabulary, and spelling instruction.* Columbus, OH: Pearson.

Lapp, D., Block, C.C., Cooper, E.J., Flood, J., Roser, N., & Tinajero, J.V. (Eds.). (2004). *Teaching all the children: Strategies for developing literacy in an urban setting.* New York: Guilford.

Mason, P., & Schumm, J.S. (Eds.). (2003). *Promising practices for urban reading instruction.* Newark, DE: International Reading Association.

Young, T.A., & Hadaway, N.L. (Eds.). (2006). *Supporting the literacy development of English learners.* Newark, DE: International Reading Association.

Websites

International Reading Association: www.reading.org (information for teachers, reading specialists, coaches, and so forth)

LD Online: www.ldonline.org (information and links for parents and teachers of struggling readers)

PBS Kids: www.pbskids.org/cgi-registry/lions/think.pl/games (information and practice games and activities to develop early reading skills for young children)

Reading Rockets: www.readingrockets.org (information about teaching reading to all kinds of kids)

Schwab Learning: www.schwablearning.org (information for parents of struggling readers)

Tumple Talking Books: www.tumblebooks.com/talkingbooks/ (online picture books read aloud with text presented simultaneously; words are tracked in color during oral reading)

POSTREADING QUESTIONS

◆ What are the key components of the Interest-Based Model of Reading, and how could you integrate these components to enhance your students' success?

◆ What would be the benefits of using an interest-based model? What problems might you encounter, and how would you deal with them?

◆ How could you integrate open-ended questions into your reading curriculum? How could this type of questioning help your students? How would you encourage students to create their own higher level questions? Why would this be important to their development as readers and thinkers?

◆ What is the role of testing in your district and your curriculum? How could you use test and assessment results to help improve student outcomes, both in terms of reading skills and beliefs?

REFERENCES

Blachowicz, C., & Fisher, P.J. (1996). *Teaching vocabulary in all classrooms*. Columbus, OH: Merrill.

Botelho, M.J. (2007). Naming practices: Defining critical and multicultural literacies. *Orbit, 36*(3), 27–30.

Burns, P.C., Roe, B.D., & Ross, E.P. (1992). *Teaching reading in today's elementary schools* (5th ed.). Boston: Houghton Mifflin.

Chall, J.S. (1983). *Stages of reading development*. New York: McGraw-Hill.

Chall, J.S. (1994). Patterns of adult reading. *Learning Disabilities: A Multidisciplinary Journal, 5*(1), 29–33.

Chall, J.S. (1996). *Stages of reading development* (2nd ed.). Fort Worth, TX: Harcourt Brace.

Chard, D.J., Vaughn, S., & Tyler, B.J. (2002). A synthesis of research on effective interventions for building reading fluency with elementary students with learning disabilities. *Journal of Learning Disabilities, 35*(5), 386–406.

Chow, P., & Cummins, J. (2003). Valuing multilingual and multicultural approaches to learning. In S.R. Schecter & J. Cummins (Eds.), *Multilingual education in practice: Using diversity as a resource* (pp. 32–60). Portsmouth, NH: Heinemann.

Cohen, S. (2003). *The mysteries of Internet research*. Fort Atkinson, WI: Upstart Books.

Cooper, E. (2007). *Poverty is not destiny—All high school students are college ready*. Speech presented at the 52nd Annual Convention of the International Reading Association, Toronto, ON, Canada.

Csikszentmihalyi, M. (1991). Literacy and intrinsic motivation. In S.R. Graubard (Ed.), *Literacy: An overview by 14 experts* (pp. 115–140). New York: Hill and Wang.

Cummins, J. (1994). The acquisition of English as a second language. In K. Spangenberg-Urbschat & R. Pritchard (Eds.), *Kids come in all languages: Reading instruction for ESL students* (pp. 36–62). Newark, DE: International Reading Association.

Cummins, J., Chow, P., & Schecter, S.R. (2006). Community as curriculum. *Language Arts, 83* 297–307.

De Temple, J.M., & Snow, C.E. (2001). Conversations about literacy: Social mediation of psycholinguistic activity. In L. Verhoeven & C.E. Snow (Eds.), *Literacy and motivation: Reading engagement in individuals and groups* (pp. 55–70). Mahwah, NJ: Erlbaum.

Fink, R.P. (1995/1996). Successful dyslexics: A constructivist study of passionate interest reading. *Journal of Adolescent & Adult Literacy, 39*, 268–280.

Fink, R.P. (1998). Literacy development in successful men and women with dyslexia. *Annals of Dyslexia, 48*, 311–346.

Fink, R.P. (2002). Successful careers: The secrets of adults with dyslexia. *Career Planning and Adult Development Journal, 18*(1), 118–135.

Fink, R.P. (2003). Reading comprehension struggles and successes: Case study of a leading scientist. *The Primer, 31,* 19–30.

Fink, R. (2006). *Why Jane and John couldn't read—And how they learned: A new look at striving readers.* Newark, DE: International Reading Association.

Fink, R. (2007). What successful adults with dyslexia teach educators about children. In K.W. Fischer, J.H. Bernstein, & M.H. Immordino-Yang (Eds.), *Mind, brain, and education in reading disorders* (pp. 264–281). Cambridge, UK: Cambridge University Press.

Fischer, K.W., & Knight, C.C. (1990). Cognitive development in real children: Levels and variations. In B. Presseisen (Ed.), *Learning and thinking styles: Classroom interaction* (pp. 43–67). Washington, DC: National Education Association.

Flippo, R.F. (1997). *Reading assessment and instruction: A qualitative approach to diagnosis.* Fort Worth, TX: Harcourt Brace.

Foorman, B.R., Francis, D.J., Beeler, T., Winikates, D., & Fletcher, J.M. (1997). Early interventions for children with reading problems: Study designs and preliminary findings. *Learning Disabilities: A Multidisciplinary Journal, 8,* 63–71.

Fountas, I.C., & Pinnell, G.S. (1999). *Matching books to readers: Using leveled books in guided reading, K–3.* Portsmouth, NH: Heinemann.

Fountas, I.C., & Pinnell, G.S. (2001). *Leveled books for readers, grades 3–6: A companion volume to* Guiding Readers and Writers. Portsmouth, NH: Heinemann.

Gardner, H. (1983). *Frames of mind: The theory of multiple intelligences.* New York: Basic Books.

Gerber, P.J., & Reiff, H.B. (1991). *Speaking for themselves: Ethnographic interviews with adults with learning disabilities.* Ann Arbor: University of Michigan.

Gresham, F.M. (2002). Responsiveness to intervention: An alternative approach to the identification of learning disabilities. In R. Bradley, L. Danielson, & D.P. Hallahan (Eds.), *Identification of learning disabilities: Research to practice* (pp. 467–521). Mahwah, NJ: Erlbaum.

Hidi, S., & Renninger, K.A. (2006). The four-phase model of interest development. *Educational Psychologist, 41*(2), 111–127.

Just, M.A., & Carpenter, P.A. (1987). *The psychology of reading and language comprehension.* Boston: Allyn & Bacon.

Kucan, L. (2007). "I" poems: Invitations for students to deepen literary understanding. *The Reading Teacher, 60,* 518–525.

Lefly, D.L., & Pennington, B.F. (1991). Spelling errors and reading fluency in compensated adult dyslexics. *Annals of Dyslexia, 41,* 143–162.

Levstik, L.S., & Barton, K.C. (1997). *Doing history: Investigating with children in elementary and middle schools.* Mahwah, NJ: Erlbaum.

Li, X., & Zhang, M. (2004). Why Mei still cannot read and what can be done. *Journal of Adolescent & Adult Literacy, 48,* 92–101.

Lima, C.W., & Lima, J.A. (1993). *A to zoo: Subject access to children's picture books* (4th ed.). New Providence, NJ: Bowker.

Lipstein, R.L., & Renninger, K.A. (2007). "Putting things into words": The development of 12–15-year-old students' interest for writing. In G. Rijlarsdaam (Series Ed.) and P. Boscolo & S. Hidi (Volume Eds.), *Studies in writing, Volume 19: Writing and Motivation* (pp. 113–140). Oxford: Elsevier.

Mascolo, M.F., Li, J., Fink, R., & Fischer, K.W. (2002). Pathways to excellence: Value presuppositions and the development of academic and affective skills in educational contexts. In M. Ferrari (Ed.), *The pursuit of excellence through education* (pp. 113–146). Mahwah, NJ: Erlbaum.

McKeown, M.G., & Curtis, M.E. (Eds.). (1987). *The nature of vocabulary acquisition.* Hillside, NJ: Erlbaum.

McLaughlin, M., & Allen, M.B. (2002). *Guided comprehension: A teaching model for grades 3–8.* Newark, DE: International Reading Association.

Ogle, D.M. (1986). K-W-L: A teaching model that develops active reading of expository text. *The Reading Teacher, 39,* 564–570.

Orton Dyslexia Society Research Committee. (1994, Fall). A new definition of dyslexia. *Perspectives, 20*(5), p. 4.

Parr, J.M., & Maguiness, C. (2005). Removing the *silent* from SSR: Voluntary reading as social practice. *Journal of Adolescent & Adult Literacy, 49,* 98–107.

Pearson, P.D., Hiebert, E.H., & Kamil, M.L. (2007). Vocabulary assessment: What we know and what we need to learn. *Reading Research Quarterly, 42,* 282–296.

Peebles, J.L. (2007). Incorporating movement with fluency instruction: A motivation for struggling readers. *The Reading Teacher, 60,* 578–581.

Recht, D.R., & Leslie, L. (1988). Effect of prior knowledge on good and poor readers' memory of text. *Journal of Educational Psychology, 80,* 16–20.

Renninger, K.A. (1992). Individual interest and development: Implications for theory and practice. In K.A. Renninger, S. Hidi, & A. Krapp (Eds.), *The role of interest and development* (pp. 361–395). Hillsdale, NJ: Erlbaum.

Renninger, K.A. (2000). Individual interest and its implications for understanding intrinsic motivation. In C. Sansone & J.M. Harackiewicz (Eds.), *Intrinsic and extrinsic motivation: The search for optimal motivation and performance* (pp. 373–404). New York: Academic.

Renninger, K.A., & Hidi, S. (2002). Student interest and achievement: Developmental issues raised by a case study. In A. Wigfield & J.S. Eccles (Eds.), *Development of achievement motivation* (pp. 173–195). New York: Academic.

Richek, M.A. (2005). Words are wonderful: Interactive, time-efficient strategies to teach meaning vocabulary. *The Reading Teacher, 58,* 414–423.

Richek, M.A. (2007). *The world of words: Vocabulary for college students.* Boston: Houghton Mifflin.

Roswell, F.G., & Chall, J.S. (1992). *Diagnostic assessments of reading and trial teaching strategies (DARTTS).* Chicago: Riverside Publishing.

Rumelhart, D.E. (1980). Schemata: The building blocks of cognition. In R.J. Spiro, B.C. Bruce, & W.F. Brewer (Eds.), *Theoretical issues in reading comprehension* (pp. 33–58). Hillsdale, NJ: Erlbaum.

Ryan, R.M., & Deci, E.L. (2000). Intrinsic and extrinsic motivation: Classic definitions and new directions. *Contemporary Educational Psychology, 25,* 54–67.

Samuels, S.J. (2002). Reading fluency: Its development and assessment. In A.E. Farstrup & S.J. Samuels (Eds.), *What research has to say about reading instruction* (3rd ed., pp. 166–183). Newark, DE: International Reading Association.

Samuels, S.J., & Farstrup, A.E. (Eds.). (2006). *What research has to say about fluency instruction.* Newark, DE: International Reading Association.

Schiefele, U. (1996). Topic interest and levels of text comprehension. In K.A. Renninger, S. Hidi, & A. Krapp (Eds.), *The role of interest in learning and development* (pp. 151–212). Hillsdale, NJ: Erlbaum.

Silvey, A. (2004). *100 best books for children.* Boston: Houghton Mifflin.

Snow, C.E., Burns, M.S., & Griffin, P. (Eds.). (1998). *Preventing reading difficulties in young children.* Washington, DC: National Academy Press.

Story-Huffman, R. (2002a). *Caldecott on the Net: Reading & Internet activities.* Fort Atkinson, WI: Upstart Books.

Story-Huffman, R. (2002b). *Newbery on the Net: Reading & Internet activities.* Fort Atkinson, WI: Upstart Books.

Tatum, A.W. (2003). Breaking down barriers that disenfranchise African-American adolescents in low-level tracks. In P.A. Mason & J.S. Schumm (Eds.), *Promising practices for urban reading instruction* (pp. 98–118). Newark, DE: International Reading Association.

Torgesen, J.K., Wagner, R.K., & Rashotte, C.A. (1997). Prevention of remediation of severe reading disabilities: Keeping the end in mind. *Scientific Studies of Reading, 1*(3), 217–234.

Verhoeven, L., & Snow, C.E. (2001). Introduction—Literacy and motivation: Bridging cognitive and sociocultural viewpoints. In L. Verhoeven & C.E. Snow (Eds.), *Literacy and motivation: Reading engagement in individuals and groups* (pp. 1–20). Mahwah, NJ: Erlbaum.

Walczyk, J.J., & Griffith-Ross, D.A. (2007). How important is reading skill fluency for comprehension? *The Reading Teacher, 60,* 560–569.

Whitehead, F., & Maddren, W. (1974). *Children's reading interests* (Schools Council Working Paper No. 52). London: University of Scheffield Institute of Education, Schools Council Research Project into Children's Reading Habits.

Winner, E. (1996). *Gifted children: Myths and realities.* New York: Basic Books.

Young, J.P. (2000). Boy talk: Critical literacies and masculinities. *Reading Research Quarterly, 35,* 312–337.

Using Student Interests
to Motivate Learning

Kurt W. Fischer and Maria Fusaro

Inspiring Reading Success: Interest and Motivation in an Age of High-Stakes Testing, edited by Rosalie Fink and S. Jay Samuels. © 2008 by the International Reading Association.

Lydia, a fifth grader, really wants to know how the human body works, but she cannot read at all well. She has trouble with rhymes and with sounding out words—she has dyslexia—and so reading is hard for her to learn. Her teacher notices her interest in the body and shows her a few books on the topic with great illustrations and a lot of text as well. Lydia latches onto the books and spends hours poring over them. Her teacher then shows her a website about the human body, where Lydia spends many more hours exploring and learning about the topic. The illustrations guide her, but to learn what she wants to know, she has to read the text, too. With weeks and months working with books and websites about the human body, her reading skills improve dramatically. She still has difficulty sounding out words, but through all her work on books and websites and with the support of her teachers and parents, she moves forward in learning to read.

James, also a fifth grader, feels compelled to know about lawn mowers, but he too cannot sound out words and cannot read well. (James's story was told to us by our colleague L. Todd Rose, who worked with James and his family.) To pursue his obsession, he takes the manual for his family's lawn mower and works to understand it, but soon his father discovers what he is doing and takes the manual away, scolding him for reading it instead of the book that his teacher assigned for class. The boy sneaks back into the garage to find the manual and squirrels it away in his room together with a flashlight. After he goes to bed, he hides under his blanket with the manual and flashlight to try to learn about the lawn mower. When his parents see the light under the blanket, they discover what he is doing, scold him again, and take away both the manual and the flashlight, telling him to read the assigned book when he is supposed to instead of reading the "stupid manual" under the covers.

Happily, a counselor learns about James's situation and speaks with his parents, encouraging them to let him read manuals, books, and websites about lawn mowers instead of forcing him to read a book that he does not find interesting. Learning about lawn mowers is important to him, and he spends many hours working on reading to get the information about lawn mowers that he wants. A month and a half later when the boy's reading is assessed, he has already made enormous progress in learning to read. When Fink (2006) studied highly successful adults who were dyslexic and had great difficulty learning to read as children, she found that they were all characterized by what Lydia and James showed—a passionate interest in learning about a topic for which books were an outstanding source of information. Fink interviewed adults with dyslexia who had compensated for their reading difficulties and excelled in careers that require reading and writing. Several adults described learning to read—always late, usually around age 12 or so—by delving into books and text on a topic of personal interest. Interest-driven reading helped these struggling readers to learn about their passionate interest, and in the process they used their special knowledge and interest to build reading skills. In this way they were able to construct meaning from the text even though their basic skills (letter identification, word recognition, phonological analysis, rhyming) remained weak. When a reader has background knowledge, context-reliant reading can be effective and accurate. The passion provides a powerful mechanism for motivating dyslexic students (and others) to tackle the difficult task of learning to read as well as many other key skills that schools teach, such as writing, mathematics, and even self-regulation of learning.

Driven to Learn: Epistemic Motivation

Fortunately, Lydia and James are not unusual in their passion. Human beings have a basic mechanism that motivates learning, called *epistemic motivation*, which drives people to pursue control and knowledge of events and topics that fascinate and engage them. Most students develop strong interests in topics that they really want to learn about—not only lawn mowers or the body, but bugs, earthworms, airplanes, dolls, soccer, the U.S. Civil War, video games, music, and many other things. They work spontaneously to learn about these special interests, and along the way they learn much else that can be important, such as reading, arithmetic, organizing objects and information, and much more.

This mechanism appears first in infants, who will work hard to re-create and control an interesting event that they accidentally create, showing what is called a circular reaction (Fischer & Connell, 2003), described first by J.M. Baldwin (1894) and elaborated by Piaget (1952), Wallon (1970), and Rovee-Collier (Rovee-Collier, Sullivan, Enright, Lucas, & Fagen, 1980) among others. In a classic example from Piaget, an experimenter ties a string from a 6-month-old infant's foot to a toy on a mobile hanging over her crib. At first, the toy moves at random, based on the child's normal bodily motion. The sight of the moving toy is interesting to the child, and she continues to look at it. As the child begins to sense the contingency between kicking the foot and seeing the toy move, she gropes with her foot movements more intentionally to affect the mobile. She repeats the actions leading up to the interesting sight in an effort to sustain it. With practice, she refines her action, as she learns effective ways to move her foot to make the toy jiggle.

Her behavior is circular in that she repeats the kicking action many times with variations in order to reproduce the interesting sight of the mobile moving. The contingency between her action and the event elicits interest, which motivates her to continue performing the kicking action, thus building a simple skill. In this early instance of epistemic motivation, the cycle of acting and reacting to the outcome leads the infant to master the skill of kicking to make the mobile move.

Although circular reactions have been primarily discussed in reference to infants, the same learning mechanism operates for older children (Fischer & Connell, 2003; Wallon, 1970). Lydia wants to understand how the human body works, just as an infant wants to understand how the toy jiggles. To construct a better understanding of the body, Lydia asks questions of more knowledgeable people and clicks on one Web link after another, looking for relevant information. She already has some understanding of the body, based on personal experiences such as being sick and then feeling better, and discussing family members' and friends' various physical strengths and ailments. But there is more that Lydia wants to understand. She asks, How can her heart possibly beat day and night? What happens to food after she eats it? Why can't her classmate see some colors the way she does? Rather than merely highlighting gaps in Lydia's knowledge of biology, her questions also reveal that there are many things she already knows. For instance, putting together ideas such as that a heart needs to beat for a person to live and that the body's organs need energy from food to function, she discovers an intriguing puzzle: Wouldn't the body run out of energy overnight if the heart is constantly working?

> The drive to learn is a basic feature of the human condition, in which each learner, embedded in an environment of social and informational supports, seeks to master interesting parts of his or her world.

As this example illustrates, Lydia builds on what she already knows about the way the body works and is motivated to answer the new questions that she encounters or discovers as she continues to explore the sources of information about the body. Lydia examines images on the Web that demonstrate how the body's energy needs depend on a person's activity level. This circular reaction involves much more diverse variations than the infant's kicking his foot to move a mobile. Although her actions are more complex than those of the infant in his crib, the pattern of behavior similarly shows a drive to explore interesting situations and leads to learning. Each of Lydia's experiences helps to restructure her understanding of the heart (or other aspects of body functioning), leading to a more complex and differentiated view of how body organs function. The cycle of seeking new information, raising new questions, and accommodating her understanding will lead to increased understanding of many different body functions.

The purpose of this chapter is to describe a natural motivational process that promotes development of skills and knowledge of the world and to show how it can be harnessed to help children master the skills that they are supposed to learn in school. This type of process helps explain how students like Lydia and James can learn to read through their passionate interest in the human body and lawn mowers, respectively. The drive to learn is a basic feature of the human condition, in which each learner, embedded in an environment of social and informational supports, seeks to master interesting parts of

TABLE 3.1
Additional Resources on Student Interest and Motivation

Report from the National Academy of Sciences on motivation and learning in young children: *Eager to Learn: Educating our Preschoolers:*
www.nap.edu/books/0309068363/html/

Usable Knowledge website, which presents research that is relevant for teachers and other educational leaders, including many pieces on learning and development (materials include text, videos, audios, and illustrations):
www.uknow.gse.harvard.edu

Information about the DESIGNS program and the role of goals in learning, on the website of the American Association for the Advancement of Science:
www.project2061.org/events/meetings/technology/tech2/schwartz-sadler.htm

Article on epistemic motivation:
Fischer, K.W., & Connell, M.W. (2003). Two motivational systems that shape development: Epistemic and self-organizing. *British Journal of Educational Psychology: Monograph Series II, 2,* 103–123.

his or her world. This epistemic motivation leads children (and adults) naturally toward higher levels of complexity in their understanding of the world (Barron, 2006; Fischer & Bidell, 2006; Fischer & Connell, 2003).

Viewing development as a dynamic and self-organizing process helps us to see how motivation drives cognitive change in self-initiated and classroom-based learning experiences, such as learning about lawn mowers or the human body. In the process of text-based exploration of a topic of interest, a student's reading skills become more advanced. James and Lydia both became more skilled readers as they practiced reading in the domains of their interest—lawn mowers (machines) and the human body (biology). Fink's (2006) work indicates that this pattern is the normal way that dyslexic students become skilled adult readers and writers. We propose that it also characterizes a large part of learning in all students and that it captures the most powerful way to improve learning in schools in general: *Engage students in topics that they naturally want to learn about, and use those topics to help them learn what they need to know more broadly.* (See Table 3.1 for additional resources on student interest and motivation.)

Dyslexia: Alternative Pathways to Reading

Reading in alphabetic systems is based in analyzing the sounds of words and coordinating those sounds with the letters of the alphabet. Difficulty analyzing the sounds of words is one of the primary causes of dyslexia (Fischer, Bernstein, & Immordino-Yang, 2007). This task is especially challenging in English because of the extensive irregularities in spelling.

Overcoming this barrier is challenging for dyslexic students, as suggested in Figures 3.1 and 3.2 (Knight & Fischer, 1992). The normative pathway for learning to read involves integrating identification of letters with the sounds of words (a skill that is important in rhyming) and connecting the letters and sounds to the meaning of the words, as illustrated in Figure 3.1. The integration of these three domains leads to a straightforward learning pathway that culminates in effective word reading.

Students with dyslexia, however, have difficulty integrating letters, sounds, and meaning, as shown for one pathway in Figure 3.2. Problems with sound analysis as well as other difficulties interfere with integrating the three domains, and so the task of learning to read is much more difficult: The alphabet becomes less a useful tool for reading and more a barrier to learning to read. The pathway in Figure 3.2 diagrams the simplest of a number of pathways for dyslexic reading difficulties. Fink's (2006) research with highly successful adult dyslexics demonstrates that epistemic motivation can help students to overcome this major barrier by building on their intrinsic interests. If a child is obsessed with manuals for lawn mowers, then he will work at decoding letters and words so that he can learn about lawn mowers, finding ways to learn to read despite his difficulties with integrating the domains. Fink's successful adults described many ways that they had learned this decoding despite their dyslexia. In this way, children's passionate interests are a legitimate and desirable means for them to learn to read.

FIGURE 3.1
Normative Pathway for Learning to Read: Integrating Reading, Letter Identification, and Rhyming

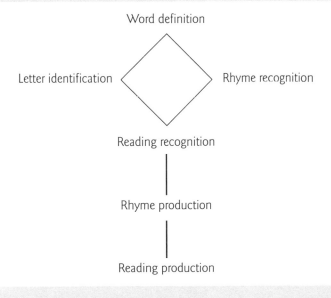

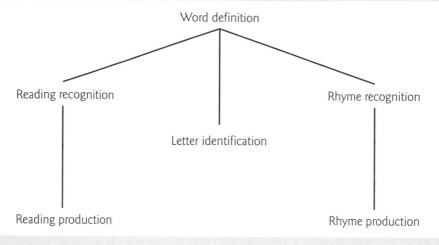

Epistemic Motivation During the School Years: Moving Beyond Boring

Schools and parents need to build on the natural process of epistemic motivation, not stamp it out and put forced learning in its place. Too many times parents and teachers do not take advantage of students' natural interests to motivate their learning but instead try to force students to learn in a narrowly prescribed way, as when James's father told him to stop reading the lawn mower manual and instead read the novel assigned by his teacher. It is no accident that when students are asked to characterize their school experience, so many of them from all over the world use one simple word—*boring* (Suárez-Orozco, Suárez-Orozco, & Todorova, in press).

Infancy is a fascinating period of life in part because infants are not easily bored. For them, so much of what they experience for the first time is novel and interesting. Indeed, they often prefer to look for a longer time at objects or scenes that are totally or partially new to them versus those that they have already encountered and come to understand. If a toy is presented to an infant repeatedly, he will eventually lose interest in it and look away. But when a different toy is presented, his attention will typically reengage, which is reflected in longer durations of time spent looking at the object. The tendency to orient toward and gaze at novel entities seems to be an (obligatory) early mechanism of learning during infancy (Fantz, 1966; Haith, 1980). The infant is tuned in to novelty, which provides the basis for constructing knowledge about the physical and social world. Though it may be less obvious later in life and sometimes overshadowed by other goals, this eagerness to learn new things is a lifelong human propensity.

Many educators, researchers, and policymakers have recognized the significance of fostering children's motivation to learn in the early years of life. In the report *Eager to Learn: Educating Our Preschoolers*, the National Research Council's Committee on Early Childhood Pedagogy argues that "Educators have an opportunity and an obligation to facilitate this propensity to learn and to develop a receptivity to learning that will prepare children for active engagement in the learning enterprise throughout their lives" (Bowman, Donovan, & Burns, 2001, p. 2). This report adopts a constructivist perspective in line with our own, viewing young children as constructing their understanding of the world by interacting with people and objects. They do not learn well by passively receiving knowledge (merely listening or seeing sources of information without grabbing hold of it to manipulate it on their own). The authors of *Eager to Learn* call on educators to foster curiosity and an eagerness to learn among preschoolers, capitalizing on their spontaneous interests, topics, and events that draw children in and motivate them to learn and explore. In the domain of reading and early literacy, the national report *Preventing Reading Difficulties in Young Children* (Snow, Burns, & Griffin, 1998) similarly highlights motivation to read among preschoolers, kindergartners, and beginning readers. This report emphasizes the roles that families and preschool teachers play in encouraging and modeling reading and in providing positive early literacy experiences.

It is noteworthy that the bulk of recent national reports on reading emphasize the earliest grade levels, reserving discussion of older students for a focus on students with learning difficulties. We believe that a rich and active account of learning and motivation is useful not only for describing the early childhood period but that it applies forcefully to school-age children as well. High school students, for example, have many passionate interests, beginning with peer relations, status, self, and sex and extending to music, sports, control of their own lives, and understanding their own cultural history. Some teachers and schools manage to engage these interests and use them to help students learn what they need to know. Many more can improve students' learning by building on the drive to learn, epistemic motivation, which extends all the way from birth to death—through all of life.

Motivation to Learn: How It Works

Lydia is highly motivated to understand the human body. While we can easily recognize that epistemic motivation is involved in this type of behavior, it is less straightforward to understand what this concept actually means in this and more subtle cases. Motivation refers sometimes to individual dispositions and sometimes to ways that behavior is energized. Most basically it refers to a feedback process in which people compare the state of affairs with their goals (the states that they desire to seek or avoid) and then act to move the state of affairs closer to what they want.

Often people think about motivation, in everyday terms, as a dispositional quality—characterizing students in a general way. From this perspective, children may be viewed as more or less motivated or curious about topics covered in school. Perhaps for some students, an intrinsic desire to build knowledge may underlie effort in school, whereas other students may need more extrinsic factors to sustain attention and effort across subjects, such as requirements for being promoted to the next grade or academic qualifications for participating in sports. However, working closely with students and monitoring their learning and activities undermines the idea of fixed levels of motivation. A given student is not equally motivated, or unmotivated, across all intellectual endeavors. Motivation operates in the here-and-now, in specific contexts, as well as in the longer term. Even attainment of long-term educational goals is contingent upon completion of many smaller tasks.

Everyday understandings of motivation also suggest a kind of energy that facilitates or enhances the engine of learning or action. For example, the rate or effectiveness of learning might get a boost when the student is under conditions of high motivation. For Lydia and James, motivation seems to have a strong sustaining effect on their efforts to learn about human biology or lawn mowers, and she or he will likely do so at a faster rate than many of their peers. But this everyday explanation leaves unclear where this energy comes from and how it increases or decreases. Certainly it is not necessary to have very high motivational energy in order to learn something. Many of Lydia's classmates, for example, will eventually achieve a high level of understanding of the body, once external conditions (e.g., mandatory biology classes, personal encounters with illness) make the topic more salient for them. The energizing effect of motivation can be clarified by considering the process by which the human body and brain generate epistemic motivational states.

> The learner notices a discrepancy between her expectation and her experience, and the surprising and interesting outcome leads to the goal of extracting new information about the world....

Epistemic motivation fits the model for motivation and emotion in general, in which a person automatically and unconsciously appraises the fit between an experience and expectations (Fischer, Shaver, & Carnochan, 1990). In epistemic motivation, the learner notices a discrepancy between her expectation and her experience, and the surprising and interesting outcome leads to the goal of extracting new information about the world by repeating and manipulating relevant events (Fischer & Connell, 2003). People's representations (i.e., understandings) about the world are modified when we encounter something new and reorganize existing understandings to fit the new phenomenon. For example, in Lydia's case, the realization that one of her classmates cannot distinguish certain colors is a violation of her prior understanding of how others literally see the world. Her understanding of vision previously rested on the notion that humans' eyes all worked the same way (i.e., the same way her eyes work) with blindness being a notable exception. This discrepancy, that some people see colors in a different way, is interesting and can initiate a search for a better understanding of vision, such as seeking resources about how color-blind people see and do not see patterns of color.

Epistemic motivation is a special case of the way emotion in general organizes behavior and learning. While acting in the world, a child may notice a change in the environment: a moving toy, a flash of light, a pleasant melody. How will the child respond? More specifically, what set of actions and behaviors (what script) is he or she most likely to exhibit? The answer depends on the individual's emotional appraisal of the event. If the notable change is perceived to be frightening, for example, a young child may retreat from it, display a fearful facial expression, and seek an attachment figure for safety or reassurance. Emotion also organizes behavior in epistemic motivation, as with the infant's moving mobile or Lydia's interest in the vision of her color-blind peer. In these examples, the child appraises the target event as interesting and worth exploring. The action tendency, or script, associated with interest is that the child will continue to direct her attention toward the event, and repeat and vary the relevant actions that brought it about.

Piaget (1952) framed these ideas in terms of the complementary processes of assimilation and accommodation, emphasizing learning during infancy: If an experience does not quite fit the child's existing understanding (i.e., cannot be assimilated), she will try to actively modify that understanding to accommodate it. This mismatch between expectation and experience (i.e., disequilibrium) generates interest, which drives the process of reconciling the unknown with the known. This is the essence of epistemic motivation at work. The reason it is so powerful is that it evokes a strong drive to explore and control the actions and information on the topic or situation of interest.

The depth and breadth of a child's exploration depend on many factors. If a certain website proves unhelpful or too advanced, Lydia may look around for other links to explore. Her exploration is not random, however, for she progressively builds her understanding. Of course, her exploration on any given day will eventually come to an end. The learner will sometimes tire of the event or actions (e.g., no longer seeing a toy or the concept of color blindness as interesting in the moment, no longer wanting to kick to make a mobile move or read about color blindness for now). Once the novelty of the topic is gone—that is, once Lydia assimilates information and accommodates her understanding to the point of resolving the discrepancy between the known and the unknown—she will typically break out of the cycle of exploration. Also, other salient changes in the environment may distract her and break the cycle. Though a learner aims to conserve, or reinstate, interesting events, other internal and external conditions and goals can override this motivation process.

Feedback Systems: The Role of Goals

An important difference between infants and older children as well as adults is that development produces a feedback system involving multiple goals. As a result, people become able to monitor and intentionally modify their behavior to fit multiple intentions and concerns. Older children can consider how their behavior within the circular reaction of epistemic motivation relates to several goals, not just the most obvious one. The decision to change their behavior may be made with or without conscious awareness of the goals. In case of conflict, they can change their activity to fit diverse goals (Fischer & Connell, 2003).

For example, if Lydia's peers tease her for raising too many questions about the human body, she may refrain from or remain quiet about this exploration to maintain positive relationships with her friends. The goal of being liked by peers may trump her motivation to continue the learning experience. As another example, she may find that her interest in the functioning of the human body pleases an important adult in her life. The motivation to achieve the approval of the adult may provide feedback that bolsters her activity. In both cases, other goals that are not specific to understanding human biology per se feed into the motivational process.

Goals are especially important in educational contexts. A student is more likely to persist in an interesting school activity and learn from it when multiple goals converge. Indeed, optimal teaching seems to involve relating activities to multiple goals and concepts, especially in the later grades, when the knowledge that students must learn is highly complex (Schwartz & Fischer, 2006). Schwartz and Sadler (2007) evaluated a science curriculum (called DESIGNS) for seventh- and eighth-grade students. This approach introduces involvement in laboratory activities early in the learning process ("messing about" by manipulating and varying arrangements of objects and events, such as nails, batteries, and wires to make a magnet) and couples them with structured support from the teacher and from printed handouts to guide the learning process and sustain epistemic motivation. Students using the curriculum learned about electromagnets through manipulating nails, batteries, and wires to try to make the magnet work better— for example, to pick up a larger number of paper clips. The researchers compared groups of students participating in DESIGNS with two other curricula: a traditional textbook-based one that culminated in laboratory experience and a less structured, activity-based approach involving self-directed, hands-on learning about electromagnetism.

Explicit short-term DESIGNS goals provided necessary structure for the laboratory sessions, such as "build a stronger magnet" instead of simply "work with or explore the magnet," and "figure out how the wrappings of the wire around the nail affect the strength of the magnet" instead of simply "use the wire to make it stronger." These stated goals gave students a way to appraise whether they were using the laboratory materials effectively and to relate their activities and observations to the concepts about electromagnetism. Students could figure out which actions (e.g., sanding ends of the wire) moved them closer to the goal and could adjust their approach accordingly. They could use the information that they obtained to feed back to the concepts they were seeking to understand. DESIGNS generated an interest in obtaining a notable change (e.g., picking up many paper clips with the magnet) while allowing the students to build from a concrete to a more abstract understanding of electromagnetism concepts. This approach was more effective than introducing abstract concepts from the start and having students derive correct answers by following prescribed laboratory procedures. It was also more effective than having students explore wires, nails, light bulbs, and other materials without specific goals—in unstructured activities.

Conclusion: The Power of Epistemic Motivation

We have argued that humans exhibit an intrinsic drive to sustain interesting events in the world by repeating and mastering the activities that generate those events—epistemic motivation (Fischer & Connell, 2003). This is not an airy concept, but a concrete mechanism that directly activates activity to master or understand an interesting event or situation. The process applies to all instances when interest shapes our behavior by driving us to understand and master some aspect of the world. It is evident early in infancy, and it continues throughout life, whenever people find something so interesting that they naturally want to explore it and understand it or get control of it. Each of these experiences provides opportunities for students to encounter insights discrepant from their existing knowledge. The process provides a powerful mechanism for driving student learning, not only with strong students but also with students who have disabilities such as dyslexia or who are not interested in most school learning. Indeed, research by Fink (2006) shows that highly successful adults who are dyslexic build their reading skills through pursuing their passion for knowledge in an area of strong interest. Students bring strong interests to the classroom, and they also can have their interest sparked—for example, by a lively class discussion, a field trip, a class project, or an internship. Teachers and schools can use this powerful mechanism to motivate students to learn about not only idiosyncratic topics but also the fundamental knowledge that society demands of an educated adult.

POSTREADING QUESTIONS

- For each of your students, identify at least one topic or situation that captures his or her attention. The topics may or may not be traditionally academic. What are some ways to weave those topics into your reading instruction? How can you connect students with similar interests?

- What aspects of the classroom context facilitate long periods of engaged reading and learning, and what aspects hinder this type of work?

- How might classmates working together generate and act on shared states of high epistemic motivation?

Acknowledgments

Conversations with Todd Rose, Marc Schwartz, and the teachers at the Ross and Landmark Schools contributed to the arguments and examples in this chapter. Preparation of this chapter was supported by grants from the Ross School and the Harvard Graduate School of Education.

REFERENCES

Baldwin, J.M. (1894). *Mental development in the child and the race.* New York: MacMillan.

Barron, B. (2006). Interest and self-sustained learning as catalysts of development: A learning ecology perspective. *Human Development, 49,* 193–224.

Bowman, B.T., Donovan, S., & Burns, M.S. (Eds.). (2001). *Eager to learn: Educating our preschoolers.* Washington, DC: National Academy Press.

Fantz, R.L. (1966). Pattern discrimination and selective attention as determinants of perceptual development from birth. In A.H. Kidd & J.L. Rivoire (Eds.), *Perceptual development in children* (pp. 143–173). New York: International Universities Press.

Fink, R. (2006). *Why Jane and John couldn't read—And how they learned.* Newark DE: International Reading Association.

Fischer, K.W., Bernstein, J.H., & Immordino-Yang, M.H. (Eds.). (2007). *Mind, brain, and education in reading disorders.* Cambridge, England: Cambridge University Press.

Fischer, K.W., & Bidell, T.R. (2006). Dynamic development of action and thought. In W. Damon & R.M. Lerner (Eds.), *Theoretical models of human development: Handbook of child psychology* (6th ed., Vol. 1, pp. 313–399). New York: Wiley.

Fischer, K.W., & Connell, M.W. (2003). Two motivational systems that shape development: Epistemic and self-organizing. *British Journal of Educational Psychology: Monograph Series II, 2,* 103–123.

Fischer, K.W., Shaver, P.R., & Carnochan, P. (1990). How emotions develop and how they organise development. *Cognition & Emotion, 4*(2), 81–127.

Haith, M.M. (1980). *Rules that babies look by: The organization of newborn visual activity.* Hillsdale, NJ: Erlbaum.

Knight, C.C., & Fischer, K.W. (1992). Learning to read words: Individual differences in developmental sequences. *Journal of Applied Developmental Psychology, 13,* 377–404.

Piaget, J. (1952). *The origins of intelligence in children* (M. Cook, Trans.). New York: International Universities Press.

Rovee-Collier, C., Sullivan, M.W., Enright, M., Lucas, D., & Fagen, J.W. (1980). Reactivation of infant memory. *Science, 208,* 1159–1161.

Schwartz, M.S., & Fischer, K.W. (2006). Useful metaphors for tackling problems in teaching and learning. *On Campus, 11*(1), 2–9.

Schwartz, M.S., & Sadler, P.M. (2007). Empowerment in science curriculum development: A microdevelopmental approach. *International Journal of Science Education, 29,* 987–1017.

Snow, C.E., Burns, M.S., & Griffin, P. (Eds.). (1998). *Preventing reading difficulties in young children.* Washington, DC: National Academy Press.

Suárez-Orozco, C., Suárez-Orozco, M., & Todorova, I. (2008). *Learning a new land: Immigrant students in American society.* Cambridge, MA: Harvard University Press.

Wallon, H. (1970). *De l'acte à la pensée* [From action to thought]. Paris: Flammarion.

CHAPTER 4

Reading Success:
A Motivational Perspective

JANINE BEMPECHAT

Inspiring Reading Success: Interest and Motivation in an Age of High-Stakes Testing, edited by Rosalie Fink and S. Jay Samuels. © 2008 by the International Reading Association.

The latest pedagogical techniques are no match for the obstacles teachers face when they encounter students who have a low self-concept of their reading ability or believe effort to be a futile investment in learning. Like all achievement beliefs and behaviors, students' reading-related cognitions play a vital role in their eventual success as readers, predicting, among other things, their persistence, diligence, and ability to be resilient in the face of difficulty or challenge.

Students' reading-related beliefs do not develop in a vacuum. They are coconstructed with their peers and the adults in their lives—their caregivers and teachers. Further, the structure of the classrooms in which they learn (e.g., competitive, cooperative) contributes uniquely to their developing beliefs about learning. In this chapter, we examine motivational factors in learning, including attributions for success and failure, beliefs about ability and the nature of intelligence, and self-regulation skills. Our goal is to provide teachers with an understanding of the practical applications of achievement motivation research for enhancing adaptive beliefs about learning. Indeed, as we explain, advances in achievement motivation have shed new light on our understanding of reading success. In our review and analysis, we include research on students with learning disabilities, with the understanding that these include difficulties acquiring reading skills.

The Importance of Motivational Factors in Learning

Achievement motivation is the study of goal-directed behavior in educational settings. More specifically, it is the study of factors other than intellectual ability that influence the kinds of tasks that children choose to pursue, as well as the persistence they display in the pursuit of their goals (Eccles, Roeser, Vida, Fredricks, & Wigfield, 2006). These include attributions for success and failure, beliefs about ability, and self-regulation. Over the past several years, educators and researchers working with struggling readers have been calling for increased attention to be paid to the central role of motivational factors in these students' learning experiences (Bernard, 2006; Horner & O'Conner, 2007;

Pavri, 2006). Educators and researchers have recognized that, for children with learning disabilities, early difficulties in reading acquisition make issues of ability particularly salient and can herald a host of maladaptive beliefs about learning, including low confidence and diminished expectations for success. If we can understand how struggling readers experience their learning, we can do much to help them develop resiliency in the face of challenge.

Our understanding of the power of achievement beliefs to influence children's learning behavior and outcomes emerged more than four decades ago, largely as a result of the integration of social cognition theory with achievement motivation research. At mid-century, achievement motivation was conceived of largely as an innate need or drive (Atkinson, 1964). Prominent theorists, such as Bernard Weiner and Albert Bandura, recognized that the path from an inner drive to pursue a goal to its successful realization was mediated by achievement cognitions—self-perceptions of ability, attributions for success and failure, self-efficacy—and the emotions that accompany these self-judgments (Bandura, 1982; Weiner, 1985). The notion that children's academic self-evaluations could explain and even predict future achievement behavior and outcomes set the field on a novel pathway and shed much-needed light on basic questions, such as those listed at the beginning of this chapter, that had had puzzled educators for a long time.

As the field has grown, research in achievement motivation has come to be characterized broadly as a search to understand the answers to three primary questions that students ask themselves when they approach a task (Eccles, Wigfield, & Schiefele, 1998). The first, "Can I do this task?" captures students' ability-related concerns. The second, "Do I want to do this task?" speaks to students' intrinsic interest in learning a given task and the value they place on this learning. The third, "What do I have to do to succeed on this task?" represents research on how children learn to organize, plan, and self-regulate their performance. These three lines of inquiry are, of course, integrated and reciprocal in nature (Denissen, Zarrett, & Eccles, 2007; Dowson & McInerney, 2003). For example, children invest more effort and are more persistent in areas in which they believe they have high ability. However, because issues of ability are so salient for struggling readers, our focus in this chapter is on research related to the first question—"Can I do this task?" We demonstrate the ways in which students' self-perceptions of ability have a profound impact on intrinsic interest and the development of self-regulation skills. (For additional resources for adults and children on motivation and interest, see Table 4.1.)

Self-Perceptions of Ability

Why do we choose to pursue some tasks and not others? In this section, we consider three influential approaches to understanding achievement behavior—attribution theory, self-efficacy theory, and goal theory. These theories, while different in orientation, all highlight the central role played by children's academic self-evaluations in their subsequent orientations toward learning.

TABLE 4.1
Additional Resources for Adults and Children on Motivation and Interest

Resources for Adults
Teachers may find it helpful to assess their students' orientations for learning. Edward Deci and Richard Ryan, of the University of Rochester, have made available a variety of questionnaires that researchers and teachers can use to examine the ways in which students approach classroom learning. These useful questionnaires, along with brief theoretical and research commentary, are available at www.psych.rochester.edu/SDT/measures/selfreg.html.

As a result of their experiences with their dyslexic son, Charles Schwab and his wife developed a nonprofit organization dedicated to providing up-to-date information for parents about how they can support their children's reading. The website schwablearning.org contains a variety of user-friendly articles written by experts on topics such as organization and time management, how to help children manage homework, and managing relationships between home and school.

The U.S. Department of Education disseminates research findings and practical tips for parents and teachers who are working with students who display low or diminished motivation. Parents and teachers can learn about factors that foster and inhibit motivation, as well as information on how motivation can be enhanced in all students: www.ed.gov/parents/academic/help/adolescence/partx4.html.

The University of Michigan maintains a very informative website on children's motivation. With an emphasis on early childhood, the site provides summaries of research findings on motivation in young children, improving motivation, and parental involvement. Readers will find helpful "Tips for Parents," which include strategies for managing student frustration and making learning interesting: sitemaker.umich.edu/356.omo/home.

Resources for Children
The following Web resources represent a small sample of websites geared toward engaging children in academic activities. These sites provide games designed to foster interest in improving vocabulary, literacy, and phonics.

pbskids.org/lions/
www.randomhouse.com/kids/home.pperl
pbskids.org/readingrainbow/
www.sesameworkshop.org/sesamestreet/

Attribution Theory

According to Weiner (1985), achievement-motivated behavior is driven by the need we all have to understand the reasons for our successes and failures. His attribution theory, and the extensive body of research stemming from it, have demonstrated that individuals, including children, experience affective reactions to success or failure (e.g., pride, shame) and actively seek to understand their performance outcomes by ascribing them to four main categories of attributions: effort (or lack of effort), innate ability (or lack thereof), luck (good or bad), and other external factors (e.g., being liked or disliked by the teacher). These attributions are linked to specific emotions (e.g., lack of effort and guilt, lack of ability and pity) and vary along at least three dimensions—stability, controllability, and locus (internal or external).

For example, suppose that when presented with a poor grade on a test, a student realizes that she did not put enough time into studying. Lack of effort is a factor that is, by its very nature, unstable, controllable, and internal. According to Weiner (1985), an ascription to lack of effort will likely lead to feelings of guilt, which will increase the probability that this student will redouble her efforts in the face of the next test. Now suppose that this same student believes that her poor performance was due to the fact that she simply is not smart enough and lacks ability. This attribution to lack of ability, a factor that is perceived as stable, internal, and uncontrollable, will likely give rise to feelings of incompetence and shame and will make it less likely that this student will invest serious effort in advance of the next test. For struggling readers, the implications are clear. To the extent that they perceive little or no improvement despite great effort, they may indeed come to view their difficulties as stemming from a basic lack of innate ability. If students decided that this is indeed the case, it would make no sense for them to try harder—greater effort would be unlikely to yield any significant gains.

Students are indeed active participants in their learning, and their attempts to judge their abilities do not occur in a vacuum. From the onset of formal schooling, students become increasingly exposed to a variety of social comparison information and are developmentally poised to attend to and interpret it (Pomerantz, Ruble, Frey, & Greulich, 1995). Grades, test scores, report cards, and teacher feedback provide students with a normative sense of their performance and progress relative to others. This growing awareness of social comparison information may lead struggling readers to feel all the more incompetent as they observe their peers make progress with relative ease or, at the least, with far less effort than they themselves feel they need to invest.

Important for teachers, Weiner's research has demonstrated that children as young as 5 years old are able to infer attributions from teachers' affect (Weiner, Graham, Stern, & Lawson, 1982). In one experimental study, children ages 5, 9, and 11 were read scenarios in which teachers were described as feeling a variety of emotions, including anger and pity, toward a failing student. At all ages children correctly inferred that if a teacher conveyed anger at a failing student, it must be because that student had invested little effort in his work. Students perceived that the message implicit in the teacher's anger was that she had expected the student to succeed with the necessary effort. At the same time, only older children—9- and 11-year-olds—correctly inferred that teacher pity was likely the result of a perceived lack of ability on the failing student's part. The implicit message in this case is that the teacher understood that the student's lack of ability would preclude success.

For teachers of struggling readers, the implications for student feedback are clear. While it is very difficult to observe students' struggle to acquire proficiency, teachers need to maintain their expectations for success and convey their belief that effort can compensate for learning difficulties. They can do this by modeling effective cognitive and metacognitive skills, such as organization and planning. We discuss strategies for these in a later section on fostering adaptive achievement beliefs and behaviors.

Self-Efficacy Theory

The power of expectations to influence behavior is also central in Bandura's self-efficacy theory. According to Bandura, self-efficacy is the "core belief that one has the power to produce desired effects" (Bandura & Locke, 2003, p. 87). This focus on students' beliefs in their personal agency has helped educators understand how it is that many students may know exactly what they need to do to successfully complete a task but somehow do not manage to do so. According to Bandura, this gap between knowledge and action can be understood by examining how students evaluate their achievement experiences. They do so in the context of reciprocal interactions between individual factors (e.g., achievement beliefs), environmental factors (e.g., teacher feedback), and behavioral factors (e.g., effort; Schunk & Zimmerman, 2007). Students engage in this kind of self-evaluation throughout the process of selecting and pursuing a goal (Bandura, 1991). They make judgments of self-efficacy based on perceptions of their abilities, their prior classroom experiences, and perceptions of support they have for learning. Students actively gauge their progress, and their self-efficacy tends to increase if they believe they are advancing toward their goal. For struggling readers, it is important that, in and of themselves, setbacks do not necessarily diminish perceptions of self-efficacy, as long as students believe that they can improve by fine-tuning their learning strategy (Schunk, 1995).

From the perspective of self-efficacy theory, expectations are not merely thoughts about the probability of success. Instead, expectations encompass both an active anticipation of possible outcomes (outcome expectations) and students' judgments about whether they have the necessary ability to succeed at the task (efficacy expectations). Self-efficacy beliefs are important, then, because they have significant bearing on the extent to which children will approach tasks with a positive outlook. Indeed, a certain reasonable level of confidence in one's ability to succeed will propel students to invest effort and be persistent, and particularly so when a task presents challenges. In contrast, students who have low outcome expectations and little belief in their ability to succeed are the most at risk for learned helplessness and self-handicapping behaviors.

A variety of studies have demonstrated that students' perceptions of self-efficacy predict the goals they choose to pursue, the effort they are willing to invest in a task, and the extent to which they will persist when the task becomes difficult. For example, Pintrich and DeGroot (1990) surveyed seventh graders' self-efficacy beliefs, cognitive and metacognitive strategies (e.g., study techniques, self-regulation), and effort. Those with higher self-efficacy beliefs were more effective learners, in the sense that they were more likely to make use of relevant cognitive strategies and engage in more self-regulation, such as planning. They were also more persistent and had higher academic outcomes. The fact that cognitive strategies, but not self-efficacy beliefs, were related to grades suggests that by strengthening cognitive strategies, teachers can help students do better in school. More important, though, the results of this study suggest that by enhancing students' self-efficacy beliefs, teachers may be able to scaffold self-regulation, which can lead to higher achievement (Pintrich & DeGroot, 1990).

Goal Theory

How can struggling readers maintain a sense that they are capable of learning? Goal theorists such as John Nicholls (1989) and Carol Dweck (1999) have argued that this desire to appear capable (or avoid appearing incapable) is what guides achievement behavior. Nicholls's studies of children's developing conceptions of ability showed ways in which children come to alter their views about the nature of intelligence and the relationship between effort and ability in ways that can be debilitating for their learning. Importantly, though, his research demonstrated that, despite children's growing tendency to view ability as limited, teachers can have a profound influence in maintaining adaptive beliefs about learning.

Nicholls found that children as young as 5 years old tend to judge their ability subjectively. Through this *undifferentiated* view of ability, children tend to define ability as mastery—something that can be enhanced through effort (Nicholls, 1978). By the end of first or the beginning of second grade, however, children's views about the nature of ability begin to shift to a more normative, *differentiated* perspective. They begin to view ability as limited by capacity, and their view of the relationship between effort and ability can best be defined as compensatory. In other words, children are now more likely to believe that the harder they have to try, the "dumber" they must be.

> John Nicholls's research demonstrated that, despite children's growing tendency to view ability as limited, teachers can have a profound influence in maintaining adaptive beliefs about learning.

What accounts for this change in children's perceptions of their abilities? There is no doubt that the changing climate of classroom learning, as well as children's growing cognitive capacities to interpret this climate, have a major impact on their developing achievement beliefs (Eccles et al., 2006). As we mentioned earlier, children's growing awareness of social comparison information brings issues of ability to the fore. In a series of studies, Nicholls documented the differential effects on students' learning goals when their classrooms are structured around competitive as compared to cooperative learning. Classrooms oriented around a typical competitive model, where rewards are limited to the few highest achieving students, contribute the heightened concerns about ability (Johnson & Johnson, 1999).

Students in these classrooms tend to become *ego involved*. In other words, they focus on how they are doing relative to others and become especially concerned with demonstrating that they have ability. Not surprising, they tend to avoid challenge. For these students, the outcomes of learning—grades and test scores—take on greater significance than the process of learning itself and students come to place great importance on extrinsic reasons for learning (rewards) and avoiding challenge. In contrast, when students learn in cooperative settings, they become *task involved*, or focused on the process of learning, engaged by challenge, intrinsically interested in learning for its own sake, and less daunted by setbacks or difficulties (Nicholls, 1984, 1989).

For teachers of struggling readers, this research offers an optimistic message about the malleability of students' achievement beliefs and teachers' ability to foster task-involved learning. That is, even among students with learning disabilities, maladaptive competence-related beliefs are not necessarily unchangeable. By minimizing the salience, or heightened importance, of ability in their classrooms, teachers can help their students approach reading with greater confidence and an enhanced sense of control over their learning.

What can teachers do, though, when their students believe very strongly that they simply lack the ability to be successful readers? Dweck's approach to goal theory has focused on students' implicit theories of intelligence and the ways in which these influence their achievement beliefs and behaviors (Dweck, 1999). According to Dweck, children come to develop one of two distinct theories of intelligence. They believe that everyone can learn new things. Those who adhere to an *entity* theory believe that intelligence is fixed, limited, and limiting. They endorse statements such as "You can learn new things, but how smart you are stays pretty much the same." In contrast, those who endorse an *incremental* theory believe that intelligence is malleable and unlimited. They agree with statements such as "As long as you try, you can get smarter and smarter."

These different theories of intelligence set students on very different paths with respect to their achievement beliefs and behaviors. For example, when given a choice of tasks, entity theorists tend to opt for the one that they already know how to perform (*performance* goal), thus sacrificing opportunities to learn something new. They also tend to have lower confidence when faced with a novel task and are more susceptible to learned helplessness when confronted with challenge or difficulty. In addition, entity theorists tend to define intelligence in others in terms of the products of learning ("She's smart because she always gets A's") (Bempechat, London, & Dweck, 1991; Grant & Dweck, 2003).

In contrast, when given the choice, incremental theorists tend to select tasks from which they will learn something new (*learning* goal), even if this means they may make mistakes and appear incompetent. They tend to have higher confidence and display mastery-oriented behavior, even in the face of difficulties. Interestingly, incremental theorists tend to define intelligence in others in terms of the process of learning ("He's smart because he tries hard").

Dweck and her colleagues recently reported that students' theories of intelligence in mathematics in the seventh grade predicted their math achievement two years later (Blackwell, Trzesniewski, & Dweck, 2007). Specifically, endorsement of an incremental theory predicted increases in math achievement in junior high school, while endorsement of an entity theory predicted decreased math achievement over time. In addition, relative to entity theorists, incremental theorists were more learning goal oriented, had positive beliefs about effort, and reported nonhelpless reactions to challenge. A subsequent intervention study demonstrated that students who were taught an incremental theory of intelligence engaged in more adaptive learning behaviors, such as seeking help, and showed significant improvement in their math performance.

Summary

With social cognition as the guiding theoretical framework, our understanding of the complexities of children's achievement-related beliefs and behaviors has become more nuanced. It is clear that children's developing beliefs about the causes of success and failure, their self-efficacy beliefs, and their conceptions of ability all have a profound influence on their task choices, persistence, and resilience to learned helplessness. It is a great challenge for struggling readers to maintain adaptive beliefs about learning in the face of disabilities over which they may feel they have no control. As we describe in the following section, however, techniques aimed at fostering cognitive skills can be successfully integrated with strategies that enhance adaptive motivational beliefs and behaviors.

Fostering Adaptive Achievement Beliefs and Behaviors in Struggling Readers

As Polloway and his colleagues have noted, simultaneous educational trends in the 1980s had a direct impact on the school experiences of students with learning disabilities (Polloway, Bursuck, & Epstein, 2001). First, emerging cross-national research on the math and science achievement of U.S. students as compared to Japanese, Chinese, and European students showed that U.S. students lagged far behind their Asian and European peers (McKnight et al., 1987; Stevenson, Lee, & Stigler, 1986). As a result, increased pressure was placed on schools to enhance student achievement, in part through more sweeping high-stakes testing at the state and national levels. At the same time, the process of inclusion integrated students with learning disabilities into general education classes, where they and their teachers faced the same pressures to perform. This pressure was and continues to be nontrivial; students with learning challenges face added academic hurdles, including memory or listening deficits, organizational problems, and difficulty setting reasonable goals (Hughes, Ruhl, Schumaker, & Deschler, 2002).

Against this backdrop, how can teachers foster adaptive motivational tendencies in students whose struggles to become successful readers are likely to propel them toward low self-perceptions of ability? Building on research she conducted with Nicholls, Thorkildsen (2002) has proposed that we should promote literacy as a lifestyle or process, rather than a series of discrete tasks that have to be mastered in order to satisfy curricular goals. According to Thorkildsen, students need to see literacy as embedded in a social system and, in so doing, will come to see that being literate allows them to negotiate all manner of challenging life events. Typically, teachers dictate most of the academic tasks that students need to accomplish, including literacy tasks. This serves to undermine students' sense of agency around their learning and has a negative impact on their intrinsic motivation to learn (deCharms, 1992).

Further, as we noted earlier, competitively structured classrooms are environments in which mistakes can come to be viewed as implicit condemnations of ability. For teachers of struggling readers, Thorkildsen's message implies that these students need to be oriented toward the process of learning and not the products or outcomes of learning. Classroom learning should be structured around mastery goals so that the message to all students is that there is value in the difficulties, challenges, and setbacks that are inherent in becoming a proficient reader.

This focus on personal agency dovetails nicely with Schunk and Zimmerman's (2007) work on modeling as a means to enhance self-efficacy and self-regulation. Recall that Bandura's social cognitive theory views individuals as embedded in multiple contexts in which they are influenced by the reciprocal interactions that occur between personal, environmental, and behavioral factors. Given that students derive information about their self-efficacy from the adults and peers in their lives, Schunk and Zimmerman have argued that models can provide relevant information and model adaptive learning and self-regulatory strategies that foster reading success. These include *planning, monitoring, control, and reflection* (Pintrich & Zusho, 2002). In keeping with self-efficacy theory, these researchers note that when students watch a model perform a task, they develop an outcome expectation that is positive. This is especially the case when the modeled behavior results in success and represents something that they value. Models also influence self-efficacy by demonstrating that success is possible. Thus, over time and through effort, struggling readers can indeed enhance their self-efficacy.

Schunk and Zimmerman have proposed a four-phase social cognitive model of self-regulation. Through *observation*, students learn modeled skills at the cognitive level. Then, through the process of *emulation*, students attempt to reproduce the model's actions. This is followed by training in *self-control*, during which students acquire the ability to use their new skills independently when needed. In other words, the skill becomes internalized. Finally, through *self-regulation*, students learn to adapt their acquired skill to novel situations. This model is akin to Vygotsky's notion of scaffolding, in which "novice" learners gradually take over more responsibility for completing a task from their "expert" teachers (Rogoff, 1990; Vygotsky, 1934/1978).

Through a series of intervention studies, Schunk and Zimmerman showed that modeling is an effective way to foster self-efficacy for reading and persistence (Schunk & Zimmerman, 2007). In their recent study, they examined the effectiveness of modeled strategy instruction. For example, in one study of reading comprehension, fourth and fifth graders participated in 35-minute training sessions for 15 school days. A teacher modeled a five-step strategy to answer questions about a reading passage. Students then had to read and apply this five-step strategy to novel passages. As part of this experimental study, students were instructed to either learn how to use the steps in order to answer the question (process goal condition), put forth effort to answer the question (product goal), or simply try their best (general goal). Results showed that, relative to students in the general goal condition, those in the process and product goal conditions evaluated their self-efficacy for answering reading comprehension questions at a higher level. Further, confirming Nicholls's and Thorkildsen's work, students in the process goal condition attained higher reading comprehension scores (Schunk & Rice, 1989). Taken together, it appears that the integration of achievement motivation theory with reading research promises positive outcomes for students' achievement beliefs and achievement behaviors.

Importantly, these outcomes are not limited to the school context. Parents—children's primary partners in learning—can be similarly helped to foster adaptive achievement-related beliefs and behaviors. Parents play a major role in fostering achievement through their involvement with homework. Homework itself, however, is fraught with the potential for conflict between parents and children, even when children are developing typically with respect to their reading skills. The challenge for educators is to help parents help their children manage their homework when learning disabilities add challenge to already challenging assignments.

The Challenge of Homework for Struggling Readers and Their Parents

While controversy continues to surround the practice of assigning homework to students, there is general agreement that it fosters academic achievement, particularly in middle and secondary school, and serves as a training ground for adaptive achievement beliefs and behaviors (Bempechat, 2004; Cooper, Robinson, & Patall, 2006). However, relative to their peers without learning disabilities, those with learning disabilities, including struggling readers, experience their homework as more difficult, more boring, less fulfilling, and as taking more time to complete (Bryan, Burstein, & Bryan, 2001). Students with learning disabilities also display more difficulty completing their homework, spend less time on it, and do work of poorer quality as compared to their non-learning-disabled peers (Polloway et al., 2001). At the same time, however, learning-disabled students state that they want to be treated equally with respect to class assignments and report feeling stigmatized by assignments that are shorter, fewer in number, and less difficult than those assigned to their non-learning-disabled peers (Bryan et al., 2001). This is consistent with attribution theory, in the sense that students may perceive these differential homework assignments as evidence that their teachers may believe they have lower ability than their non-learning-disabled peers (Weiner, 2005).

It is not uncommon for parents to report conflict at home that is directly related to the stress associated with completing homework assignments (Xu & Corno, 1998). Many parents complain that teachers lack information about their children, do not communicate efficiently about their children's homework, and do not contact them about problems with their children's homework until it is too late for them to be helpful (Munk et al., 2001). However, in general, parents express the desire to help their children with homework and often see this as both an obligation and a natural aspect of parenthood as well as something that they believe teachers expect of them (Delgado-Gaitan, 1992; Hoover-Dempsey et al., 2001).

Parents with learning-disabled children, though, have added concerns. First, they report spending more time per night helping with homework. Two studies reported average estimates of 16 and 25 minutes longer, as compared to the time reported by parents of non-learning-disabled children (Harniss, Epstein, Bursuck, Nelson, & Jayanthi, 2001; Munk et al., 2001). In addition, they believe that their children's teachers do not know enough about their children's learning challenges to be truly helpful and do not initiate communication about their children's learning issues in the classroom (Munk et al., 2001).

Against this backdrop, parents' own self-efficacy beliefs are often called into question by the difficulties they experience in helping their children with homework. We know that parents who maintain positive attitudes about homework are better able to scaffold their children's learning without being intrusive and model self-regulation strategies that facilitate homework completion (Cooper & Valentine, 2001; Keith & Cool, 1992; Keith et al., 1993). However, despite their willingness to help their children, mothers of children with learning disabilities report that they disengage themselves from helping their children when conflicts arise, partly out of a concern that they may foster dependency or helplessness (Bryan et al., 2001). Recent research by Pomerantz and her colleagues on the affective and motivational impact of parental help with homework, however, suggests that this well-intentioned approach may do more harm than good.

Pomerantz and colleagues, recognizing that homework is essentially an affective experience, have examined parents' affect while they help their children with homework (Pomerantz, Grolnick, & Price, 2005; Pomerantz, Ng, & Wang, 2006). To the extent that their children need help with homework, the children may be vulnerable to learned helplessness. In this context, negative parental affect can undermine confidence as well as intrinsic interest (Pomerantz et al., 2005). In contrast, positive affect on the part of parents may serve to alleviate learned helplessness and communicate positive expectations.

In a study of over 100 elementary-age children and their mothers, Pomerantz and her colleagues asked mothers about how much homework their children had on a daily basis, how much they helped them, and what their affect was while helping. Mothers also rated their children's behavior (helpless, mastery oriented, autonomous) while completing their homework, as well as their emotional functioning. Results showed that mothers' negative affect increased on days when their assistance was high. Importantly, though, on such days, these mothers also reported twice as much positive as negative affect. Interestingly, mothers' positive affect did not decrease on days when they helped their children more. Instead, negative affect appeared related to mothers' perceptions that their children were displaying learned helpless behavior.

> When helping with homework, positive affect on the part of parents may serve to alleviate learned helplessness and communicate positive expectations.

Contrary to some parents' concerns then, this research demonstrates that, rather than backing off, parents may do more good by continuing to provide assistance, particularly if they maintain positive affect. In this study, mothers' positive affect mitigated the effect of their negative affect on their children, helped to alleviate feelings of learned helplessness, and contributed to mastery-oriented behavior and an increase in self-esteem and positive emotions on the part of the children.

For parents whose children have learning disabilities, a subsequent study (Pomerantz et al., 2006) provides more detailed support for the importance of displaying positive affect and fostering mastery-oriented behavior. This later longitudinal investigation showed that mothers' mastery-oriented practices while helping with homework predicted positive psychological functioning among children with more negative perceptions of self-concepts. Six months later, children with negative self-concepts of ability became more positive in their psychological functioning when their mothers used mastery-oriented practices more often and more negative when their mothers used such practices infrequently (Pomerantz et al., 2006). These findings dovetail nicely with Schunk and Zimmerman's (2007) work on modeling strategies and convey three key lessons for parents and teachers of children with learning disabilities. First, negative affect in parents when they try to help their children with homework is a natural but necessarily harmful outcome of an often conflictual process. Second, positive affect under these circumstances is critical for bolstering children's confidence in their ability to acquire new skills and knowledge. Third, the consistent modeling of mastery-oriented strategies can serve to enhance self-efficacy and alleviate learned helplessness.

Homework intervention research with learning-disabled students has begun to move away from a focus on strategies specific to teachers and parents (e.g., homework schedules, reward contingencies) to strategies targeting the development of self-regulation in students themselves. For example, Hughes and his colleagues designed PROJECT Strategy to teach a group of adolescents with learning disabilities the cognitive and metacognitive skills needed to independently complete homework (Hughes et al., 2002). Consisting of seven steps (whose acronym spells PROJECT) and four subsets, students were formally trained to (1) **P**repare their forms (bimonthly planners and weekly study guides); (2) **R**ecord their assignments in their planners and ask their teacher any question they might have about the work; (3) **O**rganize their assignments by breaking them into parts, estimating the number of study sessions they will need, schedule these sessions, and taking the assignments home; (4) **J**ump into their work, as a way to prevent task avoidance; (5) **E**ngage in their work by enlisting help if they encounter difficulty; (6) **C**heck; and (7) **T**urn in their work. Results of this intervention program demonstrated that these learning-disabled students were able both to learn and maintain the strategies they were taught. Further, they showed improved grades and higher teacher ratings of homework completion and engagement in learning.

In essence, intervention programs such as PROJECT Strategy mirror self-regulation training as described by Zimmerman and his colleagues and demonstrate that the integration of achievement motivation theory with intervention research has compelling practical applications.

Patterns of Adaptive Learning Scales (PALS)

Based on years of research on children's goal orientations, Midgley and her colleagues developed the Patterns of Adaptive Learning Scales (PALS), which provide teachers with an assessment tool to examine children's motivational goal orientations (Midgley et al., 2000). The PALS includes five student scales—(1) Personal Achievement Goal Orientations (mastery, performance-approach, and performance-avoid); (2) Perceptions of Teachers' Goals (teacher mastery goal, teacher performance-approach goal, and teacher performance-avoid goal); (3) Perception of Classroom Goal Structures (classroom mastery goal structure, classroom performance-approach goal structure, classroom performance-avoid goal structure); (4) Academic-Related Perceptions, Beliefs, and Strategies (academic efficacy, academic press, academic self-handicapping strategies avoiding novelty, cheating behavior, disruptive behavior, self-presentation of low achievement, skepticism about the relevance of school for future success); and (5) Perceptions of Parents, Home Life, and Neighborhood.

You will find items related to the first four subscales in the reproducible Patterns of Adaptive Learning Scales on pages 89–94, as these are the most relevant to the issues discussed in this chapter. The PALS manual, which includes detailed information about scale development and use, can be accessed at www.umich.edu/~pals/PALS%202000_V13Word97.pdf.

Conclusion

Advances in theory and research on children's achievement motivation have allowed us to gain deeper insights into the varied ways that children approach learning. The most important lesson we have learned is that children's developing beliefs about their academic competence have a profound influence on the extent to which they will seek challenge, persist in the face of difficulties, and recover from setbacks and failure. As we have discussed in this chapter, these beliefs are coconstructed in the contexts of children's homes and schools, and in interactions with the peers and adults in their lives.

By virtue of their learning difficulties, struggling readers are at risk for developing maladaptive achievement beliefs and behaviors. However, research has decisively shown that interventions designed to enhance self-efficacy and self-regulation can foster adaptive beliefs about learning. Struggling readers can indeed flourish in learning environments in which mistakes are embraced, reading difficulties are perceived as typical to the process of learning, and organizational and self-regulatory strategies are an active part of day-to-day learning.

POSTREADING QUESTIONS

◆ What stands out most to you about struggling readers' motivation to learn?

◆ What, if anything, surprised you about motivational issues encountered by struggling readers?

◆ Have any of your beliefs about struggling readers' achievement beliefs and behaviors changed as a result of reading this chapter? How?

◆ Have any of your prior beliefs about struggling readers' achievement beliefs and behaviors been confirmed by what you read?

◆ What might you do differently with children as a result of reading this chapter?

Acknowledgments
The author wishes to thank Rosalie Fink for her guidance and thoughtful feedback during the preparation of this chapter.

Patterns of Adaptive Learning Scales (PALS)

The first question is an example.

I like strawberry ice cream.

1	2	3	4	5
NOT AT ALL TRUE		SOMEWHAT TRUE		VERY TRUE

Here are some questions about yourself as a student in this class.
Please circle the number that best describes what you think.

1. I'm certain I can master the skills taught in class this year.

1	2	3	4	5
NOT AT ALL TRUE		SOMEWHAT TRUE		VERY TRUE

2. I would avoid participating in class if it meant that other students would think I know a lot.

1	2	3	4	5
NOT AT ALL TRUE		SOMEWHAT TRUE		VERY TRUE

3. It's important to me that I don't look stupid in class.

1	2	3	4	5
NOT AT ALL TRUE		SOMEWHAT TRUE		VERY TRUE

4. Even if I do well in school, it will not help me have the kind of life I want when I grow up.

1	2	3	4	5
NOT AT ALL TRUE		SOMEWHAT TRUE		VERY TRUE

5. If other students found out I did well on a test, I would tell them it was just luck even if that wasn't the case.

1	2	3	4	5
NOT AT ALL TRUE		SOMEWHAT TRUE		VERY TRUE

6. When I've figured out how to do a problem, my teacher gives me more challenging problems to think about.

1	2	3	4	5
NOT AT ALL TRUE		SOMEWHAT TRUE		VERY TRUE

7. I would prefer to do class work that is familiar to me, rather than work I would have to learn how to do.

1	2	3	4	5
NOT AT ALL TRUE		SOMEWHAT TRUE		VERY TRUE

8. It's important to me that other students in my class think I am good at my class work.

1	2	3	4	5
NOT AT ALL TRUE		SOMEWHAT TRUE		VERY TRUE

9. It's important to me that I learn a lot of new concepts this year.

1	2	3	4	5
NOT AT ALL TRUE		SOMEWHAT TRUE		VERY TRUE

10. My teacher presses me to do thoughtful work.

1	2	3	4	5
NOT AT ALL TRUE		SOMEWHAT TRUE		VERY TRUE

(continued)

From Midgley, C., Maehr, M.L., Hruda, L.Z., Anderman, E., Anderman, L., Freeman, K.E., et al. (2000). *Manual for the Patterns of Adaptive Learning Scales (PALS)*. Ann Arbor: University of Michigan. Used with permission.

11. I'm certain I can figure out how to do the most difficult class work.

1	2	3	4	5
NOT AT ALL TRUE		SOMEWHAT TRUE		VERY TRUE

12. Some students fool around the night before a test. Then if they don't do well, they can say that is the reason. How true is this of you?

1	2	3	4	5
NOT AT ALL TRUE		SOMEWHAT TRUE		VERY TRUE

13. My chances of succeeding later in life don't depend on doing well in school.

1	2	3	4	5
NOT AT ALL TRUE		SOMEWHAT TRUE		VERY TRUE

14. I sometimes annoy my teacher during class.

1	2	3	4	5
NOT AT ALL TRUE		SOMEWHAT TRUE		VERY TRUE

15. My teacher asks me to explain how I get my answers.

1	2	3	4	5
NOT AT ALL TRUE		SOMEWHAT TRUE		VERY TRUE

16. Some students purposely get involved in lots of activities. Then if they don't do well on their class work, they can say it is because they were involved with other things. How true is this of you?

1	2	3	4	5
NOT AT ALL TRUE		SOMEWHAT TRUE		VERY TRUE

17. When I'm working out a problem, my teacher tells me to keep thinking until I really understand.

1	2	3	4	5
NOT AT ALL TRUE		SOMEWHAT TRUE		VERY TRUE

18. Some students look for reasons to keep them from studying (not feeling well, having to help their parents, taking care of a brother or sister, etc.). Then if they don't do well on their class work, they can say this is the reason. How true is this of you?

1	2	3	4	5
NOT AT ALL TRUE		SOMEWHAT TRUE		VERY TRUE

19. My teacher doesn't let me do just easy work, but makes me think.

1	2	3	4	5
NOT AT ALL TRUE		SOMEWHAT TRUE		VERY TRUE

20. I don't like to learn a lot of new concepts in class.

1	2	3	4	5
NOT AT ALL TRUE		SOMEWHAT TRUE		VERY TRUE

21. I wouldn't volunteer to answer a question in class if I thought other students would think I was smart.

1	2	3	4	5
NOT AT ALL TRUE		SOMEWHAT TRUE		VERY TRUE

22. I sometimes copy answers from other students during tests.

1	2	3	4	5
NOT AT ALL TRUE		SOMEWHAT TRUE		VERY TRUE

(continued)

From Midgley, C., Maehr, M.L., Hruda, L.Z., Anderman, E., Anderman, L., Freeman, K.E., et al. (2000). *Manual for the Patterns of Adaptive Learning Scales (PALS).* Ann Arbor: University of Michigan. Used with permission.

Patterns of Adaptive Learning Scales (PALS) (continued)

23. I prefer to do work as I have always done it, rather than trying something new.

1	2	3	4	5
NOT AT ALL TRUE		SOMEWHAT TRUE		VERY TRUE

24. If I did well on a school assignment, I wouldn't want other students to see my grade.

1	2	3	4	5
NOT AT ALL TRUE		SOMEWHAT TRUE		VERY TRUE

25. One of my goals in class is to learn as much as I can.

1	2	3	4	5
NOT AT ALL TRUE		SOMEWHAT TRUE		VERY TRUE

26. One of my goals is to show others that I'm good at my class work.

1	2	3	4	5
NOT AT ALL TRUE		SOMEWHAT TRUE		VERY TRUE

27. It's very important to me that I don't look smarter than others in class.

1	2	3	4	5
NOT AT ALL TRUE		SOMEWHAT TRUE		VERY TRUE

28. Doing well in school doesn't improve my chances of having a good life when I grow up.

1	2	3	4	5
NOT AT ALL TRUE		SOMEWHAT TRUE		VERY TRUE

29. One of my goals is to master a lot of new skills this year.

1	2	3	4	5
NOT AT ALL TRUE		SOMEWHAT TRUE		VERY TRUE

30. I sometimes get into trouble with my teacher during class.

1	2	3	4	5
NOT AT ALL TRUE		SOMEWHAT TRUE		VERY TRUE

31. I sometimes cheat on my class work.

1	2	3	4	5
NOT AT ALL TRUE		SOMEWHAT TRUE		VERY TRUE

32. Getting good grades in school won't guarantee that I will get a good job when I grow up.

1	2	3	4	5
NOT AT ALL TRUE		SOMEWHAT TRUE		VERY TRUE

33. One of my goals is to keep others from thinking I'm not smart in class.

1	2	3	4	5
NOT AT ALL TRUE		SOMEWHAT TRUE		VERY TRUE

34. I sometimes behave in a way during class that annoys my teacher.

1	2	3	4	5
NOT AT ALL TRUE		SOMEWHAT TRUE		VERY TRUE

35. I like academic concepts that are familiar to me, rather than those I haven't thought about before.

1	2	3	4	5
NOT AT ALL TRUE		SOMEWHAT TRUE		VERY TRUE

(continued)

From Midgley, C., Maehr, M.L., Hruda, L.Z., Anderman, E., Anderman, L., Freeman, K.E., et al. (2000). *Manual for the Patterns of Adaptive Learning Scales (PALS)*. Ann Arbor: University of Michigan. Used with permission.

36. Even if I am successful in school, it won't help me fulfill my dreams.

| 1 | 2 | 3 | 4 | 5 |
| NOT AT ALL TRUE | | SOMEWHAT TRUE | | VERY TRUE |

37. If I were good at my class work, I would try to do my work in a way that didn't show it.

| 1 | 2 | 3 | 4 | 5 |
| NOT AT ALL TRUE | | SOMEWHAT TRUE | | VERY TRUE |

38. It's important to me that I thoroughly understand my class work.

| 1 | 2 | 3 | 4 | 5 |
| NOT AT ALL TRUE | | SOMEWHAT TRUE | | VERY TRUE |

39. I sometimes copy answers from other students when I do my class work.

| 1 | 2 | 3 | 4 | 5 |
| NOT AT ALL TRUE | | SOMEWHAT TRUE | | VERY TRUE |

40. I would choose class work I knew I could do, rather than work I haven't done before.

| 1 | 2 | 3 | 4 | 5 |
| NOT AT ALL TRUE | | SOMEWHAT TRUE | | VERY TRUE |

41. One of my goals is to show others that class work is easy for me.

| 1 | 2 | 3 | 4 | 5 |
| NOT AT ALL TRUE | | SOMEWHAT TRUE | | VERY TRUE |

42. Some students let their friends keep them from paying attention in class or from doing their homework. Then if they don't do well, they can say their friends kept them from working. How true is this of you?

| 1 | 2 | 3 | 4 | 5 |
| NOT AT ALL TRUE | | SOMEWHAT TRUE | | VERY TRUE |

43. Doing well in school won't help me have a satisfying career when I grow up.

| 1 | 2 | 3 | 4 | 5 |
| NOT AT ALL TRUE | | SOMEWHAT TRUE | | VERY TRUE |

44. Some students purposely don't try hard in class. Then if they don't do well, they can say it is because they didn't try. How true is this of you?

| 1 | 2 | 3 | 4 | 5 |
| NOT AT ALL TRUE | | SOMEWHAT TRUE | | VERY TRUE |

45. One of my goals is to look smart in comparison to the other students in my class.

| 1 | 2 | 3 | 4 | 5 |
| NOT AT ALL TRUE | | SOMEWHAT TRUE | | VERY TRUE |

46. One of my goals in class is to avoid looking smarter than other kids.

| 1 | 2 | 3 | 4 | 5 |
| NOT AT ALL TRUE | | SOMEWHAT TRUE | | VERY TRUE |

47. Some students put off doing their class work until the last minute. Then if they don't do well on their work, they can say that is the reason. How true is this of you?

| 1 | 2 | 3 | 4 | 5 |
| NOT AT ALL TRUE | | SOMEWHAT TRUE | | VERY TRUE |

(continued)

From Midgley, C., Maehr, M.L., Hruda, L.Z., Anderman, E., Anderman, L., Freeman, K.E., et al. (2000). *Manual for the Patterns of Adaptive Learning Scales (PALS)*. Ann Arbor: University of Michigan. Used with permission.

Patterns of Adaptive Learning Scales (PALS) (continued)

48. It's important to me that I look smart compared to others in my class.

1	2	3	4	5
NOT AT ALL TRUE		SOMEWHAT TRUE		VERY TRUE

49. It's important to me that I improve my skills this year.

1	2	3	4	5
NOT AT ALL TRUE		SOMEWHAT TRUE		VERY TRUE

50. I sometimes don't follow my teacher's directions during class.

1	2	3	4	5
NOT AT ALL TRUE		SOMEWHAT TRUE		VERY TRUE

51. It's important to me that my teacher doesn't think that I know less than others in class.

1	2	3	4	5
NOT AT ALL TRUE		SOMEWHAT TRUE		VERY TRUE

52. I can do almost all the work in class if I don't give up.

1	2	3	4	5
NOT AT ALL TRUE		SOMEWHAT TRUE		VERY TRUE

53. My teacher makes sure that the work I do really makes me think.

1	2	3	4	5
NOT AT ALL TRUE		SOMEWHAT TRUE		VERY TRUE

54. I sometimes disturb the lesson that is going on in class.

1	2	3	4	5
NOT AT ALL TRUE		SOMEWHAT TRUE		VERY TRUE

55. One of my goals in class is to avoid looking like I have trouble doing the work.

1	2	3	4	5
NOT AT ALL TRUE		SOMEWHAT TRUE		VERY TRUE

56. Even if the work is hard, I can learn it.

1	2	3	4	5
NOT AT ALL TRUE		SOMEWHAT TRUE		VERY TRUE

57. My teacher accepts nothing less than my full effort.

1	2	3	4	5
NOT AT ALL TRUE		SOMEWHAT TRUE		VERY TRUE

58. I can do even the hardest work in this class if I try.

1	2	3	4	5
NOT AT ALL TRUE		SOMEWHAT TRUE		VERY TRUE

The following questions are about this class and about the work you do in class. Remember to say how you really feel. No one at school or home will see your answers.

59. In our class, trying hard is very important.

1	2	3	4	5
NOT AT ALL TRUE		SOMEWHAT TRUE		VERY TRUE

(continued)

From Midgley, C., Maehr, M.L., Hruda, L.Z., Anderman, E., Anderman, L., Freeman, K.E., et al. (2000). *Manual for the Patterns of Adaptive Learning Scales (PALS)*. Ann Arbor: University of Michigan. Used with permission.

60. In our class, showing others that you are not bad at class work is really important.

1	2	3	4	5
NOT AT ALL TRUE		SOMEWHAT TRUE		VERY TRUE

61. In our class, how much you improve is really important.

1	2	3	4	5
NOT AT ALL TRUE		SOMEWHAT TRUE		VERY TRUE

62. In our class, getting good grades is the main goal.

1	2	3	4	5
NOT AT ALL TRUE		SOMEWHAT TRUE		VERY TRUE

63. In our class, really understanding the material is the main goal.

1	2	3	4	5
NOT AT ALL TRUE		SOMEWHAT TRUE		VERY TRUE

64. In our class, getting right answers is very important.

1	2	3	4	5
NOT AT ALL TRUE		SOMEWHAT TRUE		VERY TRUE

65. In our class, it's important that you don't make mistakes in front of everyone.

1	2	3	4	5
NOT AT ALL TRUE		SOMEWHAT TRUE		VERY TRUE

66. In our class, it's important to understand the work, not just memorize it.

1	2	3	4	5
NOT AT ALL TRUE		SOMEWHAT TRUE		VERY TRUE

67. In our class, it's important not to do worse than other students.

1	2	3	4	5
NOT AT ALL TRUE		SOMEWHAT TRUE		VERY TRUE

68. In our class, learning new ideas and concepts is very important.

1	2	3	4	5
NOT AT ALL TRUE		SOMEWHAT TRUE		VERY TRUE

69. In our class, it's very important not to look dumb.

1	2	3	4	5
NOT AT ALL TRUE		SOMEWHAT TRUE		VERY TRUE

70. In our class, it's OK to make mistakes as long as you are learning.

1	2	3	4	5
NOT AT ALL TRUE		SOMEWHAT TRUE		VERY TRUE

71. In our class, it's important to get high scores on tests.

1	2	3	4	5
NOT AT ALL TRUE		SOMEWHAT TRUE		VERY TRUE

72. In our class, one of the main goals is to avoid looking like you can't do the work.

1	2	3	4	5
NOT AT ALL TRUE		SOMEWHAT TRUE		VERY TRUE

From Midgley, C., Maehr, M.L., Hruda, L.Z., Anderman, E., Anderman, L., Freeman, K.E., et al. (2000). *Manual for the Patterns of Adaptive Learning Scales (PALS)*. Ann Arbor: University of Michigan. Used with permission.

REFERENCES

Atkinson, J.W. (1964). *An introduction to motivation*. New York: Van Nostrand.

Bandura, A. (1982). Self-efficacy mechanism in human agency. *American Psychologist, 37*(2), 122–147.

Bandura, A. (1991). Self-regulation of motivation through anticipatory and self-reactive mechanisms. In R. Dienstbier (Ed.), *Nebraska symposium on motivation: Vol. 38. Perspectives on motivation* (pp. 69–164). Lincoln: University of Nebraska Press.

Bandura, A., & Locke, E.A. (2003). Negative self-efficacy and goal effects revisited. *Journal of Applied Psychology, 88*(1), 87–99.

Bempechat, J. (2004). The motivational benefits of homework: A social-cognitive perspective. *Theory Into Practice, 43,* 189–196.

Bempechat, J., London, P., & Dweck, C.S. (1991). Children's conceptions of ability in major domains: An interview and experimental study. *Child Study Journal, 21*(1), 11–35.

Bernard, M.E. (2006). It's time we teach social-emotional competence as well as we teach academic competence. *Reading and Writing Quarterly, 22,* 103–119.

Blackwell, L.S., Trzesniewski, K.H., & Dweck, C.S. (2007). Implicit theories of intelligence predict achievement across an adolescent transition: A longitudinal study and an intervention. *Child Development, 78,* 246–263.

Bryan, T., Burstein, K., & Bryan, J. (2001). Students with learning disabilities: Homework problems and promising practices. *Educational Psychologist, 36,* 167–180.

Cooper, H., Robinson, J.C., & Patall, E.A. (2006). Does homework improve academic achievement? A synthesis of research, 1987–2003. *Review of Educational Research, 76,* 1–62.

Cooper, H., & Valentine, J.C. (2001). Using research to answer practical questions about homework. *Educational Psychologist, 36,* 143–153.

deCharms, R. (1992). Personal causation and the origin concept. In C.P. Smith, J.W. Atkinson, D.C. McClelland, & J. Veroff (Eds.), *Motivation and personality: Handbook of thematic content analysis* (pp. 325–333). New York: Cambridge University Press.

Delgado-Gaitan, C. (1992). School matters in the Mexican-American home: Socializing children to education. *American Educational Research Journal, 29,* 495–513.

Denissen, J.J.A., Zarrett, N.R., & Eccles, J.S. (2007). I like to do it, I'm able, and I know I am: Longitudinal couplings between domain-specific achievement, self-concept, and interest. *Child Development, 78,* 430–447.

Dowson, M., & McInerney, D.M. (2003). What do students say about their motivational goals? Towards a more complex and dynamic perspective on student motivation. *Contemporary Educational Psychology, 28,* 91–113.

Dweck, C.S. (1999). *Self-theories: Their role in motivation, personality and development*. New York: Psychology Press.

Eccles, J.S., Roeser, R., Vida, M., Fredricks, J., & Wigfield, A. (2006). Motivational and achievement pathways through middle childhood. In L. Balter & C.S. Tamis-LeMonda (Eds.), *Child psychology: A handbook of contemporary issues* (2nd ed., pp. 325–355). New York: Psychology Press.

Eccles, J.S., Wigfield, A., & Schiefele, U. (1998). Motivation to succeed. In N. Eisenberg (Ed.), *Social, emotional, and personality development* (Vol. 3, pp. 1017–1095). New York: Wiley.

Grant, H., & Dweck, C.S. (2003). Clarifying achievement goals and their impact. *Journal of Personality and Social Psychology, 85*(3), 541–553.

Harniss, M.K., Epstein, M.H., Bursuck, W.D., Nelson, J., & Jayanthi, M. (2001). Resolving homework-related communication problems: Recommendations of parents of children with and without disabilities. *Reading and Writing Quarterly, 17,* 205–225.

Hoover-Dempsey, K.V., Battiato, A.C., Walker, J.M., Reed, R.P., DeLong, J.M., & Jones, K.P. (2001). Parental involvement in homework. *Educational Psychologist, 36,* 195–209.

Horner, S.L., & O'Conner, E.A. (2007). Introduction: Helping beginning and struggling readers and writers to develop self-regulated strategies. *Reading and Writing Quarterly, 23,* 1–5.

Hughes, C.A., Ruhl, K.L., Schumaker, J.B., & Deschler, D.D. (2002). Effects of instruction in an assignment completion strategy on the homework performance of students with learning disabilities in general education classes. *Learning Disabilities Research and Practice, 17*(1), 1–18.

Johnson, D.W., & Johnson, R.T. (1999). Making cooperative learning work. *Theory Into Practice, 38,* 67–73.

Keith, T.Z., & Cool, V.A. (1992). Testing models of school learning: Effects of quality of instruction, motivation, academic coursework, and homework on academic achievement. *School Psychology Quarterly, 7*(3), 207–226.

Keith, T.Z., Troutman, G.C., Trivette, P.S., Keith, P.B., Bickely, P.G., & Singh, K. (1993). Does parent involvement affect eighth grade student achievement? Structural analysis of national data. *School Psychology Review, 22*(3), 474–496.

McKnight, C., Crosswhite, F., Dossey, J., Kifer, E., Swafford, J., Travers, K., et al. (1987). *The underachieving curriculum: Assessing U.S. school mathematics from an international perspective.* Champaign, IL: Stipes.

Midgley, C., Maehr, M.L., Hruda, L.Z., Anderman, E., Anderman, L., Freeman, K.E., et al. (2000). *Manual for the Patterns of Adaptive Learning Scales (PALS).* Ann Arbor: University of Michigan.

Munk, W.D., Bursuck, W.D., Epstein, M.H., Jayanthi, J., Nelson, J., & Polloway, E.A. (2001). Homework communication problems: Perspectives of special and general education parents. *Reading and Writing Quarterly, 17,* 189–203.

Nicholls, J.G. (1978). The development of the concepts of effort and ability, perception of own attainment, and the understanding that difficult tasks require more ability. *Child Development, 49,* 800–814.

Nicholls, J.G. (1984). Achievement motivation: Conceptions of ability, subjective experience, task choice, and performance. *Psychological Review, 91,* 328–346.

Nicholls, J.G. (1989). *The competitive ethos and democratic education.* Cambridge, MA: Harvard University Press.

Pavri, S. (2006). Introduction: School-based interventions to promote social and emotional competence in students with reading difficulties. *Reading and Writing Quarterly, 22,* 99–101.

Pintrich, P.R., & DeGroot, E.V. (1990). Motivational and self-regulated learning components of classroom academic performance. *Journal of Educational Psychology, 82,* 33–40.

Pintrich, P.R., & Zusho, A. (2002). The development of academic self-regulation: The role of cognitive and motivational factors. In A. Wigfield & J.S. Eccles (Eds.), *Development of achievement motivation* (pp. 249–284). New York: Academic.

Polloway, E.A., Bursuck, W.D., & Epstein, M.H. (2001). Homework for students with learning disabilities: The challenge of home-school communication. *Reading and Writing Quarterly, 17,* 181–187.

Pomerantz, E.M., Grolnick, W., & Price, C. (2005). The role of parents in how children approach achievement: A dynamic process perspective. In A.J. Elliot & C.S. Dweck (Eds.), *Handbook of competence and motivation* (pp. 229–278). New York: Guilford.

Pomerantz, E.M., Ng, F.F., & Wang, Q. (2006). Mothers' mastery-oriented involvement in children's homework: Implications for the well-being of children with negative perceptions of competence. *Journal of Educational Psychology, 98,* 99–111.

Pomerantz, E.M., Ruble, D.N., Frey, K.S., & Greulich, F. (1995). Meeting goals and confronting conflict: Children's changing perceptions of social comparison. *Child Development, 66,* 723–738.

Rogoff, B. (1990). *Apprenticeship in thinking: Cognitive development in a social context.* New York: Oxford University Press.

Schunk, D.H. (1995). Self-efficacy and education and instruction. In J.E. Maddux (Ed.), *Self-efficacy, education, and instruction: Theory, research, and application* (pp. 281–303). New York: Plenum Press.

Schunk, D.H., & Rice, J.M. (1989). Learning goals and children's reading comprehension. *Journal of Reading Behavior, 21,* 279–293.

Schunk, D.H., & Zimmerman, B.J. (2007). Influencing children's self-efficacy and self-regulation of reading and writing through modeling. *Reading & Writing Quarterly, 23,* 7–25.

Stevenson, H.W., Lee, S., & Stigler, J.W. (1986). Mathematics achievement of Chinese, Japanese and American children. *Science, 231,* 693–699.

Thorkildsen, T.A. (2002). Literacy as a lifestyle: Negotiating the curriculum to facilitate motivation. *Reading and Writing Quarterly, 18,* 321–341.

Vygotsky, L.S. (1978). *Mind in society: The development of higher psychological processes* (M. Cole, V. John-Steiner, S. Scribner, & E. Souberman, Eds. & Trans.). Cambridge, MA: Harvard University Press. (Original work published 1934)

Weiner, B. (1985). An attributional theory of achievement motivation and emotion. *Psychological Review*, *92*, 548–573.

Weiner, B. (2005). Motivation from an attributional perspective and the social psychology of perceived competence. In A.J. Elliot & C.S. Dweck (Eds.), *Handbook of competence and motivation* (pp. 73–84). New York: Guilford.

Weiner, B., Graham, S., Stern, P., & Lawson, M.E. (1982). Using affective cues to infer causal thoughts. *Developmental Psychology*, *18*, 278–286.

Xu, J., & Corno, L. (1998). Case studies of families doing third grade homework. *Teachers College Record*, *100*(2), 402–436.

Ten Tenets of Motivation for Teaching Struggling Readers—And the Rest of the Class

IRENE W. GASKINS

Inspiring Reading Success: Interest and Motivation in an Age of High-Stakes Testing, edited by Rosalie Fink and S. Jay Samuels. © 2008 by the International Reading Association.

PREREADING QUESTIONS

◆ What are some motivational issues that elementary and middle school students experience that you hope this chapter will discuss?

◆ What do you view as the four or five key factors to pay attention to as you strive to motivate a class? How would you address these factors?

Why do students in our classrooms do what they do? For example why does Joey's hand fly up each time his teacher poses a question, while Demetri and Amy sit placidly unresponsive? Why, after the teacher explicitly explains how to complete the evening's homework, does José submit well-elaborated, neatly written homework, while Sara's homework is incomplete and Andy's is nonexistent? Motivation, in all likelihood, is at the heart of the matter.

Much has been written about motivation and the application of theories of motivation in classrooms. This chapter explores some of those theories and presents 10 tenets of motivation gleaned from the motivation literature (see Table 5.1 for a listing of the 10 tenets) as well as classroom examples of the tenets as they relate to engaging struggling learners in academic pursuits. The chapter is divided into four sections, each devoted to a need that motivational theorists believe drives students' motivation once their basic

TABLE 5.1
Ten Tenets of Motivation

1. Develop a caring community of learners in which collaboration is valued and encouraged.
2. Explain how what students are expected to learn will be helpful to them.
3. Explain how learning works, including the role of motivation, and its impact on present and future learning.
4. Orchestrate a classroom milieu that fosters mastery goal orientation.
5. Present information, tasks, and activities in ways that are personally and/or situationally interesting.
6. Provide learning tasks and materials at the appropriate level of difficulty and with the support that is necessary for students to meet with success and feel competent.
7. Explain explicitly, for each task assigned, how to put into practice strategies that facilitate an effective use of effort, and scaffold success as needed.
8. Provide feedback to students, as compared to themselves, about their gains in knowledge and general academic progress.
9. Plan curriculum that moves quickly beyond the lower levels of knowing (accumulating information) to major concepts and essential understandings.
10. Provide choices within limits as one way to foster internal control.

From Gaskins, I.W. (2005). *Success with struggling readers: The Benchmark School approach* (p. 118). New York: Guilford. Used with permission from the publisher.

physiological and safety needs have been met. The needs highlighted in this chapter are belonging, meaningfulness, competence, and autonomy. Three of these needs (belonging, competence, and autonomy) are rooted in the self-determination theory of Ryan and Deci (e.g., Deci, 1995; Ryan & Deci, 2000), while meaningfulness is the linchpin of the expectancy-value model of achievement motivation (Anderman & Wolters, 2006), represented by such theorists as Eccles and Wigfield (e.g., Eccles, 1983; Wigfield & Eccles, 2000). Self-determination theory posits that satisfaction of the basic needs for autonomy, competence, and relatedness allows people the freedom to engage in self-determined activity. The action they take toward a goal is freely chosen (self-determined), not controlled by an outside motivator or internal pressure. The expectancy-value model of achievement motivation states that people are willing to put effort into achieving a goal if there is *both* the expectation that a successful outcome will result from the effort and the perception that there is worth (value) in achieving the goal. It is generally believed that, if teachers plan their curriculum and instruction with their students' needs and goals in mind, the likelihood increases that students will be engaged and learning will result (Alexander, 2006; Brophy, 2004).

Belonging

The start of a new school year arrives and with it the excitement of a new beginning and, for some, the trepidation of fitting in. The questions foremost in the minds of many young people are likely, Who will be in my class? Will the kids like me and include me? Will the teacher be nice or will she be mean?

First-day-of-school jitters are most often about the human need for relationships and fitting in—in a word, about belonging. Teachers have learned that in most cases it is unrealistic to expect students to put forth energy to initiate and direct their effort toward learning when they do not feel connected to their teachers and members of the classroom community (Noddings, 1992; Perry, Turner, & Meyer, 2006). In a young person's mind, especially an adolescent's, the need to belong usually takes precedence over the need for competence (e.g., Snow, Porche, Tabors, & Harris, 2007), thus the priority for the teacher is to "Develop a caring community of learners in which collaboration is valued and encouraged" (Gaskins, 2005, p. 118). This is the first tenet of motivation.

Develop a Caring Community

At Benchmark School, a grades 1–8 school for struggling readers, the process of community building begins even before summer vacation has concluded. For example, during August, lower grade school teachers send parents and students a welcoming letter with a list of students in the class, their phone numbers, e-mail addresses, and home addresses so that, if they desire prior to the beginning of the school year, students can set up play dates or communicate via phone or e-mail. In the days immediately preceding the opening of school, teachers invite students to join them in their classrooms for a get-acquainted conference, either individually or as part of a small group. Some even invite students to visit the classroom to perform a specific job, such as working with several other students to design a bulletin board or prepare a science exhibit to display in the classroom. In the case of middle school students, and as a first step in building community prior to the opening of school, students are invited by their team of teachers to a morning of games, followed by a picnic.

To ensure that teachers grasp the importance of establishing a caring community, some administrators, myself included, go so far as to announce that a teacher's most important job during the month of September is to create a learning environment in which students feel connected, safe, and cared for. These administrators know that if teachers accomplish the creation of a caring, connected learning environment, they will have laid the foundation for a successful year of instruction. One vehicle for accomplishing such a learning environment among elementary school students is a group activity called morning meeting (Kriete, 2002). At the start of the school year, morning meeting may be the occasion for students to sit cross-legged in a circle on the floor to learn one another's names and find out about each classmate's special interests, hobbies, and family. Throughout these discussions, teachers model a caring attitude by the interest they show in their students and by the responses they make to what each has to say. Teachers also encourage similar responses from their students. Later in the school year, problem solving or planning special projects may be featured during morning meeting. However, whatever the featured topic or activity, the teacher's focus is on demonstrating care for and interest in each student. The goal is for students to feel connected to each other and to their teachers.

> A teacher's most important job during the month of September is to create a learning environment in which students feel connected, safe, and cared for.

Snow and her colleagues' longitudinal study of the language and literacy development of young children (age 3 at the beginning of the study until completing or dropping out of high school) who were from low-income homes repeatedly documents how crucial a caring learning environment is, especially for adolescents and even for those adolescents with high literacy skills (Snow et al., 2007). The large size of some middle schools, compared with elementary schools, as well as the variety of teachers in middle school tend to work against adolescents receiving "the sort of attention from adults that ensures high levels of motivation, engagement with school, goal setting, and planning abilities" (Snow et al., 2007, p. 131). With each passing school year, the need to feel socially secure becomes more crucial to a student's motivation to engage in learning. This situation makes community building an increasingly important objective.

One community-building activity that has been successfully employed with middle school students at my school is an overnight outing at a camp that features challenge events that necessitate cooperation and collaboration (as found in an Outward Bound program). During the outing, members of the school or camp staff provide professional coaching on the lessons to be learned. Such outings lend themselves to opportunities to discuss ways of working together and leadership–follower issues that can be revisited throughout the school year, using the challenge events as touchstones.

Another way of helping students feel connected, especially in middle school, is to assign students a staff mentor or advisor with whom they will work for several years, a span that provides extended time for relationship building and the development of trust, both crucial to achieving success with students, especially early adolescents. Through experiences similar to the ones described above, students begin to realize that nearly everything great that they accomplish in school and in life will be accomplished with other people. Thus an important life skill is to learn, under the guidance of knowledgeable adult mentors, to navigate the sometimes unpredictable waters of belonging and achieving academic success (Gaskins, 1992).

Encourage Collaboration

In the classroom, to increase students' awareness of the value of collaborating and being a contributing member of a group, Benchmark teachers encourage students to first ask for explanations and clarification from classmates before they approach a teacher. For example, in preparation for a discussion, the teacher may say, "Turn to your partner and discuss the first question written on your discussion guide; then in a few minutes I will ask you to share your thinking with the class." As another example, when students do not understand an assignment or remember what to do for homework, Benchmark students are expected to ask a classmate.

Teachers in caring classrooms recognize the special talents that each student has and guide students to share those special abilities with others in the class. In these classrooms, you hear teachers make comments such as, "David's stuck. He can't find just the right word for his story. Peter, you're our word man. Would you see if you can help David?" Fostering collaboration sends the message that learning is a cooperative process and it reinforces the fact that "classrooms must become communities of learners rather than collections of competing individuals. In cooperative classrooms, students contribute to a collective expertise" (Turner, 1997, p. 196).

Students feel that they belong and are connected to their classmates and teachers when they have shared satisfying experiences, such as helping one another, and when each one demonstrates that he or she values and cares about the others. In addition, students feel a sense of belonging when their individual talents are recognized as essential to the group's success. A sense of belonging is the gatekeeper to motivation. It is difficult for a student to be motivated when he or she is concerned about social issues, such as fitting in. Being part of a classroom and school community in which developing a sense of belonging is a priority creates an environment where students are more likely to be motivated to learn.

Meaningfulness

A reading lesson has begun and the teacher is explicitly explaining how to monitor one's understanding by using a story frame for taking notes. As she explains the strategy, some students may be thinking, I know when I understand and don't understand. Why should I have to spend extra time thinking about a story frame and writing notes?

This is not an atypical thought. Clearly, these students see no value in the strategy the teacher is teaching for monitoring understanding. The activity holds no meaning for them. Missing from the teacher's explanation is the rationale for learning the strategy. Most students want to be convinced of how what they are asked to do will benefit them. Even more powerful is setting students up to experience the value of implementing the strategy, followed by the teacher clearly articulating what they experienced. As Brophy (2004) explains, "To be motivated to do something, we need good reasons for doing it, not just confidence that we can do it if we try" (p. 151).

Meaningfulness is a key to motivation. For students to want to learn what the teacher is presenting, students need to be able to attribute some meaning or value to the content or process being taught or find meaningfulness in the content or process because it interests them. This is true whether the teacher is teaching a process for accomplishing a task or if the presentation is about an event in history, a science concept, or a piece of children's literature. The motivational energy that drives learning is a student's perception of the meaningfulness of what he or she is being asked to learn.

Benchmark teachers engage in four actions to satisfy students' desire for meaningfulness: (1) explain the value of what is taught, (2) explain how learning works, (3) guide goal orientation, and (4) make learning interesting.

As a result of the need for meaningfulness, teachers must "explain how what students are expected to learn will be helpful to them" (Gaskins, 2005, p. 118). This is the second tenet of motivation.

Explain the Value of What Is Taught

To show students how to monitor understanding and why monitoring is a valuable strategy, a teacher might say something like the following:

> Today we are going to learn how to monitor our understanding of a story. Understanding what you read is the reason for reading. Sometimes, however—at least this is true for me—my mind wanders when I am reading and I find myself at the end of the story not quite sure what I read. How many of you have ever had that happen? [Teacher acknowledges the students who nod in agreement.] To check or monitor my understanding, I try to summarize the story. One way to do that is to think about story elements. Who can remember the major elements of a story? Here's a note card for each of you—write down as many story elements as you can remember. [Teacher circulates as students write.] Wow, you guys are amazing. Each of you remembered at least one of the story elements you learned last year. I see that you have written that the story elements are setting (place and time), characters, central story problem, and problem resolution. If I can discuss these four elements of a story, it is likely that I understood the main points of what I read. If I can't do this, I reread. Monitoring your understanding is one of the most important strategies you will ever learn. Why do you think that? [Students respond.] Yes, you're correct. You seem to be saying that knowing what you know and don't know and learning what you don't know are secrets to becoming smarter. Every day I discover things that I don't know and I get smarter by trying to figure out what I don't

know. Today we are going to begin learning a process for monitoring understanding. We will work as a group to jot down very brief notes on the sheet of paper I am giving you [see reproducible Story-Frame Notes for Monitoring Understanding on page 105]. We will write notes as we read today's story together. On the first line of the sheet it says *setting* (time and place). The second line says *characters*. The third line says *problem*. And the last line says *resolution*. Underneath each one of these words we will write our notes.

In this scenario, the teacher has made the activity meaningful by explaining why monitoring is important and how it will help students. She explains that if students recognize what they do not know and make an effort to find out (by digging in the text or asking teachers and classmates for clarification), they will increase what they know and, as a result, become smarter. She also makes the strategy personal by sharing that she uses the strategy.

Another tenet that flows from the need for meaningfulness is grounded in students' naïveté regarding how the brain works and the control they can have over this process (Schunk & Zimmerman, 2006). A basic, age-appropriate understanding of the brain's malleability and how students can take control of how the brain works provides students with a rationale for learning the processes and procedures the teacher recommends they use for achieving specific learning goals. This tenet is to "Explain how learning works, including the role of motivation, and its impact on present and future learning" (Gaskins, 2005, p. 118).

Explain How Learning Works

In teaching strategies for learning, thinking, and problem solving, teachers at Benchmark share with students how the strategies they are teaching support what psychologists know about how people learn (Gaskins, 2005). In fact, during the 1980s and 1990s, I taught two courses for students about how the mind works and how they can take control of the learning, thinking, and problem-solving processes. One course was for middle school students, Psychology 101. A second course, Learning and Thinking, was for lower school students (Gaskins & Elliot, 1991). The content of both of these courses included discussions of fixed and growth beliefs about abilities (Dweck, 2006). Emphasis was placed on three facts: (1) Ability is not fixed. (2) It is the job of educators to help students become smart by teaching them strategies for learning. (3) Becoming smarter is under the control of each student.

Over time the teachers and support teachers, who were in the classrooms while the courses were being taught, adopted the language used to describe how the mind works and shared this knowledge with their students as the rationale for why they taught specific strategies. During the years a student attends Benchmark School (on average, 4–8 years), teachers explain (with many examples) a minimum of six principles of learning as the rationale for the strategies they are teaching (Gaskins, 2005, p. 133). These principles include the following:

Story-Frame Notes for Monitoring Understanding

Name _____   Date _____

Write notes underneath each category and the page number where you found the information.

Setting   Page Number

     Place _____

     Time _____

Characters   Page Number

_____

_____

_____

Problem   Page Number

_____

_____

_____

Resolution   Page Number

_____

_____

_____

From Gaskins, I.W. (2005). Success with struggling readers: The Benchmark School approach (p. 118). New York: Guilford. Used with permission from the publisher.

Inspiring Reading Success: Interest and Motivation in an Age of High-Stakes Testing, edited by Rosalie Fink and S. Jay Samuels. © 2008 by the International Reading Association. May be copied for classroom use.

1. What people learn is based on what they already know (e.g., students access background knowledge before reading a text or solving a problem).

2. Metacognitive strategies for monitoring and controlling learning are essential to knowing when you do or do not understand and then taking action (e.g., students monitor understanding by putting what they read into their own words).

3. New information is easier to understand, remember, and use if it is attached to prior knowledge (e.g., students use what they know about an event—the development of Mesopotamia—to understand another event—the development of Egypt).

4. Organized knowledge is easier to recall than random information (e.g., students construct concept maps).

5. Information that is thoughtfully and deeply processed is likely to be understood and used (e.g., students analyze an event in history from different perspectives—economic, political, social, technological, and the physical and human factors of geography).

6. Concepts and strategies that are repeatedly practiced and applied are not easily forgotten (e.g., students make a daily effort to apply the decoding and comprehension strategies that are being taught).

In addition to knowing how the mind works, a student's goal orientation plays a significant role in determining what motivates him or her. The fourth tenet, "Orchestrate a classroom milieu that fosters mastery orientation" (Gaskins, 2005, p. 118), is a huge challenge because the mastery goal orientation that teachers often prefer for students may not be a good fit with family and cultural values.

Guide Goal Orientation

Students often demonstrate one of three distinct goal orientations (Alexander, 2006; Brophy, 2004). These goal orientations are (1) to learn or master the content presented to them (mastery orientation), (2) to receive accolades and recognition that come with academic success (performance orientation), and (3) to avoid the work that academic achievement necessitates (work-avoidant orientation). Present-day goal theory includes both the approach-avoidance distinction (i.e., to put forth effort or to avoid being effortful) and the learning-performance distinction (i.e., to desire understanding or to desire tangible rewards, such as good grades). Other theorists have also proposed that some students may have multiple goals that include those listed above plus work completion goals, social goals, and extrinsic goals (Alexander, 2006; Brophy, 2004).

Although earlier theory and research on motivation tended to classify mastery goals as good and performance goals as bad, more recent theory and research suggest that for some people in some achievement situations, performance-approach goals are complementary to learning goals. For example, Brophy's (2004) summary of the research suggests that performance-approach goals may be related to short-run retention and grades, whereas learning goals may be more closely related to long-run retention and interest in the subject. Furthermore, for many students the situation plays a role in goal orientation. For example, a student may be mastery oriented in science classes because he or she loves science and knows that a well-integrated understanding of science will prove useful to his or her becoming a medical doctor. On the other hand, the same student may be performance oriented in English and social studies classes because of the belief that achieving excellent grades is necessary to being accepted at a good college and having a chance to attend medical school. This same student may hold work-avoidant goals with respect to physical education and music classes because these classes are graded pass–fail and probably do not count in reaching the goal of attending medical school.

If we believe that the ideal goal orientation is learning oriented, then it behooves teachers to explicitly teach students how to achieve the learning tasks they assign so that students will experience how learning is accomplished and in the future be more likely to take the risks necessary to learn. Learning orientation is more likely for struggling students when teachers explicitly teach them how to learn the content being taught. Strategies for students that meet this need are discussed in the section on competence. Another aspect of meaningfulness is interest, which leads to the fifth tenet: "Present information, tasks, and activities in ways that are personally and/or situationally interesting" (Gaskins, 2005, p. 118).

Make Learning Interesting

What students find interesting, they consider meaningful to them. Interest can be divided into two categories, personal and situational (Alexander, 2006). Personal interest is interest that is durable over time and is usually related to having considerable background knowledge about the topic of interest. Situational interest is limited to the moment and can be constructed by teachers or textbooks, in some cases to the detriment of learning. For example, teachers or textbooks may add seductive details to a topic in the attempt to make the topic more interesting. However, these interesting details may be more memorable than the main points and thus interfere with the intended learning (Harp & Mayer, 1998).

Ideally teachers strive to become aware of the personal interests of their students and attempt as often as possible to customize individual reading and writing assignments to those interests. Often, however, it is necessary for students to learn concepts that they may not find personally interesting. This is a time for artistry in teaching. The teacher must frame her teaching in a manner that grabs students' attention and motivation but that is not so seductively interesting that the interest value detracts from the concept to be learned.

I can remember a time when I was invited to assist for a day in a class of fifth-grade students. The teacher had set the goal that, by the end of the school year, all her students would be able to identify the 50 states that make up the United States and name their capitals. Most of the students had discovered that learning the names of the states was not nearly the chore they had believed it might be, but learning the capitals was another matter. That task was difficult for them.

The teacher told the class that maybe I had a special strategy that I might share with them. When I visited the classroom and asked students what strategy they had used to learn the names of the states, they claimed that they had "just memorized them." I asked if this strategy was working for them in learning the capitals. About half the class was certain that they would be able to learn the state capitals by just memorization. I shared that I had learned the state capitals by using a special strategy and wondered if those who were having trouble memorizing the capitals might like me to teach it to them. Some were intrigued by my offer. Half the class elected to stay in the classroom with their teacher to independently memorize the capitals of 10 western states using individual maps of the United States. The remaining students left the classroom with me for an explanation of my special strategy for learning the capitals. I taught the mnemonic strategy of making a meaningful connection between the capital of each state and the state's name. For example, the state of California is shaped like a sack and the capital is SACramento. The capital of Oregon is Salem and Oregon is near the ocean where we can go SAILem. After discussing the importance of making a meaningful connection between the capital and state, I collaborated with the students to apply the strategy.

We returned to the classroom in less than 20 minutes. I gave each student a copy of a map of the United States, without the names of the state capitals, and they were given 10 minutes to fill in the names of as many western state capitals as they could remember. Most of the strategy group correctly filled in at least 7 of the 10 state capitals, and some could identify all 10. Students in the just-memorize-it group remembered far fewer. The just-memorize-it group was amazed that the strategy group learned so many capitals and asked the strategy students to share how they did it. Whereas originally students were not personally interested in learning the capitals, I had set up a situation that intrigued them, thus creating situational interest. The memorizers were now genuinely interested in learning how the strategy group had accomplished the task. Situational motivation was at work, and as a result multiple goals were achieved.

Competence

The teacher of a group of six third graders, reading at second-grade level, asked me to work diagnostically with her students. She was concerned about their weak comprehension of the second-grade level books they had been reading. I committed to teach the reading group for two weeks. The group was composed of three girls and three boys. I brought several second- and third-level basal anthologies to the reading table and let students scan them, and then students decided together which anthology we would use as our text. They chose a book written at the beginning third level. The group previewed the book, commenting as they looked through it about stories that might be good ones. As the girls were a major influence in choosing the book, I let the boys choose the first story we would read. They chose one about baseball, which the girls claimed they were interested in, too, as each had a brother with whom she played baseball. Fortunately, I was familiar with the story.

The students surveyed the story and, with my guidance, they collaborated to set a purpose for reading. I gave each a note card and pencil "in case you would like to jot down anything you'd like to share from the story—a difficult word, something that you didn't understand, or something you want to remember." I told the group that I would be asking them some thinking questions about which they could consult with a partner and consult their notes before answering. Jim quickly finished reading the story. It appeared that he wanted to prove that he was a good reader by seeming to be the fastest reader. I suspected that he had not read the story, so I wrote a discussion question on a card and handed it to Jim. I told him that he might want to write some notes that would help him and his partner contribute ideas to the discussion of the question. Jim read the question and returned to the text. Other students asked for a copy of the question, which I gave them, and they continued reading. Several wrote a few notes. We began the discussion, with partners conferring before participating. Someone said, "We don't agree; can we look back in the book?" I encouraged each pair to consult the book, telling students that I knew the question I gave them was going to be a hard one. When the discussion was completed, I asked students to evaluate how well they had handled this difficult story. They all agreed that, by the end of our discussion, they understood the story—and they did.

This lesson was orchestrated with appropriate scaffolding so that each student would feel competent. In the process, I learned a lot about what may have been creating some of their comprehension problems. One issue was the belief that competent readers do not experience difficulty reading any words or have any trouble comprehending what they read. Instead, the students seemed to believe that good readers read fast, do not encounter unknown words or need to reflect on the meaning of passages, and they do not ask clarification questions. As I continued to work with these students over two weeks, they began independently using some of the strategies that I had scaffolded for them during our first session—and as they did, they appeared more and more competent and motivated.

> When students feel competent, or perceive that supports are in place for them to find some measure of success, they are much more likely to take risks to participate in a learning activity.

When students feel competent, or perceive that supports are in place for them to find some measure of success, they are much more likely to take risks to participate in a learning activity. Teachers can help students feel competent by providing materials and tasks that are well matched to students' abilities, yet still allow them to experience appropriate challenge. They also can explicitly teach students how to accomplish what is assigned and then scaffold the completion of the assignment, as well as establish routines that allow students to receive immediate feedback regarding tasks completed independently. In addition, they can foster competence by guiding students to see the structure of domains and therefore to be able to separate essential understandings from details.

The scenario above about diagnostic teaching with six third graders illustrates the sixth tenet for motivation: "Provide learning tasks and materials at the appropriate level of difficulty and with the support that is necessary for students to meet with success and feel competent" (Gaskins, 2005, p. 118).

Provide Appropriate Level of Difficulty and Support

Motivation is related to students' self-concept of ability and expectation for success (Eccles et al., 1993). Therefore, students tend to enjoy and become actively engaged in activities that are well matched to their levels of knowledge and skill yet also provide challenges from which they can grow (Brophy, 2004; Vygotsky, 1934/1978). One way to accomplish this in a class with a variety of reader levels, and in cases where students would all like to read and discuss the same age-appropriate book, is for the students reading at levels below the level of the selected book to listen to a tape recording of the text, with the option to follow along in the text or to just listen. Difficulty can be further controlled by varying the sophistication of the discussion questions. A way to adjust conceptual difficulty is to have all students read an easy book to establish background knowledge for the more difficult book. In cases where students have word-recognition problems, choral reading and Readers Theatre are avenues to allow students to read fluently in a way that approximates the way that good readers read.

Feelings of competence result when students are able to handle moderately challenging tasks with appropriate effort and strategies. For that to occur, the seventh tenet of motivation needs to be in place: "Explain explicitly, for each task assigned, how to put into practice strategies that facilitate an effective use of effort, and scaffold success as needed" (Gaskins, 2005, p. 118).

Explain and Scaffold How to Do the Assigned Tasks

Durkin (1978/1979), in what has become a classic study, discovered that teachers often do not explicitly explain to students how to complete the assignments they give. Yet, if competence is the goal, then explicit explanations about how to complete specific assignments should be part of each teacher's daily plan. As outlined in Gaskins (2005), students, especially struggling readers, benefit from teachers explicitly explaining how to complete tasks such as unlocking the pronunciation of unknown words; constructing literal and inferential meanings of text; and completing a report, writing an essay, or studying for a test. In the Benchmark model of instruction (Gaskins, 2005), teachers tell students the strategy (or strategies) they are going to teach for completing a task, why the strategy will prove beneficial, when it can be used, and how to do it. Teachers model their mental processes by thinking aloud (Duffy, Roehler, & Herrmann, 1988) as they demonstrate using the strategy to complete a task and then scaffold students' efforts as they apply the strategy. It seems unfair for teachers to expect students to demonstrate competence unless they explicitly teach students the processes they need to know to successfully complete the tasks they assign.

Performance-oriented classrooms in which grades, comparisons, and competition are emphasized are not usually known for producing the most competent students. Instead, the most competent students can usually be found in classrooms that promote learning as the valued goal and in which the classroom ambience fosters among students the courage to be open and to welcome change and new ideas (Dweck, 2006). For competence to occur, however, students need to be flexible enough to learn from their mistakes and to be open to feedback. An eighth motivation tenet deals with this issue: "Provide feedback to students, as compared to themselves, about their gains in knowledge and general academic progress" (Gaskins, 2005, p. 118).

Provide Immediate Feedback

In mastery-oriented classrooms, teachers praise actions and choices that lead to efforts and achievements instead of praising talent and ability (Dweck, 2006). They help students see how much they have grown, as compared to themselves.

Learning activities that appeal to students provide them with many opportunities to be involved in making responses and receiving immediate feedback. Most students prefer activities in which they interact with the teacher or other students or have an opportunity to manipulate materials as part of the learning activity. In general, they prefer that the means of learning be active, for example, participating in a debate or discussion, rather than a more passive activity such as listening or reading where there is little chance for feedback.

Another means of creating the opportunity for students to receive immediate feedback is by circulating, as students are independently completing written responses or other written assignments, and stopping by students' desks to discuss what they have written and to provide constructive input. When teachers are occupied with other students, students can be encouraged to request feedback from a seatwork buddy (e.g., a student who sits next to the student and has read the same text) or use a rubric to gain a sense of how they are progressing.

Competence is facilitated when teachers go beyond questions that require regurgitation of basic facts found in the text to questions that stimulate students' higher levels of thinking. This leads to the ninth tenet of motivation: "Plan curriculum that moves quickly beyond the lower levels of knowing (accumulating information) to major concepts and essential understandings" (Gaskins, 2005, p. 118).

Focus on Big Ideas

In classrooms where higher levels of knowing are the expectation, knowledge is regarded as both a framework within which understandings can be organized and as the grist for problem solving (Alexander, 2006). Big ideas, major concepts, and essential understandings are the magnets that enable students to remember and understand what is taught in school and to generate new knowledge. In view of the current knowledge explosion, teachers cannot possibly teach students everything they will need to know to be considered competent. Instead, the goal should be to guide students in discovering the essential understandings that provide the structure for each domain (Erickson, 2001). An example of an essential understanding in science is that all systems are interrelated—make a change in one part of the system and it affects all the other parts. An example of an essential understanding in social studies is that humans take action to meet their needs. Instruction based on core essential understandings such as these is the approach to instruction that we have emphasized at Benchmark during the past 17 years (Gaskins, 2005; Gaskins, Guthrie, et al., 1994; Gaskins, Satlow, Hyson, Ostertag, & Six, 1994).

Autonomy

The school day has begun. Students have greeted the teacher and one another. Lunch boxes, coats, homework, and books have been put in their proper places and 13 students are seated at their desks, each reading one of the three books they keep in their desks for interludes in their daily schedule. Of the three books each student has selected, one is an easy book (often from a series), one is a "just-right" book (slightly below or at their instructional level), and the other is a challenge book (a difficult book they have always wanted to read or that they consider prestigious among peers). As students complete each book, they choose another of the same category from the library. This arrangement puts students in charge of not only choosing the book they will read but also the level of the book. Students like to periodically pull out their challenge book to see if they are ready to tackle it but usually find that they are more comfortable with an easy or just-right book. The choice is theirs.

People like choice. Having choices is one way people meet their need for autonomy, which leads to the 10th tenet for motivation: "Provide choices within limits as one way to foster internal control" (Gaskins, 2005, p. 118).

Provide Choices

Autonomy is a fundamental need of humans (Ryan & Deci, 2000). It is the desire to experience a sense of control, "an internal locus of causality" (Schunk & Zimmerman, 2006, p. 359). Autonomy is at the core of self-determination theory, which relates intrinsic motivation to freedom to make choices and take responsibility for one's actions (Schunk & Zimmerman, 2006). In a recent elaboration of self-determination theory, rather than emphasizing a dichotomy between intrinsic and extrinsic motivation, Deci and Ryan (2002) speak of mixed forms of motivation that lie on a continuum between the extremes. For example, from an intrinsic motivation point of view, a student may find inherent satisfaction in learning math concepts, yet earning a good grade in math may also be important to the student. Alexander (2006) believes that Deci and Ryan's continuum "shows that there is no good/bad dichotomy between extrinsic and intrinsic motivation as it pertains to optimal learning. Extrinsic motivation that is coupled with perceived internal control can, like true intrinsic motivation, help optimize learning" (p. 204). Further, as Brophy (2004) explains, "the key to understanding motivational dynamics is not an intrinsic vs. extrinsic motivation dichotomy, but the degree to which the person perceives rewards or other extrinsic features of the situation as informational versus controlling" (p. 206). Autonomy is feeling you are in control rather than being controlled.

Foster Internal Control

Teacher actions that foster internal control begin with a teacher's inclination to work from the student's perspective, especially when problems arise. When viewed from a student's perspective, problems such as misbehaving, not turning in homework, and applying minimum effort to class participation or other class activities may stem from a variety of reasons for being unmotivated, such as the perception that school is not a place where autonomy needs can be met because the teacher controls everything. As a result, there are few opportunities for student decision making, an especially important issue with adolescents (Eccles et al., 1993).

A few tactics that can lessen this notion include allowing students to have a say in establishing the rights and responsibilities of class members; monitoring students' progress as compared to themselves rather than applying rewards and punishments, social comparisons, or pressure; teaching students problem-solving strategies and guiding them in applying them to situations that arise, rather than imposing teacher solutions; providing the opportunity for students to complete assignments in more than one way; listening to students by inviting questions and ideas; and encouraging student initiative. As often as possible, give students choices and put them in charge of determining how to meet academic goals—then be there to provide them with the support they need to be successful.

In these days of No Child Left Behind, there seems little time for students to be autonomous. The curriculum is prescribed, the timing for using the curriculum is prescribed, what counts as progress is prescribed, and the rewards, if any, are extrinsic. Yet, the goal of most schools is for students to be intrinsically motivated, self-regulated, and able to determine for themselves what their goals are and how to fulfill them. The teacher's role is to be the guide, coach, and mentor. The No Child Left Behind agenda does not seem compatible with autonomy and intrinsic motivation. Autonomy-supportive practices need to be put in place to produce motivated, self-determined, and self-regulated students. The foundation is laid by developing a classroom ethos that provides opportunities for autonomy.

Conclusion

Knowing how to teach literacy well is necessary, but not sufficient, for creating students who read, understand what they read, and are successful in school and in life (see Table 5.2 for additional resources for teachers of struggling readers). Many other variables interact to determine success. One of those variables is motivation.

In the recent longitudinal study reported by Snow and colleagues (2007), the authors note the paradox of students (all from low-income families) who do well on reading tests in fourth grade and beyond but who are not successful in middle school and high school. They conclude that teaching students to read is not enough and that teachers need to deal with

TABLE 5.2
Additional Resources for Teachers of Struggling Readers

Gaskins, I.W. (2005). *Success with struggling readers: The Benchmark School approach*. New York: Guilford.

Gaskins, I.W., & Elliot, T.T. (1991). *Implementing cognitive strategy instruction across the school: The Benchmark manual for teachers*. Cambridge, MA: Brookline Books.

Gaskins, R.W. (1992). When good instruction is not enough: A mentor program. *The Reading Teacher, 45,* 568–572.

Kriete, R. (2002). *The morning meeting book: Strategies for teachers series #1*. Portland, ME: Stenhouse.

TABLE 5.3
Student Needs and Teacher Actions That Foster Motivation

Belonging

Arrange class activities that foster students getting to know and to work with each other in a caring, noncompetitive milieu.

Provide students with mentors.

Encourage students to consult and collaborate with classmates.

Discover and then use each student's strengths.

Meaningfulness

Explain the value of what is taught.

Explain how learning works.

Guide goal orientation.

Make learning interesting.

Competence

Provide appropriate level of difficulty and support.

Share personal experiences using strategies.

Explain and scaffold how to do the assigned tasks.

Provide immediate feedback.

Focus on big ideas.

Autonomy

Analyze student behaviors from the student's perspective.

Allow students to have a say in establishing rights and responsibilities.

Monitor students' progress as compared to themselves.

Teach and guide problem-solving strategies.

Provide opportunities for students to complete assignments in more than one way.

Invite students' questions and ideas.

Encourage student initiative.

Give students choices within limits.

Put students in charge of determining how to meet learning goals.

the many factors, in addition to literacy skills, that influence students' ultimate success in school. Snow and her colleagues call for more far-reaching interventions, for example with respect to motivation, feeling that students need motivation to succeed that is joined with an understanding of what it takes to succeed. In addition, they believe that students need to be shown the relationship between school success and their own long-term goals.

In this chapter, I have discussed the importance of motivation to succeed in school and suggested that once students' basic physiological and safety needs have been met, another set of needs plays a dominant role in determining each student's motivation to respond to instruction. These are the needs for belonging, meaningfulness, competence, and autonomy. Ten tenets of motivation were discussed as guidelines teachers can use to create an environment in which students' needs will be met, thereby enhancing their motivation to learn. Table 5.3 contains the four needs discussed in this chapter and provides specific examples of teacher actions that help meet students' needs for belonging, meaningfulness, competence, and autonomy. These teacher actions may address multiple need categories. For example, explaining strategies may build competence and, as a result, build autonomy; sharing personal experiences may make strategies meaningful and build connectedness with the teacher. The result of these actions should be improved motivation.

POSTREADING QUESTIONS

◆ What teacher actions do you feel are necessary to establish a classroom in which students have a sense of belonging? A sense of meaningfulness? A sense of competence? A sense of autonomy?

◆ What is your rationale for choosing these actions?

Acknowledgments

I appreciate the suggestions of Emily Galloway, Robert Gaskins, and Eric Satlow on an earlier version of this chapter.

REFERENCES

Alexander, P.A. (2006). *Psychology in learning and instruction*. Upper Saddle River, NJ: Pearson Education.

Anderman, E.M., & Wolters, C.A. (2006). Goals, values, and affect: Influences on student motivation. In P.A. Alexander & P.H. Winne (Eds.), *Handbook of educational psychology* (2nd ed., pp. 369–389). Mahwah, NJ: Erlbaum.

Brophy, J. (2004). *Motivating students to learn* (2nd ed.). Mahwah, NJ: Erlbaum.

Deci, E.L. (with Flaste, R.). (1995). *Why we do what we do: The dynamics of personal autonomy*. New York: Putnam.

Deci, E., & Ryan, R. (Eds.). (2002). *Handbook of self-determination research*. Rochester, NY: University of Rochester Press.

Duffy, G.G., Roehler, L., & Herrmann, B.A. (1988). Modeling mental processes helps poor readers become strategic readers. *The Reading Teacher, 41,* 762–767.

Durkin, D. (1978/1979). What classroom observations reveal about reading comprehension instruction. *Reading Research Quarterly, 14,* 481–533.

Dweck, C.S. (2006). *Mindset: The new psychology of success.* New York: Random House.

Eccles, J.S. (1983). Expectancies, values, and academic behaviors. In J.T. Spence (Ed.), *Achievement and achievement motives* (pp. 75–146). San Francisco: Freeman.

Eccles, J.S., Wigfield, A., Midgley, C., Reuman, D., Iver, D.M., & Feldlaufer, H. (1993). Negative effects of traditional middle schools on students' motivation. *The Elementary School Journal, 93,* 553–574.

Erickson, H.L. (2001). *Stirring the head, heart, and soul: Redefining curriculum and instruction* (2nd ed.). Thousand Oaks, CA: Corwin Press.

Gaskins, I.W. (2005). *Success with struggling readers: The Benchmark School approach.* New York: Guilford.

Gaskins, I.W., & Elliot, T.T. (1991). *Implementing cognitive strategy instruction across the school: The Benchmark manual for teachers.* Cambridge, MA: Brookline Books.

Gaskins, I.W., Guthrie, J.T., Satlow, E., Ostertag, J., Six, L., Byrne, J., et al. (1994). Integrating instruction of science, reading, and writing: Goals, teacher development, and assessment. *Journal of Research in Science Teaching, 31,* 1039–1056.

Gaskins, I.W., Satlow, E., Hyson, D., Ostertag, J., & Six, L. (1994). Classroom talk about text: Learning in science class. *Journal of Reading, 37,* 558–565.

Gaskins, R.W. (1992). When good instruction is not enough: A mentor program. *The Reading Teacher, 45,* 568–572.

Harp, S.F., & Mayer, R.E. (1998). How seductive details do their damage: A theory of cognitive interest in science learning. *Journal of Educational Psychology, 90,* 414–434.

Kriete, R. (2002). *The morning meeting book: Strategies for teachers series #1.* Portland, ME: Stenhouse.

Noddings, N. (1992). *The challenge to care in schools: An alternative approach to education.* New York: Teachers College Press.

Perry, N.E., Turner, J.C., & Meyer, D.K. (2006). Classrooms as contexts for motivating learning. In P. Alexander & P. Winne (Eds.), *Handbook of educational psychology* (2nd ed., pp. 327–348). Mahwah, NJ: Erlbaum.

Ryan, R.M., & Deci, E.L. (2000). When rewards compete with nature: The undermining of intrinsic motivation and self-regulation. In C. Sansone & J. Harackiewicz (Eds.), *Intrinsic and extrinsic motivation: The search for optimal motivation and performance* (pp. 13–54). New York: Academic.

Schunk, D.H., & Zimmerman, B.J. (2006). Competence and control beliefs: Distinguishing the means and ends. In P. Alexander & P. Winne (Eds.), *Handbook of educational psychology* (2nd ed., pp. 349–307). Mahwah, NJ: Erlbaum.

Snow, C.E., Porche, M.V., Tabors, P.O., & Harris, S.R. (2007). *Is literacy enough? Pathways to academic success for adolescents.* Baltimore: Paul H. Brookes.

Turner, J.C. (1997). Starting right: Strategies for engaging young literacy learners. In J.T. Guthrie & A. Wigfield (Eds.), *Reading engagement: Motivating readers through integrated instruction* (pp. 183–204). Newark, DE: International Reading Association.

Vygotsky, L.S. (1978). *Mind in society: The development of higher psychological processes* (M. Cole, V. John-Steiner, S. Scribner, & E. Souberman, Eds. & Trans.). Cambridge, MA: Harvard University Press. (Original work published 1934)

Wigfield, A., & Eccles, J.S. (2000). Expectancy-value theory of achievement motivation. *Contemporary Educational Psychology, 25,* 68–81.

Teaching Fluency Artfully

Timothy Rasinski

Inspiring Reading Success: Interest and Motivation in an Age of High-Stakes Testing, edited by Rosalie Fink and S. Jay Samuels. © 2008 by the International Reading Association.

The rationale for testing children in reading is, on the surface, quite admirable and appropriate—to identify those students who are experiencing difficulty in reading, to monitor growth in reading, and to hold education professionals accountable for their work with students. However, in the current environment in which the futures of students, their teachers, and their schools are dependent on students' performance on certain narrowly defined tests, the focus of schooling in general and reading instruction in particular has shifted to improving performance on the tests themselves and away from authentic academic achievement and motivation for learning. I, along with many other professionals, am deeply troubled by this shift and its ultimate effects on students, teachers, and the role of schools.

I feel there are better ways to increase reading achievement (authentic achievement as well as achievement on tests) and at the same time inspire a love of reading and learning. In this chapter, I focus on fluency, my particular area of interest in reading, and share my vision of how fluency can be taught effectively and, at the same time, inspire and motivate students to learn and love learning.

I have been involved in the study and teaching of reading fluency for over 25 years. As a teacher of struggling readers in Nebraska, USA, I was fascinated by my students who were highly intelligent, well spoken, and inquisitive, yet had significant difficulty learning to read. I wondered how it could be that students with such high learning potential could do so poorly when it came to reading. I thought that the topic of cognitive and learning styles could help explain and offer insight into teaching these children more effectively. I had intended to study learning styles in my doctoral program.

However, while in my doctoral studies at the Ohio State University, I was directed by my advisor and mentor, Dr. Jerome Zutell, to a series of professional articles, most notably Chomsky (1976), Samuels (1979), Schreiber (1980), and Allington (1983), that were an epiphany for me. These scholars wrote about an idea that I had heard applied to reading in only the most general ways—that idea was reading fluency. From those initial articles I dove into the topic, abandoned learning styles as my major interest, and focused my dissertation study on developing and testing a model of reading fluency (Rasinski, 1985).

My initial study (and subsequent work) in fluency gained some attention and recognition from the International Reading Association and the College Reading Association, resulted in some publications (Rasinski, 1989a, 1989b, 1990a, 1990b, 1991), and spurred my continued interest in and study of reading fluency. Other scholars also used the 1980s and 1990s to enhance our understanding of reading fluency, its importance, and how it might be taught most effectively (Chall, 1996).

Nevertheless, despite the increasing interest in reading fluency among certain literacy scholars, fluency was largely ignored by the field, especially by those involved in reading curriculum and instruction. A widely reported international study of factors associated with success in learning to read (Postlethwaite & Ross, 1992), for example, did not include reading fluency among the factors under consideration. I recall attending national meetings of professional literacy organizations in which I or others presented papers on reading fluency or reported on recent studies on reading fluency in which the entire audience, including the presenter and chairperson of the session, was less than five people. Zutell and I found that as of the mid-1990s reading fluency continued to be benignly ignored in instructional materials for elementary students and teachers in training.

The Turning Point for Fluency

The turning point for reading fluency came with the publication of the report of the National Reading Panel (National Institute of Child Health and Human Development, 2000). In the summary report, the National Reading Panel identified five important instructional factors that were positively and empirically linked to student achievement in reading. One of the factors was reading fluency. The panel defined reading fluency and presented research-based methods for nurturing fluency in students.

Reading fluency is defined in two components—the ability to read words in print automatically, and the ability to read text with appropriate and meaningful expression (prosody). Automaticity in reading refers to the ability of readers to decode words in print effortlessly, using minimal amounts of a reader's limited cognitive resources, so that those same cognitive resources can be used for the more important goal of reading—comprehension (LaBerge & Samuels, 1974). When a reader achieves automaticity in word decoding, comprehension can take place at the same time.

Expressive or prosodic reading takes fluency to the next level in which a reader embeds prosodic features, such as pitch, volume, emphasis, and phrasing that make the reading sound like authentic oral language, and adds additional meaning to the reading (Schreiber, 1980, 1987, 1991; Schreiber & Read, 1980). (See the reproducible Multidimensional Rubric for Assessing the Prosodic Features of Reading Fluency on page 120.) To be able to read with appropriate expression, readers need to attend to the meaning of the text while reading.

In addition to identifying the components of reading fluency, the panel also identified methods for providing effective instruction in reading fluency. Chief among these methods were guided repeated reading and assisted reading. Repeated reading involves

Multidimensional Rubric for Assessing the Prosodic Features of Reading Fluency

NAME _____

Fluency Rubric

	1	2	3	4
Expression and volume	Reads in a quiet voice as if to get words out. The reading does not sound natural like talking to a friend.	Reads in a quiet voice. The reading sounds natural in part of the text, but the reader does not always sound like he or she is talking to a friend.	Reads with volume and expression. However, sometimes the reader slips into expressionless reading and does not sound like he or she is talking to a friend.	Reads with varied volume and expression. The reader sounds like he or she is talking to a friend with his or her voice matching the interpretation of the passage.
Phrasing	Reads word by word in a monotone voice.	Reads in two or three word phrases, not adhering to punctuation, stress, and intonation.	Reads with a mixture of run-ons, midsentence pauses for breath, and some choppiness. There is reasonable stress and intonation.	Reads with good phrasing, adhering to punctuation, stress, and intonation.
Smoothness	Frequently hesitates while reading, sounds out words, and repeats words or phrases. The reader makes multiple attempts to read the same passage.	Reads with extended pauses or hesitations. The reader has many "rough spots."	Reads with occasional breaks in rhythm. The reader has difficulty with specific words and/or sentence structures.	Reads smoothly with some breaks, but self-corrects with difficult words and/or sentence structures.
Pace	Reads slowly and laboriously.	Reads moderately slowly.	Reads fast and slow throughout reading.	Reads at a conversational pace throughout the reading.

Score _____

Scores of 8 or more indicate that the student is making adequate progress in fluency.
Scores below 8 indicate that the student may need additional instruction in fluency.

Adapted from Zutell, J., & Rasinski, T.V. (1991). Training teachers to attend to their students' oral reading fluency. *Theory Into Practice, 30*, 211–217.

Inspiring Reading Success: Interest and Motivation in an Age of High-Stakes Testing, edited by Rosalie Fink and S. Jay Samuels. © 2008 by the International Reading Association. May be copied for classroom use.

students in reading a reasonably brief text several times until it can be read with sufficient fluency. In a landmark study, Samuels (1979) found that when students read a passage several times, each successive reading rendered higher levels of word recognition, reading speed, and comprehension. More important, however, when students moved on to new texts that were as challenging or more challenging than the one before, improvement in word recognition, reading speed, and comprehension were also noted. Guided assisted reading involves students reading a text while simultaneously hearing the text read aloud in a fluent manner. As readers do their best to examine and read a passage visually (and orally), they are, at the same time, hearing an oral rendering of the same text. The oral assist can come in the form of reading with another person or while reading and listening to a recorded version of the same passage. Early studies of both forms of assisted reading, reading with a partner (Heckelman, 1969) and recorded assistance (Chomsky, 1976), demonstrated promising results. In Chomsky's study, for example, done at much the same time as Samuels's study on repeated reading, young readers who were making very little progress in reading now demonstrated significant improvement when repeatedly reading a passage while listening to a prerecorded version of the same passage. Later reviews of the research (see Chard et al., 2002; Kuhn & Stahl, 2000; Rasinski & Hoffman, 2003) have confirmed these results to the point where repeated and assisted reading are now accepted as the main instructional tools for fluency instruction.

During roughly the same time period, other research, aimed at improving reading assessment, done largely by special educators and school psychologists, made significant progress. Deno (1985; Deno, Mirkin, & Chiang, 1982) found that reading rate, as measured through one minute of reading and then counting the number of words read correctly, was strongly correlated with other more elaborate and more general measures of reading achievement. This form of assessment, originally referred to as Curriculum Based Measurement, suggests that reading rate is a measure of automaticity in reading, and because of automaticity's theoretical and increasingly empirical link to reading comprehension, it is a reasonable proxy for measures of reading comprehension and overall reading achievement. Deno's work in this form of Curriculum Based Measurement has found further expression in Good and Kaminski's (2005) Oral Reading Fluency component of their Dynamic Indicators of Basic Early Literacy (DIBELs) as well as in other reading assessment systems (e.g., Aimsweb).

The result of all this fine work in reading fluency has been the development of instructional methods and systems for teaching reading fluency that rely heavily on repeated and assisted readings. Moreover, the criterion variable that is usually employed for measuring growth in fluency is reading rate. An ever-growing body of studies, often sponsored or supported by the publishers of fluency materials, have demonstrated strong growth in reading rate as a result of the fluency treatment and, to a lesser extent, improvements in reading comprehension.

I certainly accept the research that has led to these developments. I believe the research, some of it my own, has demonstrated the efficacy of repeated and assisted reading and the use of reading rate as a measure or indicator of automaticity and general reading achievement. However, at the same time, I find myself concerned with the direction that fluency instruction has evolved over the past several years.

In particular I am disturbed by the mechanical approach in which fluency instruction is often implemented in classrooms and intervention settings around the United States. Students are asked to engage in repeated and assisted reading of informational texts (because of the importance of providing students with new information and of reinforcing other content areas of the curriculum) with the major goal of increasing students' reading speed. Once a certain reading rate is achieved, students move on to another slightly more challenging text to read repeatedly until the criterion rate is achieved. Similarly, major oral fluency assessments involve students reading passages with the sole purpose of reading the passage quickly. Prosody or expression is seldom assessed. Reading comprehension, too, is seldom assessed, and if it is assessed, it is done so in ways that could be best described as superficial.

This overemphasis on reading speed as the key criterion for reading fluency development and assessment is a major concern. I find that students (and teachers) are beginning to view reading instruction as an exercise in reading fast. A few weeks before writing this chapter, I conducted a reading diagnostic clinic at Kent State University. Of the eight children that we tested, three of them, when confronted with a passage to read orally, asked the diagnostician if they should read the passage as fast as possible. Often when visiting elementary classrooms I have the opportunity to talk with students and ask individual children to name the best reader in their class. Then upon their naming a classmate, I ask them to tell me why they think that student is such a good reader. With increasing frequency, I am getting the answer that the nominated reader is a fast reader—that is what makes him or her so good at reading. Clearly, teachers and students have been unduly influenced by those who think that reading fluency is nothing more than learning to read text quickly.

In addition to this concern about reading speed, I find myself wondering if informational text is the best choice for developing reading fluency. Although informational text is important and may certainly be one of the most important types of texts for students to read, it generally is not written for oral expressive reading, one of the key elements of fluency that is often ignored instructionally and in assessment.

Fluency as an Art Form—Performance, Rehearsal, and Repeated Reading

I certainly subscribe to the notions that reading fluency is composed of automaticity in word recognition and expressive or prosodic reading of text. Moreover, I agree that guided repeated reading and assisted reading are valuable and effective instructional methods for developing fluency. I also agree that reading speed is an indicator or way to measure automaticity (but most definitely not a guide or recipe for teaching automaticity).

At the same time, however, I find myself asking, How can teachers engage students in repeated and assisted reading in ways that are authentic and that focus attention on meaning and at the same time nurture both areas of fluency—automaticity and expressive reading? Current methods in vogue have students repeatedly read informational texts for the main purpose of reading the passage ever more quickly. I find such an approach not terribly authentic when viewed in light of the major purpose of reading, neither engaging nor intrinsically motivating beyond students trying to outpace their previous reading and the readings of their classmates and focusing primarily on developing automaticity at the expense of expression. The problem has become not so much how to teach reading fluency but more how to teach it in authentic and engaging ways.

To this end I found myself further asking, what would make anyone want to repeatedly practice any set of activities—whether in sports, music, or the other performing arts? The answer I found myself drawn to is *performance*. Football teams practice the same plays at the end of the year that they practiced at the beginning of the season to ensure high levels of performance during the games. Musical groups, whether a local jazz band or a symphonic orchestra, repeatedly practice their music because of the next performance— the gig Saturday night at the Blue Note or the concert at Carnegie Hall. And, of course, actors practice or rehearse their lines because of the eventual performance they will make, either on stage or film.

In the same way, then, performance in reading is a very natural reason for readers to engage in guided repeated reading. Readers do not practice their texts to read ever more quickly; they read to bring the words to life with their voices. Thus, expression or prosodic reading becomes a focus of the repeated reading. And, although quick reading is not central to the repeated reading in this approach, repeated reading has been shown to lead to greater automaticity and speed, so word-recognition automaticity and reading speed can be expected to mature as students engage in this form of guided and assisted repeated readings.

Texts With Voice

What kinds of texts lend themselves to artistic performance and rehearsal? I have come to the conclusion that texts written with *voice* work especially well in this regard. Texts written with voice are texts that are meant to be read or performed with voice or expression. For the most part, then, the criterion of *voice* puts most informational texts in a secondary position. Informational texts tend to be written in a disembodied third-person voice with the intent to convey as much information as possible in as tightly and logically organized a manner as possible. While I am not attempting to denigrate the importance of informational texts (I feel they are as important as any text form and will probably gain in importance in coming years), I do not feel that they would be my primary choice for developing reading fluency through rehearsal and performance. I often ask teachers and students with whom I work how easy it might be to perform an informational passage on the topic of evaporation or addition, for example. I am usually greeted with a great deal of skepticism, to say the least.

If informational texts are not the primary source of texts for practice and perform-ance, what are? Certainly narrative or story material is often written with compelling voice that lends itself to prosodic interpretation. However, the very nature of most nar-ratives makes them lengthier than one would want for repeated reading by developing readers. We have overcome this problem quite easily by providing students with short seg-ments of stories that are especially well suited for expressive performance.

Beyond narrative texts, I have found several other text forms or genres that meet the criterion of voice. These other text forms include scripts (Readers Theatre), mono-logues, dialogues, poetry, rhymes, song lyrics, oratory or rhetoric, jokes and riddles, letters, journals, and diaries. Other forms, I am sure, exist, but this corpus, I believe, establishes a strong foundation of text types that are meant to be practiced and eventually performed.

Repeated and assisted readings are done by students with the eventual goal of per-formance for an audience always in mind. An audience will not find a performance sat-isfying if the readers read the passages quickly; rather, it is the expressive reading that will make the reading satisfying for listeners.

The general routine that teachers follow in using this voiced approach to fluency instruction usually begins with the introduction of a text early in the week. Students, alone or in small groups, are assigned a text that they will eventually perform for an au-dience (see Table 6.1 for a list of websites that provide voiced texts). Then daily periods of practice or repeated reading follow. Early in the week the teacher or other instructor provides more support for the students by modeling, coaching, and giving feedback and encouragement. Over the course of the week (and the school year), the responsibility for the reading shifts from the teacher to the students themselves, with the teacher mov-ing further into the background as students take greater control of their reading. Eventually, by the end of the week students perform their assigned reading for their classmates or other audience (e.g., students from other classrooms, parents, school prin-cipal, other teachers) that the teacher may invite into the classroom.

The simplicity of this routine is part of the allure of this approach to fluency. Every week the routine is essentially the same, so students know what they need to do and take increasingly greater control over the process. The performance is the motivator for the practice in much the same way that the stage play or concert is the motivator for performing artists.

Theoretically, this more artful approach to teaching fluency should result in similar improvements in reading fluency that previous studies examining repeated readings have reported. Rehearsing texts for future performance is essentially a form of repeated reading, albeit in a more natural and authentic manner that employs the rehearsal for both automaticity and for expressive and prosodic purposes.

Beyond theory, however, an emerging body of research is reporting remarkable gains in reading fluency and overall reading performance with this artful approach to fluency. Martinez, Roser, and Strecker (1999), for example, report second graders making gains of over a year in reading achievement (overall reading level as measured by an informal reading inventory) in 12 weeks of implementation of a Readers Theatre curriculum.

TABLE 6.1
Useful Websites for Finding Voiced Texts

Readers Theatre

Aaron Shepard's RT Page: Scripts and Tips for Reader's Theater
www.aaronshep.com/rt

FictionTeachers.com
www.fictionteachers.com/classroomtheater/theater.html

Free Online Scripts
hrsbstaff.ednet.ns.ca/phillie/AR7/freescripts.htm

Gander Academy: Readers Theatre
www.cdli.ca/CITE/langrt.htm

Internet Resources for Conducting Readers Theatre
www.readingonline.org/electronic/elec_index.asp?
HREF=carrick/index.html

Literacy Connections: Readers' Theatre
www.literacyconnections.com/ReadersTheater.html

MargiePalatini
www.margiepalatini.com

Readers' Theatre
www.vtaide.com/png/theatre.htm

Reader's Theatre Basics
bms.westport.k12.ct.us/mccormick/rt/RTHOME.htm

Readers' Theatre Collection
www.readerstheatre.ecsd.net/collection.htm

Reader's Theater Scripts and Plays
www.teachingheart.net/readerstheater.htm

ReadingLady
www.readinglady.com

Scripts for Schools
loiswalker.com/catalog/guidesamples.html

StoryCart.com
www.storycart.com

Timeless Teacher Stuff
www.timelessteacherstuff.com

Tony Palermo's Ruyasonic: Audio Theatre/Radio Drama Resources
ruyasonic.com/rdr_main.htm

Poetry

American Poems—Your Poetry Site
www.americanpoems.com

Children's Poetry Archive
www.poetryarchive.org/childrensarchive/home.do

Story It: Language Art Resources for Children and Their Teachers: Poems for Children—The Classics
www.storyit.com/Classics/JustPoems/classicpoems.htm

Songs

Bus Songs.com: Children's Songs From Camp, Parties, TV, and the Nursery
www.bussongs.com

The Children's Music Archive
judyanddavid.com/cma.html

NIEHS Kids Pages: Sing-Along Songs
www.niehs.nih.gov/kids/music.htm

NIEHS Sing-Along Songs Index
www.niehs.nih.gov/kids/music.htm#index

Songs for Children
www.head-start.lane.or.us/education/activities/music/index.html

The Teacher's Guide Children's Songs Page
www.theteachersguide.com/ChildrensSongs.htm

Folk Songs and Songs of America

English Folk Song Lyrics
classic-sf.co.uk/folk-lyrics

Military Songs
www.ftmeade.army.mil/songs.html

Patriotic Songs
www.scoutsongs.com/categories/patriotic.html

Popular Songs in American History
www.contemplator.com/america

Speeches and Oratory

American Oratory: The Power of Rhetoric in the United States
www.americanrhetoric.com

These gains, as well as gains in reading rate, were approximately twice that of a control group of second graders not engaged in repeated reading of Readers Theatre scripts. On top of this, the authors report that students found such reading intrinsically motivating and enjoyable. One student, Omar, wrote this in his journal: "Readers theater is the funnest reading I've ever did before!" (p. 333).

Griffith and Rasinski (2004) report similar outstanding results among fourth graders engaged in weekly performance of Readers Theatre scripts, poetry, and other performance texts, some of which were authored by the teacher and students. Three years of data suggest that struggling readers in Lorraine Griffith's fourth-grade class made over two years gain in reading achievement during the year they were in her classroom. Gains in reading rate among her struggling readers approached 60 words per minute, whereas the normal academic year growth in reading rate among fourth graders is less than 30 words per minute. Moreover, students found Griffith's approach highly engaging and motivating. They relished the opportunity to perform for others and were thrilled by the progress they saw themselves making. One of Griffith's students, Taylor, was identified as an at-risk student when he entered fourth grade. By spring he had noticed that his reading was more like students in the top reading group. He went to Mrs. Griffith "and said with a certain level of impertinence, 'What am I doing in this reading group…?'" (Griffith & Rasinski, 2004, p. 137). During the following summer vacation Taylor read the Lord of the Rings trilogy by J.R.R. Tolkien.

In a study of parents engaged in repeated and assisted reading of short rhymes over a 12-week period with their first-grade children identified as at-risk in reading, Rasinski and Stevenson (2005) report significant gains in word recognition and reading rate when compared with a control group of students receiving the same reading curriculum in school, but not the repeated and assisted reading at home. Indeed, by November of the school year these at-risk students receiving the fluency treatment had already achieved the January benchmark for reading fluency. Moreover, most of the parents and children reported finding value in the repeated and assisted reading activities and loving the opportunities to read together for a few minutes every evening.

Biggs, Homan, Dedrick, and Rasinski (in press) engaged struggling middle-grade students in a repeated reading treatment in which students learned lyrics to songs presented to them in a computer-based "learn to sing" program. Again, these students made remarkable and significant results in reading comprehension in a 12-week implementation. The average gain in reading comprehension was over a year.

Repeated and assisted reading protocols are effective in improving reading fluency and overall reading achievement, regardless of the text employed. However, careful attention to the type of text used and the purpose for the repeated reading can result in treatments that emphasize expression and prosodic fluency as well as automatic word-recognition fluency and, importantly, can result in fluency instruction protocols that are more authentic, natural, and intrinsically motivating for students and teachers engaged in such instruction.

Unexpected Benefits of an Artful Approach to Fluency

My initial forays into the use of scripts, poetry, songs, and other texts were aimed specifically at improving students' reading fluency. However, as I became more involved in this artful approach to teaching fluency, it became apparent to me that there were other benefits nurtured by this approach that I had not anticipated but that may be as important as the improvement in fluency itself. This more expansive view of fluency began with a visit to a teacher's classroom.

Until recently Kathy Perfect was a fourth-grade teacher in an elementary school in northeast Ohio. Her passion is poetry and she wanted her students to develop a similar love for and appreciation of poetry. In her class, students regularly heard her read poetry and would also perform poetry on their own. One of my most memorable classroom experiences was the time I visited her class on a Friday afternoon to hear students perform the poems they had selected earlier in the week. The class had one of its regular poetry cafés that Kathy organized for her students. A parent or two supplied appropriate treats, and students came to class ready for a day of poetry, with many dressed in black and wearing berets, toting bongos and tambourines, and declaring "Carpe diem" to one another and anyone else within earshot.

I was impressed by the level of expressiveness students invoked in their performances—meaning was carried through voice, inflection, tone, phrasing, emphasis, and even dramatic pause. Clearly, these students had been enthusiastically rehearsing their selected verses for some time. Although fluency in reading was apparent, Kathy's reason for having the students practice was the poetry itself. She noted to me and to students that no one would enjoy a poem if it were read in a halting fashion, either too fast or too slowly. It had to be read with just the right voice for each poem to be savored by the listening audience.

It became apparent to me that these students were learning just what Kathy wanted them to learn—a love for poetry. This experience also helped me remember fondly my own school experiences with poetry when my elementary classmates and I read and recited "In Flanders Field" every Armistice Day (now called Veteran's Day) and Walt Whitman's "O Captain! My Captain!" when we celebrated Abraham Lincoln's birthday. It dawned on me then that there exists a variety of genres beyond narrative and exposition that are text forms that legitimately need to be read, reread, studied, and appreciated. Further, such texts add a welcome dimension of depth and variety to the reading classroom. In addition to narrative and exposition, students need opportunities to engage with what poet laureate Robert Pinsky (as cited in Keillor, 2004) calls "rhythmical words" meant to be read aloud. Such texts allow for deeper exploration of the English language and how meaning is made and communicated in other written forms. That is all good news.

The bad news is that in our desire to load the curriculum with informational and narrative texts, these other text forms have been left behind. Proof of this comes to me quite often when I visit classrooms and ask students about poems, songs, speeches, and other such texts that were a regular part of my school experience; the students I meet usually report complete ignorance of such texts—nursery rhymes; poetry by Walt Whitman,

Emily Dickinson, and Langston Hughes; patriotic songs and songs about the United States and its folk heroes; speeches such as "The Gettysburg Address" and "Ain't I a Woman" are completely foreign to these students. They have not had a chance to explore the wonderful depth of language that such texts offer. What a shame.

An artful approach to fluency instruction, then, widens the scope of what counts as legitimate reading material—these other forms and genres add to the palette of text choices provided to the teacher and students. Moreover, these other text forms (I like the term *rhythmical words* that poet Pinsky uses), such as poetry, speeches, songs, and scripts, provide opportunities to explore and appreciate the richness of the language and ways in which writers use language to express meaning. Rhythm, rhyme, alliteration, assonance, imagery, metaphor, and simile are just some of the ways in which writers of rhythmical words express meaning. Moreover, they do so in texts that are often compact but rich with these and other elements of writing style.

> An artful approach to fluency instruction, then, widens the scope of what counts as legitimate reading material—these other forms and genres add to the palette of text choices provided to the teacher and students.

The use of this richer palette of texts permits students and teachers to explore meaning in different ways, too. Reading comprehension itself can be taught to a greater depth with these other texts. For example, the interpretation and creation of metaphor (and simile) are sophisticated comprehension and thinking skills found in the reading curriculum in every state. And yet, these can be difficult skills to teach, as metaphors are not often used in informational text and they may be so few and complex in narrative that they may not be easily or efficiently studied in the classroom. Creators of poems, songs, speeches, and scripts often create metaphors in a relatively compact text that lends itself to analysis and discussion.

When Walt Whitman writes "O Captain, my Captain...;" or Emily Dickinson, "There is no frigate like a book...;" or Langston Hughes, "Well son, I'll tell ya, life for me ain't been no crystal stair...," the metaphor or simile is easily accessible for students to comprehend, discuss, and create others on their own. This past year, I observed fifth graders read Hughes's "Mother to Son" in which Hughes uses climbing a flight of stairs as a metaphor for life. After having made the requisite comparisons between life and stair climbing, the teacher had students name other common events in life. Watching the Super Bowl, cooking supper, and making a cross country trip were volunteered. The teacher then asked students to get into small groups and discuss how such events could be used as a metaphor for life. After brief discussions in which the analyses were made, the teacher asked students then to write, rehearse, and perform their own metaphorical poems, similar to Langston Hughes. Some of the results were breathtaking (see, for example, Carlos's poem on page 131; all students' names are pseudonyms).

Comprehension is also fostered through response to text—how we think, how we act, how we are changed, how we are moved—by what we read. Rosenblatt (1978) notes that there are two types of responses that human beings make to text: efferent, or response from the head, and aesthetic, or response from the heart. Both forms of response are important and both should be nurtured in the classroom. However, since high-stakes testing focuses almost exclusively on the efferent side of education, efferent responses in reading increasingly tend to dominate the classroom scene. The aesthetic side of reading is not part of high-stakes testing and is thus too often benignly neglected in classrooms.

The types of texts I promote through an artful approach to fluency tend to lend themselves more toward the aesthetic response. I think all of us can remember listening to a song, a poem, a speech, or a play and being moved to tears or a response that was felt as much from our hearts as it was from our heads. Allowing students to respond to texts in this aesthetic way is important; it allows us to make connections to who we are as humans, our feelings, fears, and fantasies, not just what we know and what we need to know. I think Robert Pinsky (Keillor, 2004) summed it up best when he wrote, "[T]here's something about reciting rhythmical words aloud—it's almost biological—that comforts and enlivens human beings" (n.p.).

Not only do rhythmical texts have the power to touch the heart; they have the ability to unite many hearts. I often ask teachers and students why it is that the military services have songs, why it is that we have patriotic songs, why it is that there were songs used during the U.S. Civil War, the Civil Rights era, or the union movement? One answer, of course, is to inspire. Another answer is to unite. Rhythmical words have an ability to pull people together who share the sentiments expressed in the text.

That sense of unity is not only important for the military services and the citizens of a country; it is also important for children in school. Students need to learn that they are part of a larger whole, that they are members of their school, their community, their country. Songs, and other rhythmical texts, are the kinds of texts that can nurture that unity, and that is another reason they have a legitimate and necessary place in our schools. The rituals behind performing the Preamble to the Constitution, singing a patriotic song, or reciting the Pledge of Allegiance help bind our students to the larger community that they are called to serve and support.

In our summer reading clinic at Kent State, our students learn and practice a different patriotic song every other day. Then on the day before the Fourth of July, all the students, their teachers, and their family members gather around the flagpole in front of the school for a patriotic sing-along. All participants have a songbook in their hands and are encouraged to sing and read at the same time. When we sing "Grand Old Flag," "This Land Is Your Land," "God Bless America," and many other patriotic songs, we engage in authentic reading and singing, but we also celebrate who we are as citizens of the United States.

Similarly, rhythmical texts that I advocate for fluency instruction have the ability to celebrate the differences between us—our cultural and ethnic backgrounds. Cultures often mark themselves through song, poetry, script, and rhetoric. These texts can be used, then, for celebrating the various cultures that reside in our classrooms.

Being of Polish descent, I am able to share with my students folk songs in Polish that I grew up with. Other students of Irish, Italian, German, Jewish, African, Hispanic,

Chinese, Japanese, Iranian, and other cultures can find rhythmical texts that, as a group, we can learn, practice, perform, and celebrate. In this way we value the cultures and backgrounds that students bring with them to the classroom.

Writing, the other side of the literacy coin, of course is an important part of the school curriculum. As in reading, the types of writing that tend to dominate the school curriculum are narratives and the various forms of exposition or informational writing. While not denying that these forms are important and should be emphasized, other forms of writing, the ones I advocate, should be used in an artful approach to fluency. Writing rhythmical words should also be nurtured in school.

I feel that the best way to learn to write narrative and informational text is to examine the best forms of these available to students and encourage students to emulate those forms in their own writing. An important part of the analyses of such texts is the repeated reading of those texts so that students can get inside the form and structure of the text.

Students should also be given opportunities and encouragement to write poetry, song lyrics, scripts, speeches, and other rhythmical words. The repeated readings of rhythmical texts allow students entry into the structure and nuances of the particular text. Students can then emulate that text or text structure in their own writing. In our reading and writing program for struggling readers, we invite students to turn the narratives they read in guided reading into poems, scripts, monologues, dialogues, letters, journal entries, and the like. This past summer clinicians in our reading clinic worked with students to create a fictional dialogue between the book characters Junie B. Jones and Ramona Quimby. What would their conversation be like if they were seated next to each other on a school bus? During February, fifth graders worked on dialogues between different presidents. Many students opted to create a conversation between the two Georges—George Washington and George W. Bush. Creating such dialogues required good understanding of the content and ability to write with voice.

Students practice their written transformations and eventually perform them for an audience. We also invite and encourage them to write their own versions (or parodies) of the rhythmical texts that they practice and perform. These can be as simple as a silly version of Yankee Doodle written by Jason (age 10), a student in our summer reading clinic:

Yankee Doodle went to town
Riding on a camel.
Hit a bump and hurt his rump
And now he rides side saddle.

Tyler (age 7) wrote this version of Diddle Diddle Dumpling:

Diddle diddle dumpling my son Fred
Slept all day on his bed
Woke up at midnight and dreamed there's a monster under my bed
Diddle diddle dumpling my son Fred.

And Elizabeth (age 8) wrote her own version of Diddle Diddle Dumpling:

> Diddle diddle dumpling, my girl Mag.
> Had a dog and his name was Tag.
> He chewed on a bone and he chewed on a rag.
> Diddle diddle dumpling, my girl Mag.

All three students practiced their creations and read them at a weekly poetry slam in their classrooms.

On the other hand, students' text transformations can be as sophisticated as writing their own metaphorical version of Hughes's "Mother to Son." Below is 12-year-old Carlos's version of Hughes's classic poem.

> Father to Son
> Well, son, I'll tell you:
> Life for me ain't been no Super Bowl game.
> It's had lots of fumbles,
> And interceptions,
> And plenty of fourth downs and ten to go,
> And times when I was down by three touchdowns late in the fourth quarter—
> Desperate.
> But all the time
> I've kept on plugging away,
> And getting field goals,
> And even a touchdown now and then.
> And sometimes having to sit on the bench
> When I knew I could make the play.
> So boy, don't you give up on the game.
> Don't you go to the showers
> 'Cause you find the game can be kind of tough.
> Don't you get blocked now—
> For I'm still playing son,
> I'm still getting in the game,
> And life for me ain't been no Super Bowl game.

Clearly, Carlos understood the meaning of Hughes's original text and was, through a deep analysis of the text, able to write a similar version that used the Super Bowl as the central metaphor. When Carlos performed the text for his classmates, two other boys were so moved by it that they asked if they could have a copy to perform on their own.

The reproducible Readers Theatre script on pages 132–135 is a rewritten version of the classic tale The Three Billy Goats Gruff. It was rewritten by second graders who had

Readers Theatre Script

The Three Billy Goats Gruff (With Attitude!)

Parts: (6) Little Billy Goat Gruff, Middle-Size Billy Goat Gruff, Big Billy Goat Gruff, Troll, Narrators 1 and 2

Narrator 1:   Welcome to our show. Our play today is The Three Billy Goats Gruff.

Narrator 2:   As Little Billy Goat Gruff strolls through the fields he sees a run-down, rickety, old bridge. On the other side of the bridge is a meadow with green, green grass and apple trees.

Little BGG: I'm the littlest billy goat. I have two big brothers. I want to go across this bridge to eat some of that green, green grass and apples so that I can become big like my two brothers.

Narrator 1:   Little Billy Goat Gruff starts across the bridge.

All: [Softly] Tripity, trapity, tripity, trapity, tripity, trapity.

Narrator 2:   Just as Little Billy Goat Gruff came to the middle of the bridge, an old troll popped up from underneath.

Troll: Who is that walking on my bridge? Snort Snort.

Little BGG: It's only I, Little Billy Goat Gruff.

Troll: Arrrgh. I'm a big, bad troll and you are on *my* bridge. I'm going to eat you for my breakfast. Snort Snort.

Little BGG: I just want to eat some green, green grass and apples in the meadow. Please don't eat me Mister Troll. I'm just a little billy goat. Wait until my brother comes along. He is much bigger and tastier than me.

Troll: Bigger? Tastier? Well, alright. I guess I will. Go ahead and cross the bridge. Arrrgh.

Little BGG: Thank you very much, you great big, ugly old troll.

Troll: What did you call me? Come back here right now! Grrrr.

Little BGG: Oh, nothing. Bye!

(continued)

Adapted by second-grade students, Kent State University Summer Reading Clinic, Camp Read-A-Lot.

Inspiring Reading Success: Interest and Motivation in an Age of High-Stakes Testing, edited by Rosalie Fink and S. Jay Samuels. © 2008 by the International Reading Association. May be copied for classroom use.

Readers Theatre Script (continued)

All: [Softly] Tripity, trapity, tripity, trapity, tripity, trapity.

Narrator 1: Little Billy Goat Gruff ran across the bridge. He ate the green, green grass and apples. The troll went back under his bridge and went to sleep.

Narrator 2: Before long Middle-Size Billy Goat Gruff walks up to the rickety, old bridge. He too sees the meadow with the green, green grass and apple trees.

Middle-size BGG: I'm the middle-size billy goat. I have a big brother and a little brother. I want to go across this bridge to eat some green, green grass and apples so that I can be big like my brother.

Narrator 1: Middle-Size Billy Goat Gruff starts across the bridge.

All: [A bit louder, as Middle-Size BGG is bigger] Trip trip, trap trap, trip trip, trap trap, trip trip, trap trap.

Narrator 2: Just as the Middle-Size Billy Goat Gruff came to the middle of the bridge, an old troll popped up from under the bridge.

Troll: Grrrr. Who is that walking on my bridge? Arrrgh.

Middle-size BGG: It is I, Middle-Size Billy Goat Gruff.

Troll: Grrrr. I'm a big, bad troll and you are on my bridge. I'm going to eat you for my lunch. Snort Snort.

Middle-size BGG: I just want to eat some green, green grass and apples in the meadow. Please, please don't eat me Mister Troll. I'm just a middle-size billy goat. Why don't you wait until my brother comes along. He is much bigger and much much tastier than I am.

Troll: Bigger? Tastier? Hmmmmm. Alright, I think I will. Go ahead and cross the bridge.

Middle-size BGG: Thank you very much, you great big, really ugly, and dirty old troll with bad breath.

Troll: What did you call me? Grrrr. You come back here right this very instant!

Middle-size BGG: Oh, nothing. See ya!

(continued)

Adapted by second-grade students, Kent State University Summer Reading Clinic, Camp Read-A-Lot.

All:	[A bit louder] Trip trip, trap trap, trip trip, trap trap, trip trip, trap trap.
Narrator 1:	Middle-Size Billy Goat Gruff ran across the bridge. He ate the green, green grass and apples. The troll went back under his bridge and once again fell fast sleep.
Narrator 2:	After a while, Big Billy Goat Gruff sees the run-down, rickety, old bridge. On the other side of the bridge is a meadow with green, green grass and apple trees.
Big BGG:	I'm the biggest billy goat. I have two brothers. I want to go across this bridge to eat some green, green grass and apples just as they did.
Narrator 1:	So Big Billy Goat Gruff starts across the bridge.
All:	[Even louder this time] TRIP, TRAP, TRIP, TRAP, TRIP, TRAP.
Narrator 2:	Just as Big Billy Goat Gruff got to the middle of the bridge, an old troll popped up from under the bridge.
Troll:	Grrr. Who is that walking on my bridge?
Big BGG:	It is I, Big Billy Goat Gruff.
Troll:	Grrrr. I'm a big, bad troll and you are on my bridge. I'm going to eat you for my supper. Snort Snort.
Big BGG:	Oh really? [Smiles at audience] Well then, come right on up here and have a feast then. [Again smiles at audience]
Narrator 1:	The troll climbs onto the bridge. Big Billy Goat Gruff lowers his head and charges the troll! Garump. Big Billy Goat Gruff knocks the troll clean off the bridge and into the icy cold water!
Troll:	Glug Glug Glug. Grrrrr. Grrrr. Brrr.
Big BGG:	Brothers, that ugly old bully won't bother us again. I butted him with my horns and knocked him off the bridge and into the icy cold water. I've done my job and from now on we can come and go in peace. Now, I'm going to go and eat some of that green, green grass and some apples.
All:	[Loud] TRIP, TRAP, TRIP, TRAP, TRIP, TRAP.

(continued)

Adapted by second-grade students, Kent State University Summer Reading Clinic, Camp Read-A-Lot.

Readers Theatre Script (continued)

Narrator 2:   Big Billy Goat Gruff crosses the bridge and joins his brothers. He ate the green, green grass and apples.

Little Billy
Goat: Munch Munch Munch.

Little and
Middle-Size
Billy Goat: Munch Munch Munch.

All Three
Billy Goats
Together: Munch Munch Munch. This green, green grass is great for lunch!

Narrator 1:   And that mean, ugly, old troll? He never came back to the bridge. He learned that being mean never pays.

Troll: This water feels like ice. Brrr Brrr Brrr. Next time I'll try being nice!

All: The End.

Adapted by second-grade students, Kent State University Summer Reading Clinic, Camp Read-A-Lot.

Inspiring Reading Success: Interest and Motivation in an Age of High-Stakes Testing, edited by Rosalie Fink and S. Jay Samuels. © 2008 by the International Reading Association. May be copied for classroom use.

read the original version of the story and thought that the Billy Goats needed to be portrayed with a bit more attitude in their voices. They had also been performing scripts written by others. The teacher felt that this was a wonderful opportunity to engage students in writing, using the original story as a scaffold and model. The subsequent four days that involved practicing and eventually performing the script were a natural and engaging lesson in reading fluency.

One more point is worth mentioning when it comes to writing. One of the most challenging aspects to master in writing is voice—writing in such a way that a reader can imagine the face and hear the voice of the author. I know as a writer that I myself regularly struggle with voice. The texts that I have been advocating in this chapter for use with fluency, these more artful texts, are written with voice. Because they are written with voice, readers who read them to an audience need to read them with the voice they hear in the text.

When we ask students to examine such texts, we are asking them to examine them for the sense of voice embedded in them by the author. At the same time, when we ask students to write in the style of a Langston Hughes, a George M. Cohan, or a Sojourner Truth, we are asking them to write with a voice similar to one that the original author used. One of Lorraine Griffith's fourth-grade students, Elizabeth, reported that when she writes she tries to "hear the voice in her head" and put that voice on paper. No doubt Elizabeth learned to write with voice by first learning to read with voice. And no doubt she learned to read with voice through numerous rehearsals on texts that themselves were rich with the author's voice.

Another important consequence I have observed over and over again in students who engage in repeated and assisted reading of rhythmical texts meant to be performed is a greater sense of confidence. Most of the students for whom fluency instruction is most beneficial are struggling readers—students who have little confidence in their ability to read. This lack of confidence bleeds into other curricular areas and into other aspects of life. Students begin to believe that they do not have the ability to accomplish what needs to be accomplished in and out of school.

In reading, lack of confidence often manifests itself in not only slow and halting reading, but also in what I call "mumble" oral reading in which students often curl their bodies inward, put their hands in their pockets, lean against a nearby wall if standing, and fail to make eye contact with whomever may be listening to their reading. Once this lack of confidence begins to manifest itself in students, it often becomes a self-fulfilling prophecy in which students meet with less and less success in their academic endeavors.

Repeated and assisted practice, especially when that practice is aimed at a performance for an audience, a performance in which the performers can take justifiable pride, is a wonderful antidote to the loss of confidence that comes from repeated episodes of public disfluent reading that are often found in oral round-robin reading. Through repeated and assisted reading, less fluent readers learn that they can read as well as their more fluent classmates; they just need to practice a bit more. And, when these readers perform for an audience, even an audience of one, they can receive the affirmation of their efforts through the praise of others. As one young reader who engaged in a Readers Theatre curriculum and was attending rehearsal wrote, "I never thought I could be a star, but I was the BEST reader today" (Martinez et al., 1999, p. 333).

As you can probably infer, woven through this discussion of the additional benefits of this artful approach to fluency is perhaps the most important consequence of all—motivation to read and write (Worthy & Prater, 2002). Students find the texts and activities described in this chapter inherently motivating. They are reading for authentic purposes—to perform, to publish, to make meaning, to love language in all its forms, to celebrate themselves and others, to foster community and collaboration, to develop a sense of self-efficacy in themselves, and to touch the hearts of others for whom they may perform. I have watched students so motivated to make their oral reading performance memorable for an audience that they engage in sustained, intense, and self-regulated rehearsal of a text for more than an hour. Although such outcomes are often dismissed as secondary fluff by some educational critics, I contend that these motivational and aesthetic outcomes are central to the ultimate aims of education—to educate the whole child.

Conclusion: Beyond Fluency—Authenticity and Engagement

I began my professional journey in reading by wondering, How is it that there are some children who are otherwise highly intelligent who have difficulty in learning to read? This initial question led me to investigate reading fluency as one important answer to that wondering.

Deeper work into reading fluency, however, led me down a path that I had not intended. Fluency is best developed through assisted and repeated readings of texts. Repeated and assisted reading is best and most legitimately employed when readers intend to perform for an audience. Certain texts lend themselves better to performance than others. These texts are often the ones that are associated with the artistic side of reading—poetry, song, rhetoric, plays, and the like.

The use of these texts to nurture fluency is an engaging and authentic way to get students into fluency instruction. Students will want to practice if they know they will eventually be performing a text for an audience. Thus, I think of these artistic texts and their artistic uses as an ideal approach for teaching fluency.

My journey into fluency also led me to see that the use of these texts not only develops reading fluency, an area that has become a focal point for high-stakes testing of students; these texts are also ideal for developing some other important but often neglected areas of the elementary and middle school curricula—a wider variety of texts for reading instruction using texts or genres that have become secondary in most reading curricula, an appreciation of language that is found in these texts, deeper and more heartfelt or aesthetic understandings of the meanings authors intend to create through such texts, more varied responses to those texts, opportunities to write in various forms, opportunities to create a sense of unity among classmates, an appreciation of the differences that classmates bring to school, and, of course, greater opportunities to develop that internal confidence in one's own abilities that is essential to future growth (see Table 6.2).

TABLE 6.2
Voiced Texts for Fluency and Performance

Scripts (Readers Theatre)
Dialogues
Monologues
Poetry
Nursery rhymes
Songs
School cheers
Jokes and riddles
Oratory
Letters
Journals and diaries
Well wishes
Rituals

Confucius has said that "a journey of a thousand miles begins with a single step." It is important that the first step be taken, for unless it is taken, we will not know what we will find in all those remaining miles. I for one am glad that I took that initial step into reading fluency and then traveled that road for many more miles. I find it deeply satisfying to know that in that journey I found that it is possible to teach reading and reading fluency in ways that show measurable academic progress while at the same time nurturing the aesthetic side of reading and language that is of equal, yet often neglected, importance.

POSTREADING QUESTIONS

◆ According to this chapter, what is the relationship between intrinsic motivation to read and an arts-enhanced reading curriculum?

◆ What is your perception of the relationships between arts-enhanced reading instruction, intrinsic motivation, and outcomes on state-mandated test scores in reading?

◆ Do you think you may choose to use some of the arts-enhanced practices described in this chapter with your own students? If so, which ones and why? If not, why not? What problems might you encounter? What benefits do you think your students might gain?

REFERENCES

Allington, R.L. (1983). Fluency: The neglected goal of the reading program. *The Reading Teacher, 36,* 556–561.

Biggs, M., Homan, S., Dedrick, R., & Rasinski, T. (in press). Using an interactive singing software program: A comparative study of middle school struggling readers. *Reading Psychology, An International Quarterly*.

Chall, J.S. (1996). *Stages of reading development* (2nd ed.). Fort Worth, TX: Harcourt Brace.

Chard, D.J., Vaughn, S., & Tyler, B. (2002). A synthesis of research on effective interventions for building fluency with elementary students with learning disabilities. *Journal of Learning Disabilities, 35*, 386–406.

Chomsky, C. (1976). After decoding: What? *Language Arts, 53*, 288–296.

Deno, S.L. (1985). Curriculum-based measurement: The emerging alternative. *Exceptional Children, 52*, 219–232.

Deno, S.L., Mirkin, P., & Chiang, B. (1982). Identifying valid measures of reading. *Exceptional Children, 49*, 36–45.

Good, R., & Kaminski, R. (2005). *Dynamic indicators of basic early literacy skills* (6th ed.). Eugene, OR: Institute for the Development of Educational Achievement.

Griffith, L.W., & Rasinski, T.V. (2004). A focus on fluency: How one teacher incorporated fluency with her reading curriculum. *The Reading Teacher, 58*, 126–137.

Heckelman, R.G. (1969). A neurological impress method of reading instruction. *Academic Therapy, 4*, 277–282.

Keillor, G. (2004). For the week of October 18, 2004. *The Writer's Almanac*. Retrieved April 22, 2007, from writersalmanac.publicradio.org/programs/2004/10/18/index.html

Kuhn, M.R., & Stahl, S.A. (2000). *Fluency: A review of developmental and remedial practices* (CIERA Rep. No. 2-008). Ann Arbor, MI: Center for the Improvement of Early Reading Achievement.

LaBerge, D., & Samuels, S.J. (1974). Toward a theory of automatic information processing in reading. *Cognitive Psychology, 6*, 293–323.

Martinez, M., Roser, N., & Strecker, S. (1999). "I never thought I could be a star": A Readers Theatre ticket to reading fluency. *The Reading Teacher, 52*, 326–334.

National Institute of Child Health and Human Development. (2000). *Report of the National Reading Panel. Teaching children to read: An evidence-based assessment of the scientific research literature on reading and its implications for reading instruction: Reports of the subgroups* (NIH Publication No. 00-4754). Washington, DC: U.S. Government Printing Office.

Postlethwaite, T.N., & Ross, K.N. (1992). *Effective schools in reading: Implications for educational planners*. The Hague, The Netherlands: International Association for the Evaluation of Educational Achievement.

Rasinski, T.V. (1985). *A study of factors involved in reader-text interactions that contribute to fluency in reading*. Unpublished doctoral dissertation, Ohio State University, Columbus.

Rasinski, T.V. (1989a). Adult readers' sensitivity to phrase boundaries in texts. *Journal of Experimental Education, 58*, 29–40.

Rasinski, T.V. (1989b). Fluency for everyone: Incorporating fluency in the classroom. *The Reading Teacher, 42*, 690–693.

Rasinski, T.V. (1990a). *The effects of cued phrase boundaries on reading performance: A review*. Bloomington, IN: ERIC Clearinghouse on Reading and Communication Skills. (ERIC Document Reproduction Service No. ED313689)

Rasinski, T.V. (1990b). Effects of repeated reading and listening-while-reading on reading fluency. *Journal of Educational Research, 83*, 147–150.

Rasinski, T.V. (1991). Investigating measures of reading fluency. *Educational Research Quarterly, 14*(3), 37–44.

Rasinski, T.V., & Hoffman, J.V. (2003). Theory and research into practice: Oral reading in the school literacy curriculum. *Reading Research Quarterly, 38*, 510–522.

Rasinski, T., & Stevenson, B. (2005). The effects of Fast Start reading: A fluency-based home involvement reading program, on the reading achievement of beginning readers. *Reading Psychology: An International Quarterly, 26*, 109–125.

Rosenblatt, L. (1978). *The reader, the text, and the poem: The transactional theory of literary work*. Carbondale: Southern Illinois University Press.

Samuels, S.J. (1979). The method of repeated readings. *The Reading Teacher, 32*, 403–408. (Reprinted in *The Reading Teacher, 50*, 376–381)

Schreiber, P.A. (1980). On the acquisition of reading fluency. *Journal of Reading Behavior, 12*, 177–186.

Schreiber, P.A. (1987). Prosody and structure in children's syntactic processing. In R. Horowitz & S.J. Samuels (Eds.), *Comprehending oral and written language* (pp. 243–270). New York: Academic.

Schreiber, P.A. (1991). Understanding prosody's role in reading acquisition. *Theory Into Practice, 30*, 158–164.

Schreiber, P.A., & Read, C. (1980). Children's use of phonetic cues in spelling, parsing, and—maybe—reading. *Bulletin of the Orton Society, 30*, 209–224.

Worthy, J., & Prater, K. (2002). "I thought about it all night": Readers Theatre for reading fluency and motivation. *The Reading Teacher, 56*, 294–297.

Zutell, J., & Rasinski, T.V. (1991). Training teachers to attend to their students' oral reading fluency. *Theory Into Practice, 30*, 211–217.

CHAPTER 7

Building Engaging Classrooms

Ana Taboada, John T. Guthrie, and Angela McRae

Inspiring Reading Success: Interest and Motivation in an Age of High-Stakes Testing, edited by Rosalie Fink and S. Jay Samuels. © 2008 by the International Reading Association.

In this chapter, our aim is to describe classroom practices that support students' intrinsic motivation. Our premise is a simple one. Teaching the cognitive skills required for reading is important, but it is not enough. We need to systematically support motivation of all kinds daily in our classrooms. To explore this topic, we first present a vignette of a classroom in which the teacher creates a highly motivating environment to support students' literacy. We then zoom into five motivations consisting of (1) interest in reading, (2) mastery goals, (3) control and choice, (4) social interaction, and (5) self-efficacy. We present essential aspects of these motivations and recommend classroom practices to increase and support each one. We discuss these practices bearing in mind all children, but we devote special attention throughout the chapter to English-language learners (ELLs), given that this is the fastest growing population in U.S. public schools (Francis, Rivera, Lesaux, Kieffer, & Rivera, 2006). We conclude each section with questions that reflect on the extent that these practices are occurring in our classrooms.

Motivating Literacy: A Picture From the Classroom

Matthew, David, and Manuela are students in Jennifer's fourth-grade class. They enjoy science and learning about animals and strange insects in the wild. The class is working on a month-long unit on animals' and plants' survival in the woodlands. Jennifer has carefully chosen this unit as part of her goal of integrating reading and science. With this in mind, she looked at language arts and science standards that were aligned with this unit. Science standards included investigating how plants and animals in an ecosystem interact with one another and their environment, animals' behavioral and structural adaptations, organization of communities, life cycles, habitats, and niches. Language arts standards included reading objectives for expository texts such as summarizing, distinguishing facts from concepts, using text organizers, formulating questions, and drawing conclusions. Reading objectives for narrative texts included identifying major events and details in stories, reacting to story characters, and reading expressively. Jennifer's challenge was to choose a unit that met district standards while providing her diverse group of students with engaging reading experiences.

Matthew, David, and Manuela are representative of the diversity in Jennifer's class and the different experiences, motivations, and literacy skills that students bring to the act of reading. Matthew's reading is on grade level. He is a good student who likes to please his teacher by promptly completing assignments. He enjoys hands-on activities and reading stories in class but is more reticent about spending time writing and reading on his own. Like some other students in his class, Matthew treasures external rewards such as good grades and teacher recognition. David, a struggling reader, is slowly learning to enjoy stories when they are read to him and likes books on topics with which he is familiar. He has difficulty comprehending, struggling with finding main ideas and supporting details in nonfiction text. He enjoys the vivid pictures and large font headings in these texts and does well on short, concise tasks such as identifying words and topics in the index and table of contents. However, David dislikes more challenging tasks such as summarizing a section of a book or retrieving information from several books to answer broad, conceptual questions. David rarely reads on his own because he struggles with connecting information and making inferences. For David, reading a page of expository text and recalling the many details is a mountain he cannot climb. Answering traditional comprehension questions that test for factual, detailed information has turned him off from these texts. Jennifer is pleased that the woodlands is a topic that piques David's interest.

Manuela is a shy, quiet, English-language learner (ELL). She came to Jennifer's class from another district a month after the beginning of the school year. She had difficulty catching up with her classmates in many areas of the curriculum. This is Manuela's third year in U.S. public schools. Her conversational English allows her to communicate effectively in social situations; however, she struggles with reading both informational and narrative texts on grade level because her academic vocabulary is limited. Books that are accessible to most fourth graders are a bit too difficult for her and this turns her away from reading. In addition, Manuela is self-conscious of her limitations with the English language; her sense of competence is diminished, so she avoids oral reading and participation in whole-class discussions at all costs. Jennifer's knowledge of the strengths and limitations of her students along with an understanding of motivation practices allows Jennifer to create a literacy learning environment in which she can support students like Matthew, David, and Manuela to become engaged, intrinsically motivated readers.

During week 2 of the woodland unit, students explored the small woodland area behind their school, with the goal of closely observing insects and plants that live in and under a dead log. Jennifer had previously scooped out a few appropriate logs. Students took magnifying glasses and note pads to take notes and draw pictures of some of the many bugs and plants that reside under these dead logs. Students were brimming with excitement and curiosity to become "watchful scientists." They used their naked eyes, as well as magnifying glasses, to look at these creatures. Jennifer provided some guidelines for their observation, such as a few open-ended questions and diagrams. Students spent time observing, recording, and drawing what they saw. They also wrote their own questions about the plants and animals in the log. Jennifer reminded students of the conceptual question for the week: "How do the 'hidden worlds' contribute to animal and plant survival in the woodlands?"

The next day, students shared their observations and questions in a whole-group discussion. Jennifer listed student responses on construction paper and placed them in different corners of the classroom. She then had students turn to the book *A Dead Log* (Green, 1999), with the purpose of reading to answer some of their questions. Although the book's reading level was a bit difficult for students like Manuela and David, Jennifer modeled use of text features and how to search for specific information. She then provided a higher scaffold for those students who needed it. For example, she specifically asked students which sections in the table of contents they should first check to learn more about the specimens they observed in the woods. Jennifer referred students to the posted observations and questions and indicated that by reading the identified sections they would start answering some of their questions. Students began to notice how they could expand their learning by connecting their observations to information in their books. Matthew suddenly noticed with astonishment, "I knew these were beetles, but I did not know these ones I saw were called centipedes and that toads could live inside the log, too! We did not see any of those!" He avidly flipped the pages of the book and was excited about the many other animals that live in a log that he did not know about. Because all students were using the same book, Jennifer briefly reviewed activating background knowledge for the whole group, pointing out how their observations serve as background knowledge for reading. She then moved on to questioning, the week's reading strategy. Jennifer reminded students of the goal of questioning as a reading strategy: understanding text better and setting a goal for reading.

Students then broke into small groups with the goal of reading a few more sections in their book and sharing one interesting fact with one another. Jennifer then asked David to share his interesting fact from the book and pose a question in relation to it. Jennifer had books on centipedes and snails that David used to build the answer to his questions. Jennifer carefully selected books from the library with slightly below grade reading level that were on topics within the theme for students like David and Manuela. Books used for small-group instruction were labeled *team sets* to indicate their use during small-group activities. Some team-set titles included *Centipedes* (Cooper, 1996), *Insects (True Books: Animals)* (Stewart, 2000), *Millipedes* (Schaffer, 1999), and *Beetles (Incredible Insects)* (Gerholdt, 1996). Small groups continued working on questioning as the reading strategy for the week. Jennifer scaffolded students' questioning by providing a questioning rubric so students could ask different level questions. Students learned to differentiate factual from conceptual or higher level questions in the context of big ideas and concepts such as adaptation, feeding, locomotion, niche, and reproduction.

While Matthew and David were busy putting sticky notes next to facts and big ideas on their books and jotting down questions, Jennifer led Manuela's group and continued with the expressive reading lessons she started some weeks ago. Because Manuela needed to gain understanding and enjoy the pace of fluent, oral reading, Jennifer focused on vocabulary and expressive reading instruction for ELLs in her class using *Insectlopedia*, a poetry book by Douglas Florian (1998). Jennifer modeled fluent and expressive reading; she varied the tone of her voice and her intonation to emphasize feelings and emotions.

She also pointed out how repetitive words are used to create meaning and rhythmic effects in a poem. ELLs delved into words and their rhyming patterns to learn exotic insect names as part of the academic vocabulary. They entered some of these words into their word logs. These logs consisted of individual booklets with entries for word meanings, synonyms, word use in a sentence, and antonyms whenever possible. With these systematic word entries, students became more familiar with using dictionaries and book glossaries and discussing word meanings with one another. Before they moved to expository texts again, students formed pairs and provided feedback to each other on rate, intonation, prosody, and other aspects of expressive reading. Students formed pairs, and feedback was recorded on a fluency chart and provided in a nonthreatening context by avoiding exposure to the whole group. On the chart, student pairs indicated for each other whether they had read with intonation, read by clearly pronouncing words, respected punctuation, and so forth. In this way, students returned to the poems with more confidence about what expressive reading sounds like. When they were ready, students read their favorite poem expressively to kindergartners. A real audience boosted these students' motivation for reading expressively.

> When they were ready, students read their favorite poem expressively to kindergartners. A real audience boosted these students' motivation for reading expressively.

Later in the day, students accessed bookmarked Internet websites on beetles, sow bugs, snails, centipedes, and other woodland insects. Students gathered information on survival concepts for each of these insects. For homework, they read a chapter book called *Bug Boy* (Sonenklar, 1998). Students were gripped by the adventures of a boy who can turn into a bug and see the world from a bug's perspective. Homework choices included reacting to the main character's adventures, identifying survival concepts in the story, or writing an alternative ending to Bug Boy's intrepid undertakings. Toward the end of the week, small groups presented their research on the selected insects in one of three formats: poster, PowerPoint presentation, or a short chapter book in which they described and illustrated their findings. Students were excited about this weekly project; they were on their way to becoming experts on a topic they experienced firsthand, asked questions about, read extensively on, discussed with others, and learned about in depth. These fourth graders were thrilled to be sharing their knowledge. Literacy took on a full, new dimension for them. They were on the path to becoming engaged readers.

We have all met teachers like Jennifer, teachers who provide their students with thoughtful, meaningful, motivating literacy instruction. However, the question remains: What motivation practices did Jennifer and teachers like her use to support students' engaged reading?

In the remainder of the chapter, we describe each of five motivations: interest in reading, mastery goals, choice and control, social interaction, and self-efficacy. In each section we present essential characteristics and attributes of each motivation in relation to reading and describe classroom practices that support each of the motivations.

Interest in Reading

The first motivation we would like to address is interest in reading. John Dewey viewed interest as such a significant influence on a child's education that he devoted a whole volume to its discussion (Dewey, 1913). For Dewey, teaching that incorporates a child's interest allows the child to find purpose and spirit in his learning. He stated, "[I]f we can secure interest in a given set of facts or ideas, we may be perfectly sure that the pupil will direct his energies towards mastering them" (p. 1). Interest, for Dewey, is a dynamic, propulsive force that projects the child toward the object of his interest. Interest is also personal; it signifies a direct concern: "to be interested in any matter, is to be actively concerned with it" (p. 16).

As educators, we know that for students to be intrinsically motivated to read we need to take their interests into account. But how can we do that? It is certainly a bit ambitious to think that we can create a literacy curriculum that takes every student's interests into account all the time. We all face time and curriculum constraints that make this a difficult endeavor. However, as with other motivations, there are certain principles and practices that can help us better understand the nature of children's interests and use these to support engaged, motivated reading.

Let us first look a little deeper into the nature of interest. Researchers have generally distinguished between situational and personal interest (Hidi, 2000, 2001; Hidi & Renninger, 2006). Situational interest consists of affective reactions and attention to particular content or tasks. Personal interest refers to a broader, more enduring predisposition toward a domain, classes of objects, events, or ideas (Renninger & Hidi, 2002). Personal interest has also been referred to as a reader's personal identification with the content of text (Schiefele, 1999). For example, David's interest in observing centipedes and other insects under the log are an example of situational interest, while his interests in wild animals, race cars, and biographies of baseball players exemplify his personal interests.

Studies have also shown that when students read texts related to their interests, they processed information at deeper levels and comprehended text better than when the texts were not related to their interests (Krapp, 1999; Renninger, Hidi, & Krapp, 1992; Schiefele & Krapp, 1996). In addition, personal interest correlated more highly with deep-level learning than with surface-level learning from texts (Schiefele, 1996; Schiefele & Krapp, 1996). Situational and personal interests overlap and are not completely unrelated. What is important when trying to support students' internal motivation for reading is to create instructional conditions in which students' situational interest can be expanded into personal interests. When children are part of literacy instruction that capitalizes on their concrete, task-specific interests to nurture their broader, more personal interests, their enthusiasm and excitement for reading flourishes.

Supporting Student Interest in the Classroom

The instructional implications of research on interest are forthright: Students' reading engagement can be increased if students are afforded opportunities to pursue their interests through books. Thus, we first need to *provide texts relevant to students' lives and experi-*

ences. If the majority of the topics and texts students encounter at school are irrelevant to their world, it will be hard to find these worthy of pursuit. Interests are modes of self-expression. Our interests are part of who we are as individuals, the culture we belong to, and the environment in which we live. When children start exploring and defining their interests, they are defining aspects of the self that is developing.

When ELLs are given opportunities to read books that relate to their cultures and mores, their cultural background and experiences become relevant to them. A portion of their lives is brought to their attention. A connection between their interests and reading is established. As part of a social studies unit, Jennifer's ELLs were invited to share their clothing, language, musical instruments, food, writing systems, and artifacts with their classmates. Jennifer also had students read a novel or another form of narrative from an author of their culture. They were asked to share their reactions to the novel with the class. Mystery, fantasy, and adventure books are genres that are high interest for children. Upper elementary and middle school students find stories such as *Julie of the Wolves* (George & Schoenherr, 1972) especially appealing. Other genres, like biographies of prominent scientists such as *John Muir: My Life With Nature* (Muir & Cornell, 2000), can be nicely integrated into science themes as well, and students can use them as opportunities to explore their own interests through learning about other people's lives and interests.

Second, teachers who take into account children's interests for literacy instruction *help students establish real-world connections.* Few experiences provide a more concrete source of meaning and pique one's curiosity than handling a beetle hidden under the bark of a log. Real-world connections create an immediate, direct basis for interest to which few students can remain indifferent. Whenever possible, provide real-world experiences that connect to students' reading and provide texts that connect to these experiences. Jennifer's students expanded the learning initiated with the logs by reading about types of beetles, ferns, fungi, and other specimens. They also related their own experience to a boy's discoveries of the world that lies hidden under a rock by reading *Under One Rock: Bugs, Slugs, and Other Ughs* (Fredericks & Dirubbio, 2001). This connection not only lets children expand their knowledge, but it boosts their interests by creating shared experiences between their own experiential learning and that of characters in books.

Third, effective teachers *enable students to expand their interests.* One way they do this is by extending children's specific, situational interests into personal ones. When Jennifer provided Matthew with the opportunity to read and learn about toads and other woodland animals, she was taking Matthew's situational interest (as aroused by the woodland walk experience) and connecting it to his questions and his reading on other woodland animals. She was expanding his specific, situated interest to a more sustained personal interest in the topic. Similarly, when Jennifer set up individual research projects during which students gathered information on their chosen insect from the Internet and selected books, she was inviting them to explore their situational interests closely and establishing a longer term course to develop them further.

Fourth, *create opportunities for students to ask their own questions.* When students pose their own questions in relation to a text, topic, or experience, they are expressing their curiosities, wonderment, and knowledge about the world and life around them. Learning to formulate questions is a powerful tool that links students' interests to literacy. To promote the quality and the motivational benefits of questions, we recommend a questioning rubric (Taboada & Guthrie, 2006; see reproducible Motivating Literacy: Reflection Questions for Teachers on pages 149–150). In this rubric, there are relatively lower and relatively higher level questions. Level 1 questions merely ask for a simple fact or yes–no answer. At level 2, questions seek an answer to a concept and demand a descriptive statement. Level 3 questions seek to understand an important concept, rather than just a simple fact, but they probe for the concept more deeply than at level 2 by using knowledge within the question. Level 4 questions request knowledge about relationships among high-level concepts in the topic domain and a system of relationships in the subject area. For example, the weekly question, "How do the 'hidden worlds' contribute to animal and plant survival in the woodlands?" is an example of a level 4 question.

Last, *afford students opportunities to use different modes of self-expression.* Communicating their interests in personally significant modes and media is at the core of engaging literacy. Again, prime examples of students' self-expression of their interests in reading are seen in classrooms with large numbers of ELLs. For some of these students, the use of posters (e.g., of the forest layers), graphic organizers, diagrams, or models (e.g., of the solar system) are valuable modes of expressing conceptual knowledge in ways that remove some of the language load of other types of oral presentations. Ultimately, we know we have captured students' interests when the books and literacy experiences they participate in promote the desire to keep learning.

Questions to Consider When Promoting Interest in Your Classroom

- What do I know about my students' reading interests?
- To what extent do I include books that are interesting by virtue of their content, appearance, illustrations, and layout as part of my literacy instruction?
- How often do I create learning experiences that capitalize on my students' situational interests so as to pique their curiosities?
- How do I link my students' situational interests with their reading to help them develop a more stable, personal interest in a topic?
- How can students' school-based reading interests extend to their lives beyond school?
- How can students' non-school-based interests be woven into their academic interests?
- How often do I use real-world interactions to connect to students' interests in reading?
- Can I increase the ways that students' interests are personalized through their literacy activities (e.g., such as fostering their own questions, promoting relevant writing projects)?

Motivating Literacy: Reflection Questions for Teachers

Interest in Reading

- How do I help students identify and read books that are interesting to them?
- How can I help students link their learning experiences to books in a new way?
- How can I use my students' cultural backgrounds and experiences as a platform to develop their interests and curiosities for reading?
- What do I know about my students' reading interests?
- How can I learn more about my students' reading interests?

Mastery Goals

- How do I help students focus on big, conceptual ideas for their reading and learning?
- Are students exposed to a range of fiction and nonfiction books that reflect the theme under study?
- To what extent are reading strategies embedded in content instruction, as opposed to being taught in isolation?
- How are English-language learners and struggling readers afforded opportunities to develop expertise on a topic through reading?
- How do I link English-language learners' vocabulary learning to their conceptual learning in a theme?

Control and Choice

- How can I add choice menus to different aspects of literacy instruction?
- How often do I let students choose books to read on their own?
- How are literacy activities planned and structured so that students have opportunities to choose subtopics within a theme or overall unit?
- How many book choices are students afforded in relation to a topic that they need to research?
- Are all students' voices honored in my class, irrespective of their language or knowledge status?
- What opportunities do English-language learners and struggling readers have to share and display their new understandings?
- What are all the meaningful choices that I give students?

(continued)

Inspiring Reading Success: Interest and Motivation in an Age of High-Stakes Testing, edited by Rosalie Fink and S. Jay Samuels. © 2008 by the International Reading Association. May be copied for classroom use.

Motivating Literacy: Reflection Questions for Teachers (continued)

Social Interaction

- To what extent does the climate in my classroom reflect a true collaborative environment?
- How are open discussions structured so that the majority of students can participate?
- How do I ensure that English-language learners and struggling readers are afforded opportunities to collaborate as equal partners with other students in the class in literacy projects?
- How can book clubs and other types of independent reading activities be organized so that students have time to share their reactions to books in autonomous ways?
- Do all my students feel accepted in the classroom?
- How do I show my students they are important to me?

Self-Efficacy

- How do I help my students establish initial confidence in reading?
- How do I help students develop self-efficacy in their use of specific reading strategies?
- How are texts and reading strategies aligned so English-language learners and struggling readers can develop oral fluency, develop vocabulary, and build knowledge from text?
- To what extent is the feedback provided to different students in my classroom contingent on the specific task they have at hand? How does this feedback help them become aware of their strengths and improve their weaknesses?
- How are literacy activities arranged so students can see their own progress?
- How often do my students form their own goals for reading?

Mastery Goals

When students read with the purpose of learning new material deeply because learning feels rewarding in itself, they are using mastery goals for reading. Research in motivation has portrayed students who have mastery goals for reading as seeking to understand a text deeply, rather than reading to gain teacher approval, get good grades, and outperform others (Pintrich, 2003). Students who read to earn these external incentives are portrayed as having performance goals for reading, rather than mastery goals. Students with mastery goals for reading get involved in their books and embrace the challenge of learning new ideas from texts and tasks that lead them to increased competence in reading. Those with mastery goal orientations are not merely aiming to finish an assignment or a book; they are intrinsically motivated to learn about new topics and willing to master new concepts and ideas. These students enjoy the novelty and challenge that come with new learning and are willing to spend the time and effort required to conquer new content.

Supporting Mastery Goals in the Classroom

As teachers, we want to foster mastery goals for our students' reading. How can we do this? How can we foster students' desire to read for deep understanding? A few classroom practices can help us in the process. First, teachers who motivate through mastery goals *emphasize conceptual ideas for learning.* When students are provided with opportunities to learn about substantial, conceptual ideas, rather than merely factual bits of information, they read to understand concepts and to establish connections among topics (Vansteenkiste, Lens, & Deci, 2006). For example, Jennifer selected a few survival concepts that represent important ideas in ecology such as adaptation, feeding, locomotion, niche, and reproduction. By definition, concepts are abstractions that can be applied to several topics within a domain, yet these cannot be taught in a vacuum. Teachers like Jennifer use conceptual themes to make concepts more concrete for their students. Conceptual themes, such as "The Hidden World of Woodlands," provide a content basis to learn about big ideas such as survival concepts. Likewise, in social studies the theme "Children at Work Around the World" provides a content basis to learn about concepts such as child labor, human rights, children's rights, education, and slavery.

The breadth and depth of knowledge afforded by conceptual themes provides a very suitable framework for fostering students' mastery goals in reading. When teachers use conceptual themes, students know that they are learning important ideas and that their reading is meaningful because they are reading to build knowledge. One way that Jennifer makes this explicit is through the posting of broad, weekly questions that students refer to throughout the week. An example of a weekly question in science is "How do the 'hidden worlds' contribute to animal and plant survival in the woodlands?" In social studies, when studying child labor, a weekly question could be, "What conditions exist in poor countries that facilitate child labor?" Broad, conceptual questions such as these provide students with opportunities to read from multiple sources toward meaningful and relevant ideas such as exploitation, forced labor, injustice, health, and labor laws. Conceptual ideas can also be taught through projects that allow students to manipulate ideas in different forms. For example, as a culminating project for this theme, students have researched the role of the United Nations on child labor and have reenacted moral arguments against child labor and the lack of legislation in certain developing countries. With such projects, students can apply, argue, connect, organize, defend, and transform ideas. All these processes enable them to form mastery orientations for learning.

Motivating teachers *scaffold mastery goals* to help students gain deeper understanding from their reading. These teachers understand that if learning is to be meaningful and relevant, it must also feel achievable to their students. So they provide students with short-term goals, perhaps even daily goals, which contribute to the longer term, broader goals. They keep in mind that teaching toward big ideas requires scaffolding them, phasing them in, and making them accessible to all students. For example, as part of the broad, weekly questions, Jennifer had daily goals that included "Build a graphic organizer on how ants communicate and explain it to the class," "Practice the poem 'The Daddy Long Legs' [Florian, 1998] and read it expressively to a classmate," and "Locate three new words in the *Millipedes* book and explain how they relate to two survival concepts." These short-term goals provide students with manageable tasks that are relevant to the bigger, broader ideas identified for the theme. Precisely because the core of mastery goals is deep text understanding, students are encouraged to show their understanding through multiple performances such as explaining, connecting, defending, enacting, and transforming ideas.

Mastery-oriented teachers often *use real-world interactions* as a way to provide students with direct and relevant experiences. Real-world interactions were discussed as a source of students' interests, but they also have a specific role in promoting deep understandings. Hands-on experiences provide students with opportunities to connect their sensory and observation skills to the more abstract world of books. When Jennifer's fourth graders turned over a log and observed, touched, and drew the creatures underneath it, they read about these creatures with a renewed attention. The detailed observations that came from the live experience promoted specific questions and an awareness of these creatures that was not there before. They were not just reading about a remote, unknown insect that was merely described in a book. Rather, they established a connection between the here-and-now of the bugs and plants under the log and the wealth of information in the trade books on their classroom shelves. They expanded their learning of the specifics of the observation through reading. A real-world interaction provides a source of relevance and renewed attention that can promote deeper understanding of content in the books related to it. Furthermore, real-world interactions help level the playing field for students with diverse skills and abilities.

Given that ELLs and struggling readers are the students who wrestle with the abstractness of print, real-world specimens and hands-on activities have the power of making facts and concepts concrete and instructive by removing some of the language load of other media. For most students and for these in particular, hands-on activities are a tangible route for learning that can serve to ignite curiosities and connect them to books. However, real-world interactions, while a great source of fun and experiential learning, do not support engaged reading by themselves. They serve to pique students' curiosity, but they must be a springboard to reading. Jennifer supplied an abundance of books on woodland-related topics to follow up on students' observations. Our experiences have indicated that 1 hour of real-world interaction can sustain 10 hours of engaged reading on a topic (Guthrie et al., 2006).

Finally, when teachers adopt a mastery approach to their teaching they enable students to *attribute success to effort*, rather than to their innate ability. Because success in mastery-oriented classrooms consists of deep understandings, rather than merely getting grades or outdoing others, students are aware that their efforts count and tend to persevere in the face of difficulty (Weiner, 1994). Students who are reading to build knowledge about important, broad ideas can do so through varied options that allow them to achieve success in multiple, effortful ways. When students view deep understandings as part of the effort needed to succeed, they will be more motivated to read with a purpose. By the same token, when teachers help students perceive effort as key to their reading they will provide literacy tasks that are meaningful, achievable, and with an appropriate challenge level that requires students' effort and persistence.

Questions to Consider When Promoting Mastery Goals in Your Classroom

- How often do I align district standards (e.g., in language arts) with concepts or big, conceptual ideas that will help students form mastery goals?

- How do I go about selecting conceptual themes that embed important concepts that lend themselves to extensive reading and learning?

- Can I increase my selection of expository and narrative books on a theme so students can have breadth and depth of reading within the theme?

- How do I organize books according to subthemes or subtopics that are relevant to the big ideas in the theme?

- To what extent are reading strategies embedded in content instruction, as opposed to being taught in isolation?

- How often do students have multiple opportunities to convey to others their learning on big ideas and participate in higher order thinking?

- How are real-world interactions used as a source of meaningful learning and a launch to engaged reading?

- How do I provide students with alternative modes to perform their understandings so they can show mastery in literacy?

- To what extent do the literacy practices in my classroom let students attribute success to their efforts?

Choice and Control

We all enjoy some degree of choice in our lives. If we as adults appreciate the opportunities to make choices, certainly children do. This appreciation comes from the fact that choice offers us a certain degree of control and autonomy. Research has indicated that there is a natural human need for feeling autonomous and having some control over the decisions and steps we take (Deci & Ryan, 1987). Furthermore, when students are given choices and have some control over their academic work, their motivation increases (Cordova & Lepper, 1996; Deci, Schwartz, Sheinman, & Ryan, 1981; Guthrie, Wigfield, & Von Secker, 2000; Gutman & Sulzby, 2000). Children enjoy choosing what book to read, what character in a novel they can react to, or what section of text they can read next. Choice gives students a sense of ownership over the reading process and literacy tasks they encounter. When students can choose what questions to ask, they dive into their books to find the answers with a renewed interest and personal curiosity. Choice is empowering because it gives students control over alternatives, alternatives that are meaningful to students' personal experiences as well as to the content of the curriculum. Meaningful choices that consist of options that are academically significant and account for students' individualities act as an intrinsic motivator.

Supporting Choice and Control in the Classroom

First, motivating teachers *give choices that are academically relevant and personally meaningful* for students. There are multiple ways for teachers to support choice in their classrooms. The challenge rests in knowing what types of choices support internal motivation and foster engaged reading. Academically relevant choices are linked to the main goals and elements of the curriculum and units that students are learning. If a unit or a theme has well-delineated concepts of study, academically relevant choices contribute to students' learning of these concepts.

Jennifer's fourth graders felt empowered when they chose which woodland insect to read about, what information to record during their observations, what questions to ask, which poem to read expressively to others, and which animal to research for the culminating project. Students knew these choices were relevant to what they were learning. In addition, these choices were also personally meaningful (e.g., David pursued his curiosities and posed his own questions about centipedes). This gave students an initial sense of control over their learning, which was followed with students reading to find answers to their questions, making reading a personal, focused experience as well. When given such opportunities, students can become "experts" on a topic or a book. Developing expertise gives students ownership over their reading. Specifically, it gives struggling readers and ELLs the unique opportunity to be consulted by their peers for their expertise on a topic. In this way, choice presents students with opportunities to embrace new academic challenges and tests the boundaries of their academic competencies (Stipek, 2002).

A second practice that effective teachers like Jennifer are mindful of is *scaffolding choices for students*. Some students can handle more challenging options; others first need to be guided through micro-choices. For example, Jennifer knows that Matthew is reading on grade level and works well on his own. She is also aware that he succeeds at highly structured tasks but has a hard time following open-ended tasks such as writing an essay or a book chapter. With this in mind, Jennifer provided Matthew a choice of five woodland animals for his next writing assignment. He chose to write about foxes, selected two books from a menu of five, and decided on *defense* and *communication* as the ecological concepts to write about. Jennifer guided him to look at pictures, the table of contents, and index before making his choices. With this level of scaffolding, Matthew was ready to start on his writing. With choices of topic, books, and concepts, Matthew definitely felt he made unique contributions to his class. He was thrilled to be the expert on foxes.

> Teachers certainly vary in the degree and type of choices they give. They adjust choices to students' instructional needs and curriculum components....

David, on the other hand, has difficulty with reading strategies such as summarizing and making inferences. David chose one of his curiosities noted on the classroom chart to guide his reading on the book on centipedes. David's guided reading group was working on identifying main ideas for summary writing. Sticky notes were used all over the book to differentiate main ideas from supporting details before. The group incorporated these into the summaries. In his group, David was the only one writing a summary on centipedes' locomotion. His choices gave him the opportunity to personalize his reading as well.

Teachers certainly vary in the degree and type of choices they give. They adjust choices to students' instructional needs and curriculum components and, perhaps, even to their own teaching style. At times, however, choice can be excessive and a bit overwhelming for some students. In the past, Jennifer has had experiences in which choices have been beyond what some students could handle. Knowledge of her students and growing familiarity with the ranges of choices she could offer help her in this regard.

Third, teachers who use choice to support engaged reading give students *choices that are tied to different aspects of balanced literacy instruction* (e.g., vocabulary, fluency, strategy instruction, writing). Choices tied to vocabulary instruction include having ELLs choose what words to include in their academic vocabulary glossary. In these student-built glossaries, students include words that are specific to the domain and topic under study. Academic vocabulary, including words such as *adaptation, niche, camouflage,* and *pupa* related to this theme, were entered into their glossaries. Experienced teachers may scaffold ELLs' choices with a word bank from which students can select words. When focusing on fluency instruction, students can choose their preferred practice format for expressive reading from the following: (a) tape-recording and listening to their reading, (b) reading to a partner and receiving feedback, or (c) echo reading. Strategy instruction can include simple choices such as which paragraph to summarize and what questions to ask, or more complex ones such as which strategy to use to show understanding of the main ideas of an expository book. Writing choices can include which character to react to in the last novel read, which salient dimensions of child labor to include in a condemnation speech, or simply selection of which transition words to use from paragraph to paragraph in an essay. During independent reading time, students could also choose which book to read from a selected menu. With some planning, all components of a balanced literacy curriculum can be imbued with student choices.

Fourth, *give students ample opportunities for self-expression*. Giving students options for how to display and share their knowledge built from reading is also essential in helping them become engaged and motivated readers. Students feel a unique sense of pride when they see their work displayed, yet they also yearn for a unique way to show this work. For example, students may choose to post a letter to the editors of a local newspaper alerting the community of threatened regional species, or they may choose to participate in a debate for which their parents can participate as the audience.

Fifth, teachers who offer choice *provide students with a voice in standards of evaluation*. Given today's more stringent and prescriptive evaluation standards, teachers may contend that they cannot afford this practice for all evaluations. However, they can still select dimensions of literacy that allow students to participate in the process. Involving students in building rubrics is a highly motivating experience for them (Davis, 2003). For example, Jennifer's class discussed the components of good writing and built a rubric that included dimensions such as organization of ideas, writer's voice and style, word choice, sentence fluency, paragraph transitions, and conventions of writing (such as spelling and grammar). Students discussed each of these components and came up with poor, average, and good examples for each dimension. Using the examples, levels were assigned to each category and a classroom rubric was posted for all to use and follow. Bringing students to the evaluation process not only offers them control over their learning but also affords them active participation in different aspects of balanced literacy. Giving students a voice in the evaluation process is motivating because it empowers them to expand the boundaries of their knowledge.

Whenever possible, teachers enable students to participate in the decision-making process (Davis, 2003). Participating in decisions across the various aspects of literacy instruction gives students room to explore their academic competencies and take more control of their learning and reading. Providing students with a menu of choices in which the teacher delineates what options students have for a given topic or activity ensures that choices are academically meaningful and are within the spectrum of what students can handle. When students are given parameters (e.g., how to present the topic of a book to others) rather than always being told how they will be assessed, they create the idea in their minds that reading is not constantly tied to grades or rewards, but that it has intrinsic value and they can take their own approaches toward it. Reading is not merely a means to an end, a way to achieve high grades in language arts or science. Rather, reading becomes a way to learn new ideas, build knowledge, explore new domains, and embark in new experiences and share these with others.

Questions to Consider When Promoting Choice and Control in Your Classroom

- To what extent do I allow students to take responsibility for their own learning?

- How often do I let students choose books to read on their own?

- With what frequency are students provided with opportunities to choose topics to read and research?

- How do I scaffold opportunities to choose texts so students can expand their understanding of a topic?

- Are all students' voices honored in my class, irrespective of their language or knowledge status?

- Can I add choice menus to different aspects of literacy instruction?

- How frequently are students afforded the possibility to become experts on literacy-related topics?

- How fully do students participate in the evaluation process and have opportunities to assess their own work?

Social Interaction

Teachers who think of reading as a social event understand the importance of social interaction and collaboration in the classroom. Jennifer sees reading and writing as social events during which students come together to learn and share their knowledge and enthusiasm for literacy. Students in her class love the book club discussions, their team book chapter projects, practicing fluency in pairs, building group graphic organizers, peer practicing of reading strategies, and sharing perspectives on the last novel they read. Students are comfortable with the buzz of activity that comes from talking to one another and discussing their learning from books.

When we set up social interaction around text in the classroom, we seek to go beyond a mere exchange of opinion or fun talk in which students participate in free conversations with no specific purpose or guidance. Talk for its own sake that is not text based will probably not benefit students' reading comprehension. When we refer to social interaction, we refer to student interchanges and dialogues in a literacy situation with the purpose of supporting students' reading motivation. When students come together to share their learning and build upon one another's thinking as they seek to understand text, social interaction is motivating. One may argue that reading is a solitary activity that requires individual initiative and that many readers thrive in the privacy of the reading act. However, when reading is interwoven with learning in a classroom context, its social dimension cannot be ignored. Researchers have found that when students felt accepted, special, important, and noticed by their teachers, classmates, and friends, they felt a sense of belonging or "relatedness" to others (Furrer & Skinner, 2003; Ryan & Deci, 2000).

Students with a sense of relatedness were enthusiastic and engaged in their learning. To the contrary, students who felt they did not belong to the class appeared to teachers as frustrated and disconnected from classroom activities (Furrer & Skinner, 2003). Students' interpersonal relationships are a source of support in the face of academic challenges such as understanding complex texts and building conceptual, interconnected knowledge. Team efforts and social connections give students comfort and reassurance about conquering academic challenges and becoming engaged readers.

Supporting Social Interaction in the Classroom

When student interaction is part of the social fabric of the classroom, students participate in multiple, positive social activities in relation to literacy. Teachers nurture a positive social structure in the classroom by explaining to students the importance of speaking, listening, and respecting others and helping them establish common goals and equal status in the classroom. Teachers also create opportunities for social interactions through specific practices.

First, effective teachers *hold and promote open discussions*. These may be teacher led, but they begin with open questions—ones without a yes or no answer. They do not necessarily need to be loose or ill structured, but they need to remove the sense of being evaluated on every point that is made. Several answers are possible and are encouraged so students can interact freely. When students participate in open discussions they feel important because their ideas are recognized and supported by others. Taking leadership of some of these discussions also contributes to their feeling of control over their learning and the importance of contributing valuable knowledge to the group. In Jennifer's classroom, students participate in book clubs, literature circles, and idea circles in which all members in a group contribute an important idea in relation to a concept or central aspect of an expository book.

Second, engaging teachers *support collaborative reasoning through short- and long-term projects*. Short-term projects can consist of simple collaborations such as students coconstructing a graphic organizer on a topic or subtopic within a conceptual theme. David and other classmates in Jennifer's class collaborated on a poster-size organizer on "Centipede's Locomotion and Defense" for which they shared information from three books on centipedes. Matthew and Mark collaborated in a discussion on which main idea to include in a pair summary. Long-term projects, however, need teachers' careful planning and can take the form of culminating literacy-related items such as a team chapter book on animals in the woodlands or a poster for the school entrance displaying facts on child labor. These projects require more teacher guidance and structure to ensure that all students contribute equally and meaningfully to the team effort.

In particular, research has emphasized the benefits of having ELLs collaborate using reading strategies to improve reading comprehension in the form of modified reciprocal teaching methods (Klingner & Vaughn, 1996). Specifically, if collaboration is to support engaged reading for ELLs, these children need opportunities to be exposed to the use of the English language by their English-speaking peers, as well as to engage in oral and written communication themselves. To benefit fully from social interactions, ELLs need arrangements that go beyond mere exposure to oral language. Successful student collaboration has ELLs actively participating in oral conversations, as well as reading and writing activities, in which both academic vocabulary and conceptual knowledge are at the core.

Last, another way of supporting social interaction is by *arranging partnerships* in which both students participate in meaningful literacy tasks. In pairs, students complete literacy-related tasks to share with the whole class or team. These tasks can range from answering a broad, conceptual question by searching for information in different books to sharing expressive reading. For example, *Joyful Noise: Poems for Two Voices* (Fleischman & Beddows, 2004) is a fantastic book to foster expressiveness and rotated reading because readers are guided to poem stances to read aloud so as to collaborate gracefully in the task. Simple partnering activities give students an opportunity to be actively social around literacy endeavors. In particular, the most vulnerable learners, such as struggling readers and ELLs, benefit from partnerships that can provide a secure context where they can practice skills and strengthen knowledge before they are ready to face the whole group. Overall, social interactions should be arranged so students have a voice in the ways of working with texts and have opportunities to exchange knowledge and opinions with others. When teachers create a socially cohesive climate in which most students become active participants, students become more committed, excited, and enthusiastic about literacy.

Questions to Consider When Promoting Social Interaction in Your Classroom

- How frequently do students participate in meaningful, open discussions in relation to literacy?

- How are open discussions structured so that the majority of students can participate?

- Can I increase the opportunities that students have to collaborate on short- and long-term projects related to different aspects of balanced literacy, such as writing a team book or participating in idea circles and literature circles?

- How do I support partnerships for reading tasks as an ongoing practice in my class?

- What do I do to ensure that ELLs and struggling readers participate and benefit fully from classroom collaborations?

- To what extent do students in my class exchange viewpoints about their reading?

- How does the classroom context enable all students' voices to be honored during social collaborations?

Self-Efficacy

The last motivation we would like to address is self-efficacy. Researchers refer to self-efficacy as an individual's beliefs, judgments, and perceptions of his or her capacities for specific tasks at particular points in time (Bandura, 1977, 1986, 1991; Schunk, 1989; Zimmerman, 1995). Self-efficacy is closely related to perceptions of competence, but unlike general perceptions that apply to multiple situations, self-efficacy usually refers to perceptions of performance on specific tasks (Bandura, Barbaranelli, Caprara, & Pastorelli, 1996). Self-efficacy is different from self-esteem, which consists of a more pervasive, broader perception of one's abilities and sense of well-being. Thus, an individual can have self-efficacy for a specific sport, such as tennis, or for a hobby, such as gardening. When applied to reading, self-efficacy refers to students' confidence in their ability to read and comprehend text well. Students' self-efficacy is affected by their previous experiences with a task, by observing others' successful experiences, and by the encouragement or the verbal persuasion they receive from others (Bandura, 1977, 1982).

People, in general, do not seek to participate in activities that they know they cannot do very well. That is why students who have high self-efficacy for reading tend to look for opportunities to read more and enjoy it more than students who believe they do not have the reading skills or the ability to read well (Wigfield & Guthrie, 1997). As teachers we know that when students have experienced repeated frustrations with reading, a downward spiral sets in and they are turned off from reading. Students who often find it hard to get to the end of a page due to vocabulary or decoding difficulties, or for whom the sheer amount of text makes it impossible to identify main ideas, tend to stay away from reading and develop low self-efficacy. For these students, getting the gist of a section is a struggle. Therefore, constructing meaningful knowledge from text and connecting ideas across texts are beyond them. Furthermore, for these students, negative experiences with reading have precluded them from the joy and the challenges of deep text understanding and of successful reading experiences. They feel that most books are beyond their reach and their efforts wane; they avoid books whenever they can and just read to get by. Many struggling readers and ELLs whose English proficiency is limited fall into this downward spiral in which negative reading experiences, low self-efficacy, and lack of reading development create a dispirited scenario. Reversing this spiral is not easy, but it is possible. We present four instructional practices that address the self-efficacy of students in our classrooms.

Supporting Self-Efficacy in the Classroom

A first means toward this end is *offering students texts that match their reading levels* and their interests. Self-efficacy is built on the perception of success in reading. Students who perceive themselves as competent readers are those who have high self-efficacy for reading. To foster self-efficacy in their students, teachers first need to help students develop a positive, confident attitude toward reading.

If students are constantly faced with materials beyond their capabilities, they will not want to spend effort on reading tasks that overwhelm them. Students need to feel they can enjoy and master the text in their hands. When students feel more competent in their reading, more challenging materials can be incorporated. Schools and teachers must be ready to offer these students books that are at or near their actual reading level and that are of interest to them (Yudowitch, Henry, & Guthrie, in press).

In her classroom, Jennifer makes this possible by having books with multiple reading levels, text genres, and topics within the theme. There are class, team, and individual sets of books on the conceptual theme. Whole-class books are at the middle level of the classroom range. The students' reading levels are at grade equivalents 2 through 5. Thus, team sets used for guided reading represent this range so lower level books can be used by some students and more challenging books can be used by others. In addition, students have access to approximately 20 individual titles on subtopics on the theme that vary in reading levels and can be used for students' research projects, as well as for independent reading. Books are selected mindful of (a) the range of reading levels in the class, (b) the relevance to topics within the theme, (b) text features (e.g., table of contents, index, illustrations) and content that support cognitive strategy instruction and practice, and (c) a balance between expository and narrative texts that support conceptual learning, expressive reading, and rich literature.

For struggling readers with decoding difficulties and for ELLs who are limited in their English proficiency, but who have well-developed cognitive abilities, it is crucial to use high-interest, readable books. Using books with controlled vocabulary, low reading level, and low-interest topics are detrimental to these students' reading self-efficacy, and ultimately to their reading achievement. The breadth and criteria used for book selection in Jennifer's class allows for books that can be matched to students' reading levels and interests. These are books rich in content and vocabulary and are appealing to learners by virtue of their appearance. When teachers and schools spend the time, money, and effort on selecting texts that can be matched to students' reading levels and interests, students are more motivated to spend their own time, effort, and enthusiasm in learning from them.

A second practice for supporting students' self-efficacy consists of ensuring that students *establish initial confidence* in their reading and literacy tasks (Yudowitch et al., in press). Once we have texts that match our students, we need to give them several doable assignments. Especially for students lacking in self-efficacy and confidence, they need manageable, short reading assignments that they can accomplish successfully. Incremental levels of difficulty can be given with time, but first these students need to feel they can do it. They need to feel that they can read and that they can read well.

Teachers help students establish initial confidence with literacy by helping *students become competent in the use of reading strategies*. Reading strategies are the tools students need to excavate meaning out of text. However, not all students feel confident in using them. Teachers help these students to use strategies in three main ways. First, they provide high scaffolding for the use of a strategy by having students use it in a limited or structured context. For example, rather than having students ask a question about a whole book, teachers highlight a few sentences on a page and have students use these sentences as prompts to ask a question.

Many ELLs come from cultures in which they are not accustomed to ask questions about texts or other sources of knowledge (Haynes, 2007), so providing them with concrete steps helps them in the process. Second, teachers adjust text to the strategies students are learning. If students are learning to search information texts, teachers ensure that books have a table of contents, index, and glossary that lend themselves to searching. A third way most teachers help students develop confidence in strategy use is by providing multiple opportunities for strategy practice, both across texts and genres.

The other important avenue to foster initial confidence in reading can be paved by helping students become fluent readers. Fluency is a bridge to comprehension, but it is also a fundamental element of students' self-efficacy in reading. Many struggling readers and ELLs are highly self-conscious of their oral reading and whether or not their words sound smooth and fluent to others. When teachers pair these students with fluent readers and ensure that feedback is provided on prosody, intonation, and smooth reading, they are providing them with opportunities to become more confident readers. Fostering fluency and fostering strategic reading are initial steps in helping students gain the self-efficacy they need to become engaged readers.

Third, teachers who support their students' self-efficacy *provide specific feedback on students' progress* (Schunk, 2003). For feedback to be useful, it needs to be clear, specific, and focused on the behavior or the task, rather than on the person (Mueller & Dweck, 1998). Comments such as "good job" or "great work" are less informative than specific commendations such as "You did a good job of using the information in the book to ask questions" or "Your summary is well written; you included a main idea and a supporting detail." To develop competence and confidence in different aspects of literacy, students need to know about their progress in specific areas.

Last, to increase self-efficacy for reading teachers *offer students opportunities to develop expertise on specific topics.* As discussed, like expertise provides students with a sense of ownership over their reading, it also fosters their sense of competence. Furthermore, when students feel the pride of becoming experts on a topic, they do not need to turn to other domains for recognition, such as misbehavior (Stipek, 2002) or external rewards. Because their source of pride is their competence, students can attribute their success to their knowledge, a variable over which they have control. The downward spiral starts to reverse, and gradually these students start to see themselves as competent, self-efficacious, and engaged readers.

Questions to Consider When Promoting Self-Efficacy in Your Classroom

- To what extent is there a variety and breadth of texts in my classroom that support students' reading levels and interests?

- How do I help my students establish initial confidence in reading?

- How do I enable students to perceive reading strategies as tools to help with their reading and understanding?

- How do I scaffold ELLs' use of reading strategies so they can access text more readily?

- How do I scaffold struggling readers' use of reading strategies so they can access text more readily?

- What types of supports do ELLs and struggling readers receive to develop competence in (oral) reading fluency?

- Can I increase or improve the specificity of the feedback that I provide to my students on different aspects of balanced literacy?

- How are literacy activities arranged so students can see their own progress?

Conclusion

In this chapter, we have described five motivations and specific practices that foster children's intrinsic motivation for reading during daily classroom instruction. Support for interest in reading, mastery goals, control and choice, social interaction, and self-efficacy were presented along with examples from diverse elementary school classrooms. (See Table 7.1 for website resources for the unit described.) We encourage teachers to consider the reflective questions regarding each motivation as they think of their literacy instruction and how to support engaged reading in their classrooms. Often, the central focus of traditional language arts curriculum has been to teach students to effectively apply reading strategies without regard to students' intrinsic motivation to read. If as educators we are willing to embrace the challenge of fostering children's lifelong desire to read, it is vital to support both the cognitive capacities as well as the intrinsic motivation that sustain children's engaged reading.

POSTREADING QUESTIONS

◆ In this chapter you have read about engaging classrooms for diverse learners. Taking into account the diversity of your classroom, focus either on ELLs, struggling readers, or other students with difficulties in literacy in your classroom. Think about the specific literacy needs of these children and their motivation profiles or characteristics. Think of ways in which the motivation practices described in this chapter can support these children's reading engagement.

◆ Now take your thinking to the larger group in your classroom. Focus on the diversity of your classroom that includes all learners and readers in it. Discuss with a colleague ways in which you can provide literacy instruction that has the structure and guidance that foster student engagement, taking into account the diversity of your classroom. You may want to start by thinking about the diversity of your classroom first and reviewing the five motivations in the chapter one at a time, as a second step.

Acknowledgments
This chapter draws upon *Engaging Adolescents in Reading* (Guthrie, in press), and we acknowledge the contributions of all the authors in that volume.

TABLE 7.1
Website Resources for Life Science Unit

The following is a brief list of websites that have been used by teachers in fourth-grade classrooms supporting their students' reading engagement in life science. The headings indicate the major topic included on the website.

Various Animals

EnchantedLearning.com: www.enchantedlearning.com/coloring
- Most animals in the Woodlands and Wetlands units have specific pages with a labeled drawing and information.
- All animal webpages have conceptual information at an appropriate reading level and a labeled diagram.
- Search alphabetically or by animal type.

Hogle Zoo: hoglezoo.org/animals/world.php
- Many animals have their own pages at this zoo website, so it is a good place to start research on any animal.

Woodlands Description

Naturegrid: www.naturegrid.org.uk/woodland/woodexplore.html
- This is an excellent site at the fourth-grade reading level.
- Click on the spider to explore the woodland habitat; click on "Wildlife Library" to see information on animals and plants of the woodland.

Mammals

Mouse

Naturegrid: www.naturegrid.org.uk/woodland/mouse2.html
- This site contains low-level text about the wood mouse.

SaskSchools.ca: www.saskschools.ca/~gregory/animals/mouse.html
- This webpage displays conceptual, easy-to-read information on the meadow mouse.

Raccoon

Environmental Education for Kids: www.dnr.state.wi.us/org/caer/ce/eek/critter/mammal/raccoon.htm
- This excellent page has a moderate reading level.

University of Alberta Museum of Zoology: www.biology.ualberta.ca/uamz.hp/coon.html
- This page contains photos and higher level text.

Fox

Fox Forest: www.foxforest.com
- Text is higher level, but this website contains many pages with good conceptual information, photos, and movies about red foxes.

REFERENCES

Bandura, A. (1977). *Social learning theory*. Upper Saddle River, NJ: Prentice Hall.

Bandura, A. (1982). Self-efficacy mechanism in human agency. *American Psychologist, 37*, 122–147.

Bandura, A. (1986). *Social foundations of thought and action: Social cognitive theory*. Upper Saddle River, NJ: Prentice Hall.

Bandura, A. (1991). Self-regulation of motivation through anticipatory and self-regulatory mechanisms. In R. Dienstbier (Ed.), *Perspectives on motivation: Nebraska symposium on motivation* (Vol. 38, pp. 237–288). Lincoln: University of Nebraska Press.

Bandura, A., Barbaranelli, C., Caprara, G., & Pastorelli, C. (1996). Multifaceted impact of self-efficacy beliefs on academic functioning. *Child Development, 67,* 1206–1222.

Cordova, D.I., & Lepper, M.R. (1996). Intrinsic motivation and the process of learning: Beneficial effects of contextualization, personalization, and choice. *Journal of Educational Psychology, 88,* 715–730.

Davis, H.A. (2003). Conceptualizing the role and influence of student-teacher relationships on children's social and cognitive development. *Educational Psychologist, 38,* 207–234.

Deci, E.L., & Ryan, R. (1987). The support of autonomy and the control of behavior. *Journal of Personality and Social Psychology, 53,* 1024–1037.

Deci, E.L., Schwartz, A.J., Sheinman, L., & Ryan, R.M. (1981). An instrument to assess adults' orientations toward control versus autonomy with children: Reflections on intrinsic motivation and perceived competence. *Journal of Educational Psychology, 73,* 642–650.

Dewey, J. (1913). *Interest and effort in education.* Boston: Houghton Mifflin.

Francis, D.J., Rivera, M., Lesaux, N.K., Kieffer, M., & Rivera, H. (2006). *Practical guidelines for the education of ELLs: Research-based recommendations for instruction and academic interventions.* Portsmouth, NH: RMC Research Corporation, Center on Instruction. (U.S. Department of Education, Grant No. S283B050034A)

Furrer, C., & Skinner, E. (2003). Sense of relatedness as a factor in children's academic engagement and performance. *Journal of Educational Psychology, 95,* 148–162.

Guthrie, J.T. (Ed.). (in press). *Engaging adolescents in reading.* Thousand Oaks, CA: Corwin Press.

Guthrie, J.T., Wigfield, A., Humenick, N.M., Perencevich, K.C., Taboada, A., & Barbosa, P. (2006). Influences of stimulating tasks on reading motivation and comprehension. *Journal of Educational Research, 99,* 232–245.

Guthrie, J.T., Wigfield, A., & Von Secker, C. (2000). Effects of integrated instruction on motivation and strategy use in reading. *Journal of Educational Psychology, 92,* 331–341.

Gutman, L., & Sulzby, E. (2000). The role of autonomy-support versus control in the emergent writing behaviors of African-American kindergarten children. *Reading Research & Instruction, 39,* 170–183.

Haynes, J. (2007). *Getting started with English language learners: How educators can meet the challenge.* Alexandria, VA: Association for Supervision and Curriculum Development.

Hidi, S. (2000). An interest researcher's perspective: The effects of extrinsic and intrinsic factors on motivation. In C. Sansone & J.M. Harackiewicz (Eds.), *Intrinsic and extrinsic motivation: The search for optimal motivation and performance* (pp. 309–339). New York: Academic.

Hidi, S. (2001). Interest, reading, and learning: Theoretical and practical considerations. *Educational Psychology Review, 13,* 191–209.

Hidi, S., & Renninger, A. (2006). The four-phase model of interest development. *Educational Psychologist, 41,* 111–127.

Klingner, J.K., & Vaughn, S. (1996). Reciprocal teaching of reading comprehension strategies for students with learning disabilities who use English as a second language. *The Elementary School Journal, 96,* 275–293.

Krapp, A. (1999). Interest, motivation, and learning: An educational psychological perspective. *European Journal of Psychology of Education, 14,* 23–40.

Mueller, C., & Dweck, C. (1998). Intelligence praise can undermine motivation and performance. *Journal of Personality and Social Psychology, 75,* 33–52.

Pintrich, P.R. (2003). A motivational science perspective on the role of student motivation in learning and teaching contexts. *Journal of Educational Psychology, 95,* 667–686.

Renninger, K.A., & Hidi, S. (2002). Student interest and achievement: Developmental issues raised by a case study. In A. Wigfield & J.S. Eccles (Eds.), *Development of achievement motivation* (pp. 173–195). New York: Academic.

Renninger, K., Hidi, S., & Krapp, A. (1992). *The role of interest in learning and development.* Mahwah, NJ: Erlbaum.

Ryan, R.M., & Deci, E.L. (2000). Intrinsic and extrinsic motivations: Classic definitions and new directions. *Contemporary Educational Psychology, 25,* 54–67.

Schiefele, U. (1996). Topic interest, text representation, and quality of experience. *Contemporary Educational Psychology, 21,* 3–18.

Schiefele, U. (1999). Interest and learning from text. *Scientific Studies of Reading, 3,* 257–279.

Schiefele, U., & Krapp, A. (1996). Topic interest and free recall of expository text. *Learning and Individual Differences, 8,* 141–160.

Schunk, D.H. (1989). Self-efficacy and cognitive achievement: Implications for students with learning problems. *Journal of Learning Disabilities, 22,* 14–22.

Schunk, D.H. (2003). Self-efficacy for reading and writing: Influence of modeling, goal setting, and self-evaluation. *Reading & Writing Quarterly, 19,* 159–172.

Stipek, D. (2002). *Motivation to learn: Integrating theory and practice.* Boston: Allyn & Bacon.

Taboada, A., & Guthrie, J.T. (2006). Contributions of student questioning and prior knowledge to construction of knowledge from reading information text. *Journal of Literacy Research, 38,* 1–35.

Vansteenkiste, M., Lens, W., & Deci, E.L. (2006). Intrinsic versus extrinsic goal contents in Self-Determination Theory: Another look at the quality of academic motivation. *Educational Psychologist, 41,* 19–31.

Weiner, B. (1994). Integrating social and personal theories of achievement striving. *Review of Educational Research, 64,* 557–573.

Wigfield, A., & Guthrie, J.T. (1997). Relations of children's motivation for reading to the amount and breadth of their reading. *Journal of Educational Psychology, 89,* 420–432.

Yudowitch, S., Henry, L.M., & Guthrie, J.T. (in press). Self-efficacy: Building confident readers. In J.T. Guthrie (Ed.), *Engaging adolescents in reading.* Thousand Oaks, CA: Corwin Press.

Zimmerman, B. (1995). Self-efficacy and educational development. In A. Bandura (Ed.), *Self-efficacy in changing societies* (pp. 202–231). New York: Cambridge University Press.

LITERATURE CITED

Cooper, J. (1996). *Centipedes.* Vero Beach, FL: Rourke Publishing.

Fleischman, P., & Beddows, E. (2004). *Joyful noise: Poems for two voices.* New York: HarperTrophy.

Florian, D. (1998). *Insectlopedia.* San Diego, CA: Voyager Books.

Fredericks, A.D., & Dirubbio, J. (2001). *Under one rock: Bugs, slugs, and other ughs.* Nevada City, CA: Dawn.

George, J.C., & Schoenherr, J. (1972). *Julie of the wolves.* New York: HarperTrophy.

Gerholdt, J.E. (1996). *Beetles (Incredible insects).* Edina, MN: Abdo & Daughters.

Green, J. (1999). *A dead log.* New York: Crabtree.

Muir, J., & Cornell, J. (2000). *John Muir: My life with nature.* Nevada City, CA: Dawn.

Schaffer, D. (1999). *Millipedes.* Mankato, MN: Bridgestone Books.

Sonenklar, C. (1998). *Bug boy.* New York: Random House.

Stewart, M. (2000). *Insects (True books: Animals).* New York: Scholastic.

Author Index

VAUGHN, S., 46, 121, 158
VERHOEVEN, L., 20
VIDA, M., 76, 81
VON SECKER, C., 154
VYGOTSKY, L.S., 84, 110

W

WAGNER, R.K., 28
WALCZYK, J.J., 31
WALKER, J.M., 85

WALLACE, A., 5
WALLON, H., 64–65
WANG, Q., 86–87
WEINER, B., 77–79, 85, 153
WHITEHEAD, F., 37
WIGFIELD, A., 76–77, 81, 100, 110, 113, 153–154, 160
WINIKATES, D., 28
WINNER, E., 32
WOLTER, C.A., 100
WORTHY, J., 137

X–Z

XU, J., 85
YOUNG, J.P., 37
YUDOWITCH, S., 160
ZARRETT, N.R., 77
ZHANG, M., 46
ZIMMERMAN, B.J., 80, 84, 87, 104, 112, 160
ZUSHO, A., 84
ZUTELL, J., 120

Subject Index

Note. Page numbers followed by *f* or *t* indicate figures or tables, respectively.

VAZ, A. MCDONALD, 22t
VOCABULARY: activities for, 52–56
VOICE: and authentic fluency, 123; and choices, 156; scripts with, 132–135; texts with, 123–126, 125t
VOLUNTARY READING AS SOCIAL PRACTICE (VRSP), 46

W–Y

WEBSITES: on engagement in life science, 164t; for interest-based teaching, 58t; on motivation and interest, 78t; multicultural, 46–48, 48t; for voiced texts, 125t
WEST, THOMAS G., 22t
WHITEHOUSE, LEZLI, 23t
WHITMAN, WALT, 128
WIENER, NORBERT, 5
WOODS, TIGER, 8–9
WRITING: with voice, 136
"YELLIN, KATHLEEN" (PSEUDONYM), 23t, 37
YOUNG, GLENN, 22t